# POTTS'S
# DISCOVERY OF WITCHES

In the County of Lancaster,

REPRINTED FROM THE ORIGINAL
EDITION OF

1613.

WITH AN

INTRODUCTION AND NOTES,

BY

JAMES CROSSLEY, Esq.

# INTRODUCTION.

Were not every chapter of the history of the human mind too precious an inheritance to be willingly relinquished,—for appalling as its contents may be, the value of the materials it may furnish may be inestimable,—we might otherwise be tempted to wish that the miserable record in which the excesses occasioned by the witch mania are narrated, could be struck out of its pages, and for ever cancelled. Most assuredly, he, who is content to take the fine exaggeration of the author of *Hydriotaphia* as a serious and literal truth, and who believes with him that "man is a glorious animal," must not go to the chapter which contains that record for his evidences and proofs. If he should be in search of materials for humiliation and abasement, he will find in the history of witchcraft in this country, from the beginning to the end of the seventeenth century, large and abundant materials, whether it affects the species or the individual. In truth, human nature is never seen in worse colours than in that dark and dismal review. Childhood, without any of its engaging properties, appears prematurely artful, wicked and cruel[1]; woman, the victim of a wretched

---

[1] Take, as an instance, the children of Mr. Throgmorton, of Warbois, for bewitching whom, Mother Samuels, her husband, and daughter, suffered in 1593. No veteran professors "in the art of ingeniously tormenting" could have administered the question with more consummate skill than these little incarnate fiends, till the poor old woman was actually induced, from their confident asseverations and plausible counterfeiting, to believe at last that she had been a witch all her life without knowing it. She made a confession, following the story which they had prompted, on their assurances that it was the only means to restore them, and then was hanged upon that confession, to which she adhered on the scaffold. Few tracts present a more vivid picture of manners than that in which the account of this case of witchcraft is contained. It is perhaps the rarest of the English tracts relating to witchcraft, and is entitled "The most strange and admirable Discoverie of the three Witches of Warboys, arraigned, convicted, and executed at the last Assizes at Huntingdon, for the bewitching of the five daughters of Robert Throckmorton, Esquire,

and debasing bigotry, has yet so little of the feminine adjuncts, that the fountains of our sympathies are almost closed; and man, tyrannizing over the sex he was bound to protect, in its helpless destitution and enfeebled decline, seems lost in prejudice and superstition and only strong in oppression. If we turn from the common herd to the luminaries of the age, to those whose works are the landmarks of literature and science, the reference is equally disappointing;—

"The sun itself is dark
And silent as the moon
Hid in her vacant interlunar cave."

We find the illustrious author of the Novum Organon sacrificing to courtly suppleness his philosophic truth, and gravely prescribing the ingredients for a witches' ointment;[2]—Raleigh, adopting miserable fallacies at second hand, without subjecting them to the crucible of his acute and vigorous understanding;[3]—Selden, maintaining that crimes of the imagination may be punished with death;[4]—The detector of Vulgar Errors, and the most humane of physicians,[5] giving the casting weight to the

---

and divers other persons with sundrie Devilish and grievous torments. And also for the bewitching to Death of the Lady Crumwell, the like hath not been heard of in this age. London, Printed by the Widdowe Orwin for Thomas Man and John Winnington, and are to be sold in Paternoster Rowe at the Signe of the Talbot." 1593, 4to. My copy was Brand's, and formed Lot 8224 in his Sale Catalogue.

[2] Lord Bacon thinks (see his *Sylva Sylvarum*) that soporiferous medicines "are likeliest" for this purpose, such as henbane, hemlock, mandrake, moonshade, tobacco, opium, saffron, poplar leaves, &c.
[3] See his *History of the World*.
[4] See his *Table Talk*, section "*Witches*."
[5] Sir Thomas Browne's evidence at the trial of Amy Duny and Rose Cullender at Bury St. Edmunds in 1664, is too well known to need an extract from the frequently reprinted report of the case. To adopt the words of an able writer,

vacillating bigotry of Sir Matthew Hale;[6]—Hobbes, ever sceptical, penetrating and sagacious, yet here paralyzed, and shrinking from the subject as if afraid to touch it;[7]— The adventurous explorer, who sounded the depths and channels of the "Intellectual System" along all the "wide watered" shores of antiquity, running after witches to hear them recite the Common Prayer and the Creed, as a rational test of guilt or innocence;[8]—The gentle spirit of Dr. Henry More, girding on the armour of persecution, and rousing itself from a Platonic reverie on the Divine Life, to assume the hood and cloak of a familiar of the Inquisition;[9]—and

---

(*Retros. Review*, vol. v. p. 118,) "this trial is the only place in which we ever meet with the name of Sir Thomas Browne without pleasurable associations."
[6] Those who wish to have presented to them a faithful likeness of Sir Matthew Hale must not consult Burnet or Baxter, for that great judge, like Sir Epicure Mammon, sought "for his meet flatterers the gravest of divines," but will not fail to find it in the pages of Roger North, who has depicted his character with a strength and accuracy of outline which no Vandyck or Lely of biography ever surpassed. Would that we could exchange some of those "faultless monsters" with which that fascinating department of literature too much abounds, for a few more such instantly recognised specimens of true but erring and unequal humanity, which are as rare as they are precious. In the unabridged life of Lord Guildford by Roger North, which, with his own most interesting and yet unpublished autobiography, are in my possession in his autograph, are found some additional touches which confirm the general accuracy of the portrait he has sketched of Hale in the work which has been printed. (Vide North's *Life of Lord Guildford*, by Roscoe, vol. i. p. 119.)
[7] See his *Dialogue on the Common Laws of England*.
[8] Dr. Cudworth was the friend whom More refers to without naming, *Collections of Relations*, p. 336, edit. 1726, 8vo.
[9] There is no name in this catalogue that excites more poignant regret than that of Dr. Henry More. So exalted was his character, so serene and admirable his temper, so full of harmony his whole intellectual constitution, that, irradiated at once by all the lights of religion and philosophy, and with clearer glimpses of the land of vision and the glories behind the veil than perhaps uninspired mortality ever partook of before, he seems to have reached as near to the full standard of perfection as it is possible for frail and feeble humanity to attain. Dr. Outram said that he looked upon Dr. More as the holiest person upon the face of the earth; and the sceptical Hobbes, who never dealt in compliment, observed, "That if his own philosophy were not true, he knew of none that he

the patient and enquiring Boyle, putting aside for a while his searches for the grand Magisterium, and listening, as if spell-bound, with gratified attention to stories of witches at Oxford, and devils at Mascon.[10] Nor is it from a retrospect of our own intellectual progress only that we find how capricious, how intermitting, and how little privileged to great names or high intellects, or even to those minds which seemed to possess the very qualifications which would operate as conductors, are those illuminating gleams of common sense which shoot athwart the gloom, and aid a nation on its tardy progress to wisdom, humanity, and justice. If on the Continent there were, in the sixteenth century, two men from whom an exposure of the absurdities of the system of witchcraft might have been naturally and rationally expected, and who seem to stand

---

should sooner like than More's of Cambridge." His biographer, Ward, concludes his life in the following glowing terms:—"Thus lived and died the eminent Dr. More: thus set this bright and illustrious star, vanishing by degrees out of our sight after, to the surprise and admiration of many, (like that which was observed in Cassiopeia's chair,) it had illuminated, as it were, both worlds so long at once." At the lapse of many years I have not forgotten the impassioned fondness with which the late and most lamented Robert Southey dwelt upon the memory of the Cambridge Plato, or the delight with which he greeted some works of his favourite author which I was fortunate enough to point out to him, with which he had not been previously acquainted. The sad reverse of the picture will be seen by those who consult the folio of More's philosophical works and Glanville's *Sadducismus Triumphatus*, the greatest part of which is derived from More's *Collections*. His hallucinations on the subject of witchcraft, from which none of the English writers of the Platonic school were exempt, are the more extraordinary, as a sister error, judicial astrology, met in More with its most able oppugner. His tract, which has excited much less attention than its merit deserves, (I have not been able to trace a single quotation from it in any author during the last century,) is entitled "Tetractys Anti-astrologica, or a Confutation of Astrology." Lond. 1681, 4to. I may mention while on the subject of More, that the second and most valuable part of the memoir of him by Ward, his devoted admirer and pupil, which was never printed, is in my possession, in manuscript.

[10] See Boyle's letter on the subject of the latter, in the 5th vol. of the folio edition of his works.

out prominently from the crowd as predestined to that honourable and salutary office, those two men were John Bodin[11] and Thomas Erastus.[12] The former a lawyer—much exercised in the affairs of men—whose learning was not merely umbratic—whose knowledge of history was most philosophic and exact—of piercing penetration and sagacity—tolerant—liberal minded—disposed to take no proposition upon trust, but to canvass and examine every thing for himself, and who had large views of human nature and society—in fact, the Montesquieu of the seventeenth century. The other, a physician and professor, sage, judicious, incredulous,

"The scourge of impostors, the terror of quacks,"

---

[11] I have always considered the conclusion of Bodin's book, *De Republica*, the accumulative grandeur of which is even heightened in Knolles's admirable English translation, as the finest peroration to be found in any work on government. Those who are fortunate enough to possess a copy of his interdicted *Examination of Religions*, the title of which is, "Colloquium heptaplomeres de abditis sublimium rerum arcanis, libris 6 digestum," which was never printed, and of which very few MSS. copies are in existence, are well aware how little he felt himself shackled in the spirit of examination which he carried into the most sacred subjects by any respect for popular notions or received systems or great authorities. My MS. copy of this extraordinary work, which came from Heber's Collection, is contained in two rather thick folio volumes.

[12] Few authors are better deserving of an extended biography, a desideratum which, in an age characterised by its want of literary research, is not likely to be soon supplied, than Thomas Erastus, whose theological, philosophical, and medical celebrity entitle him to rank with the greatest men of his century. At present we have to collect all that is known of his life from various scattered and contradictory sources. John Webster, in his *Displaying of Supposed Witchcraft*, contrary to the usual candour and fairness of his judgments, speaks slightingly of Erastus. There was, however, a sufficient reason for this. Erastus had shown up the empiricism of Webster's idol Paracelsus, and was in great disfavour with the writers of the Anti-Galenic school.

who had routed irrecoverably empiricism in almost every shape—Paracelsians—Astrologers—Alchemists—Rosicrucians—and who weighed and scrutinized and analyzed every conclusion, from excommunication and the power of the keys to the revolutions of comets and their supposed effects on empires, and all with perfect fearlessness and intuitive insight into the weak points of an argument. Yet, alas! for human infirmity. Bodin threw all the weight of his reasoning and learning and vivacity into the scale of the witch supporters, and made the "hell-broth boil and bubble" anew, and increased the witch *furor* to downright fanaticism, by the publication of his *Demomanie*,[13] a work in which

"Learning, blinded first and then beguiled,
Looks dark as ignorance, as frenzy wild;"

but which it is impossible to read without being carried along by the force of mind and power of combination which the author manifests, and without feeling how much ingenious sophistry can perform to mitigate and soften the most startling absurdity. His contemporary, Erastus, after all his victories on the field of imposition, was foiled by the subject of witchcraft at last. This was his pet delusion—almost the only one he cared not to discard—like the dying miser's last reserve:—

—— "My manor, sir? he cried;
Not that, I cannot part with that,—and died."

---

[13] I cannot concur with Mr. Hallam in the extremely low estimate he forms of the literary merit of Bodin's *Demomanie*, which he does not seem to have examined with the care and impartiality which he seldom is deficient in. Like all Bodin's works, it has a spirit peculiarly his own, and is, in my opinion, one of the most entertaining books to be found in the circle of Demonology.

In his treatise *De Lamiis*, published in 1577, 8vo., he defends nearly all the absurdities of the system with a blind zealotry which in such a man is very remarkable. His book has accordingly taken its place on the same shelf with Sprenger, Remigius, Delrio, and De Lancre, and deserves insertion only in a list which has yet to be made out, and which if accurately compiled would be a literary curiosity, of the singularly illogical books of singularly able reasoners. What was left unaccomplished by the centurions of literature came ultimately from the strangest of all possible quarters; from the study of an humble pupil of the transmuter of metals and prince of mountebanks and quacks—the expounder of Reuchlin *de verbo mirifico*, and lecturer in the unknown tongues—the follower of Trismegistus—cursed with bell, book and candle, by every decorous Church in Christendom—the redoubted Cornelius Agrippa; who, if he left not to his pupil Wierus the secret of the philosopher's stone or grand elixir, seems to have communicated a treasure perhaps equally rare and not less precious, the faculty of seeing a truth which should open the eyes of bigotry and dispel the mists of superstition, which should stop the persecution of the helpless and stay the call for blood. If, in working out this virgin ore from the mine, he has produced it mixed up with the *scoria* of his master's *Occult Philosophy*; if he gives us catalogues of devils and spirits, with whose acquaintance we could have dispensed; if he pleads the great truth faintly, inconsistently, imperfectly, and is evidently unaware of the strength of the weapons he wields; these deductions do not the less entitle Wierus to take his place in the first rank of Humanity's honoured professors, the true philanthropists and noble benefactors of mankind.

In our own country, it may be curious and edifying to observe to whom we mainly owe those enlightened views on this subject, which might have been expected to proceed in their natural channel, but for which we look in vain, from the "triumphant heirs of universal praise," the recognized guides of public opinion, whose fame sheds such a lustre on our annals,—the Bacons, the Raleighs, the Seldens, the Cudworths, and the Boyles.

The strangely assorted and rather grotesque band to whom we are principally indebted for a vindication of outraged common sense and insulted humanity in this instance, and whose vigorous exposition of the absurdities of the prevailing system, in combination with other lights and sources of intelligence, led at last to its being universally abandoned, consists of four individuals—on any of whom a literary Pharisee would look down with supercilious scorn:—a country gentleman, devoted to husbandry, and deep in platforms of hop gardens,[14]—a baronet, whose name for upwards of a century has been used as a synonyme for incurable political bigotry,[15]—a little, crooked, and now forgotten man, who died, as his biographer tells us, "distracted, occasioned by a deep conceit of his own parts, and by a continual bibbing of strong and high tasted liquors,"[16]—and last, but not least assuredly, of one who was by turns a fanatical preacher and an obscure practitioner of physic, and who passed his old age at Clitheroe in Lancashire in attempting to transmute metals and discover the philosopher's stone.[17] So strange a band of Apostles of reason may occasion a smile; it deserves, at all events, a little more particular consideration before we address ourselves to the short narration which may be deemed necessary as an introduction to the republication which follows.

---

[14] Reginald Scot.
[15] Sir R. Filmer.
[16] John Wagstaffe.
[17] John Webster.

Of the first of the number, Reginald or Reynold Scot, it is to be regretted that more particulars are not known. Nearly the whole are contained in the following information afforded by Anthony à Wood, *Athenæ.*, vol. i. p. 297; from which it appears that he took to "solid reading" at a crisis of life when it is generally thrown aside. "Reynolde Scot, a younger son of Sir John Scot, of Scot's Hall, near to Smeeth, in Kent, by his wife, daughter of Reynolde Pimp, of Pimp's Court, Knight, was born in that county, and at about 17 years of age was sent to Oxon, particularly as it seems to Hart Hall, where several of his countrymen and name studied in the latter end of K. Henry VIII. and the reign of Edward VI., &c. Afterwards he retired to his native country, without the honour of a Degree, and settled at Smeeth, where he found great encouragement in his studies from his kinsman, Sir Thomas Scot. *About which time, taking to him a wife, he gave himself up solely to solid reading*, to the perusing of obscure authors that had, by the generality of scholars, been neglected, and at times of leisure to husbandry and gardening. He died in September or October in 1599, and was buried among his ancestors, in the church at Smeeth before mentioned." Retired as his life and obscure as his death might be, he is one whose name will be remembered as long as vigorous sense, flowing from the "wells of English undefiled," hearty and radiant humour, and sterling patriotism, are considered as deserving of commemoration. His *Discoverie of Witchcraft*, first published in 1584, is indeed a treat to him who wishes to study the idioms, manners, opinions, and superstitions of the reign of Elizabeth. Its entire title deserves to be given:—

"*The discouerie of witchcraft, wherein the lewde dealing of witches and witchmongers is notablie detected, the knauerie of coniurors, the impietie of inchantors, the follie of soothsaiers, the impudent falshood of cousenors, the infidelitie of atheists, the pestilent practises of Pythonists, the curiositie of figurecasters, the vanitie of dreamers, the beggerlie art of Alcumystrie, the abhomination of idolatrie, the horrible art of poisoning, the vertue and power of naturall magike, and all the conueiances of Legierdemaine and iuggling are deciphered: and many other things opened, which haue long lien hidden, howbeit verie necessarie to be knowne. Heerevnto is added a treatise vpon the nature and substance of spirits and diuels, &c: all latelie written by Reginald Scot Esquire.* 1 John, 4, 1. *Beleeue not euerie spirit but trie the spirits, whether they are of God; for many false prophets are gone out into the world, &c.* 1584."

This title is sufficient to show that he gives no quarter to the delusion he undertakes to expose, and though he does not deny that there may be witches in the abstract, (to have done so would have left him a preacher without an audience,) yet he guards so cautiously against any practical application of that principle, and battles so vigorously against the error which assimilated the witches of modern times to the witches of Scripture, and, denying the validity of the confessions of those convicted, throws such discredit and ridicule upon the whole system, that the popular belief cannot but have received a severe shock from the publication of his work.[18] By an extraordinary elevation of

---

[18] In the epistle to his kinsman Sir Thomas Scot, prefixed to his *Discoverie*, he observes:—

"I see among other malefactors manie poore old women conuented before you for working of miracles, other wise called witchcraft, and therefore I thought you also a meet person to whom I might commend my booke."—And he then proceeds, in the following spirited and gallant strain, to run his course against the Dagon of popular superstition:—

"I therefore (at this time) doo onelie desire you to consider of my report, concerning the euidence that is commonlie brought before you against them. See first whether the euidence be not friuolous, & whether the proofs brought against them be not incredible, consisting of ghesses, presumptions, &

impossibilities contrarie to reason, scripture, and nature. See also what persons complaine vpon them, whether they be not of the basest, the vnwisest, & most faithles kind of people. Also may it please you to waie what accusations and crimes they laie to their charge, namelie: She was at my house of late, she would haue had a pot of milke, she departed in a chafe bicause she had it not, she railed, she curssed, she mumbled and whispered, and finallie she said she would be euen with me: and soone after my child, my cow, my sow, or my pullet died, or was strangelie taken. Naie (if it please your Worship) I haue further proofe: I was with a wise woman, and she told me I had an ill neighbour, & that she would come to my house yer it were long, and so did she; and that she had a marke aboue hir waste, & so had she: and God forgiue me, my stomach hath gone against hir a great while. Hir mother before hir was counted a witch, she hath beene beaten and scratched by the face till bloud was drawne vpon hir, bicause she hath beene suspected, & afterwards some of those persons were said to amend. These are the certeinties that I heare in their euidences.

"*Note also how easilie they may be brought to confesse that which they neuer did, nor lieth in the power of man to doo*: and then see whether I haue cause to write as I doo. Further, if you shall see that infidelitie, poperie, and manie other manifest heresies be backed and shouldered, and their professors animated and hartened, by yeelding to creatures such infinit power as is wrested out of Gods hand, and attributed to witches: finallie, if you shall perceiue that I haue faithfullie and trulie deliuered and set downe the condition and state of the witch, and also of the witchmonger, and haue confuted by reason and lawe, and by the word of God it selfe, all mine aduersaries obiections and arguments: then let me haue your countenance against them that maliciouslie oppose themselues against me.

"*My greatest aduersaries are yoong ignorance and old custome.* For what follie soeuer tract of time hath fostered, it is so superstitiouslie pursued of some, as though no error could be acquainted with custome. But if the lawe of nations would ioine with such custome, to the maintenance of ignorance, and to the suppressing of knowledge; the ciuilest countrie in the world would soone become barbarous, &c. For as knowledge and time discouereth errors, so dooth superstition and ignorance in time breed them."

The passage which I next quote, is a further specimen of the impressive and even eloquent earnestness with which he pleads his cause:—

"In the meane time, I would wish them to know that if neither the estimation of Gods omnipotencie, nor the tenor of his word, nor the doubtfulnes or rather the impossibilitie of the case, nor the small proofes brought against them, nor the rigor executed vpon them, nor the pitie that should be in a christian heart, nor yet their simplicitie, impotencie, or age may suffice to suppresse the rage or rigor wherewith they are oppressed; yet the consideration of their sex or kind ought to mooue some mitigation of their punishment. For

good sense, he managed, not only to see through the absurdities of witchcraft, but likewise of other errors which long maintained their hold upon the learned as well as the vulgar. Indeed, if not generally more enlightened, he was,

---

if nature (as Plinie reporteth) haue taught a lion not to deale so roughlie with a woman as with a man, bicause she is in bodie the weaker vessell, and in hart more inclined to pitie (which Ieremie in his lamentations seemeth to confirme) what should a man doo in this case, for whome a woman was created as an helpe and comfort vnto him? In so much as, euen in the lawe of nature, it is a greater offense to slea a woman than a man: not bicause a man is not the more excellent creature, but bicause a woman is the weaker vessell. And therefore among all modest and honest persons it is thought a shame to offer violence or iniurie to a woman: in which respect Virgil saith, *Nullum memorabile nomen fœminea in pœna est.*

"God that knoweth my heart is witnes, and you that read my booke shall see, that my drift and purpose in this enterprise tendeth onelie to these respects. First, that the glorie and power of God be not so abridged and abased, as to be thrust into the hand or lip of a lewd old woman: whereby the worke of the Creator should be attributed to the power of a creature. Secondlie, that the religion of the gospell may be seene to stand without such peeuish trumperie. Thirdlie, that lawfull fauour and christian compassion be rather vsed towards these poore soules, than rigor and extremitie. Bicause they, which are commonlie accused of witchcraft, are the least sufficient of all other persons to speake for themselues; as hauing the most base and simple education of all others; the extremitie of their age giuing them leaue to dote, their pouertie to beg, their wrongs to chide and threaten (as being void of anie other waie of reuenge) their humor melancholicall to be full of imaginations, from whence cheefelie proceedeth the vanitie of their confessions; as that they can transforme themselues and others into apes, owles, asses, dogs, cats, &c: that they can flie in the aire, kill children with charmes, hinder the comming of butter, &c.

"And for so much as the mightie helpe themselues together, and the poore widowes crie, though it reach to heauen, is scarse heard here vpon earth: I thought good (according to my poore abilitie) to make intercession, that some part of common rigor, and some points of hastie iudgement may be aduised vpon. For the world is now at that stay (as Brentius in a most godlie sermon in these words affirmeth) that euen as when the heathen persecuted the christians, if anie were accused to beleeue in Christ, the common people cried *Ad leonem*: so now, if anie woman, be she neuer so honest, be accused of witchcraft, they crie *Ad ignem.*"

in some respects, more emancipated from delusion than even his great successor, the learned and sagacious Webster, who, a century after, clung still to alchemy which Reginald Scot had ridiculed and exposed. Yet with all its strong points and broad humour, it is undeniable that *The Discoverie of Witchcraft* only scotched the snake instead of killing it; and that its effect was any thing but final and complete. Inveterate error is seldom prostrated by a blow from one hand, and truth seems to be a tree which cannot be forced by planting it before its time. There was something, too, in the book itself which militated against its entire acceptance by the public. It is intended to form a little Encyclopædia of the different arts of imposition practised in Scot's time; and in order to illustrate the various tricks and modes of cozenage, he gives us so many charms and diagrams and conjurations, to say nothing of an inventory of seventy-nine devils and spirits, and their several seignories and degrees, that the *Occult Philosophy* of Cornelius Agrippa himself looks scarcely less appalling, at first sight, than the *Discoverie*. This gave some colour to the declamation of the author's opponents, who held him up as Wierus had been represented before him, as if he were as deeply dipped in diabolical practises as any of those whom he defended. Atheist and Sadducee, if not very wizard himself, were the terms in which his name was generally mentioned, and as such, the royal author of the *Demonology* anathematizes him with great unction and very edifying horror. Against the papists, the satire of Scot had been almost as much directed as against what he calls the "witch-mongers," so that that very powerful party were to a man opposed to him. Vigorous, therefore, as was his onslaught, its effect soon passed by; and when on the accession of James, the statute which so long disgraced our penal code was enacted, as the adulatory tribute of all parties, against which no honest voice was raised, to the known opinions of the monarch, Scot became too unfashionable to be seen on the tables of the great or in the libraries of the learned. If he were noticed, it was only to be traduced as a sciolist, (imperitus dialecticæ et aliarum bonarum artium, says Dr. Reynolds,) and to be exposed for imagined lapses in scholarship in an age when for a writer not to be a scholar, was like a traveller journeying without a passport. Meric Casaubon, who carried all the prejudices of the time of James the first into the reign of Charles the second, but who, though overshadowed by the fame of his father, was no unworthy scion of that incomparable stock, at the same time that he denounces Scot as illiterate, will only acknowledge to having met with him "at friends houses" and "booksellers shops," as if his work were one which would bring contamination to a scholar's library. Scot was certainly not a scholar in the sense in which the term is applied to the Scaligers, Casaubons, and Vossius's, though he would have been considered a prodigy of reading in these days of superficial acquisition. But he had original gifts far transcending scholarship. He had a manly, straightforward, vigorous understanding, which, united with an honest integrity of purpose, kept him right when greater men went wrong. How invaluable a phalanx would the battalion of folios which the reign of James the first produced now afford us, if the admirable mother-wit and single-minded sincerity of Reginald Scot could only have vivified and informed them.[19]

---

[19] In the intervening period between the publication of Soot's work and the advertisement of Filmer, several books came out on the subject of witchcraft. Amongst them it is right to notice "A Dialogue concerning Witches and Witchcraft, by George Giffard, Minister of God's Word in Maldon," 1593, 4to. This tract, which has been reprinted by the Percy Society, is not free from the leading fallacies which infected the reasonings of almost all the writers on witchcraft. It is, nevertheless, exceedingly entertaining, and well deserves a perusal, if only as transmitting to us, in their full freshness, the racy colloquialisms of the age of Elizabeth. It is to be hoped that the other works of Giffard, all of which are deserving of attention, independently of their

theological interest, as specimens of pure and sterling English, may appear in a collected form. The next tract requiring notice is "The Trial of Witchcraft, by John Cotta," 1616, 4to, of which a second and enlarged edition was published in 1624. Cotta, who was a physician of great eminence and experience, residing at Northampton, has supplied in this very able, learned, and vigorous treatise, a groundwork which, if pursued to its just results, for he writes very cautiously and guardedly, and rather hints at his conclusions than follows them out, would have sufficed to have overthrown many of the positions of the supporters of the system of witchcraft. His work has a strong scholastic tinge, and is not without occasional obscurity; and on these accounts probably produced no very extensive impression at the time. He wrote two other tracts—1. "Discovery of the Dangers of ignorant practisers of Physick in England," 1612, 4to; 2. "Cotta contra Antonium, or An Ant-Anthony," Oxford, 1623, 4to; the latter of which, a keen satire against the chymists' aurum potabile, is exceedingly rare. Both are intrinsically valuable and interesting, and written with great vigour of style, and are full of curious illustrations derived from his extensive medical practice. I cannot conclude this note without adverting to Gaule's amusing little work, ("Select Cases of Conscience touching Witches and Witchcraft, by John Gaule, Preacher of the Word at Great Haughton, in the county of Huntingdon," 1646, 24mo.) which gives us all the casuistry applicable to witchcraft. We can almost forgive Gaule's fundamental errors on the general question, for the courage and spirit with which he battled with the villainous witchfinder, Hopkins, who wanted sorely to make an example of him, to the terror of all gainsayers of the sovereign power of this examiner-general of witches. Gaule proved himself to be an overmatch for the itinerating inquisitor, and so effectually attacked, battled with, and exposed him, as to render him quite harmless in future. The minister of Great Haughton was made of different metal to the "old reading parson Lewis," or Lowes, to whose fate Baxter refers with such nonchalance. As the only clergyman of the Church of England, that I am aware of, who was executed for witchcraft, Lewis's case is sufficiently interesting to merit some notice. Stearne's (vide his *Confirmation of Witchcraft*, p. 23,) account of it, which I have not seen quoted before, is as follows:—

"Thus was Parson Lowis taken, who had been a Minister, (as I have heard) in one Parish above forty yeares, in Suffolke, before he was condemned, but had been indited for a common imbarriter, and for Witchcraft, above thirty yeares before, and the grand Jury (as I have heard) found the bill for a common imbarriter, who now, after he was found with the markes, in his confession, he confessed, that in pride of heart, to be equall, or rather above God, the Devill tooke advantage of him, and hee covenanted with the Devill, and sealed it with his bloud, and had three Familiars or spirits, which sucked on the markes found upon his body, and did much harme, both by Sea and Land, especially by Sea, for he confessed, that he being at Lungarfort in Suffolke, where he preached, as he walked upon the wall, or workes there, he saw a great saile of Ships passe by, and that as they were sailing by, one of his three Impes, namely his yellow one, forthwith appeared to him, and asked him what hee should doe, and he bade it goe and sinke such a Ship, and shewed his Impe a new Ship, amongst the middle of the rest (as I remember) one that belonged to Ipswich, so he confessed the Impe went forthwith away, and he stood still, and viewed the Ships on the Sea as they were a sayling, and perceived that Ship immediately, to be in more trouble and danger then the rest; for he said, the water was more boystrous neere that then the rest, tumbling up and down with waves, as if water had been boyled in a pot, and soone after (he said) in a short time it sanke directly downe into the Sea, as he stood and viewed it, when all the rest sayled away in safety, there he confessed, he made fourteen widdowes in one quarter of an houre. Then Mr. Hopkin, as he told me (for he tooke his Confession) asked him, if it did not grieve him to see so many men cast away, in a short time, and that he should be the cause of so many poore widdowes on a suddaine, but he swore by his maker, no, he was joyfull to see what power his Impes had, and so likewise confessed many other mischiefes, and had a charme to keep him out of Goale, and hanging, as he paraphrased it himselfe, but therein the Devill deceived him; for he was hanged, that Michaelmas time 1645. at Burie Saint Edmunds, but he made a very farre larger confession, which I have heard hath been printed: but if it were so, it was neither of Mr. Hopkins doing nor mine owne; for we never printed anything untill now." Hutchinson gives the explanation of this confession. What can be more atrocious than the whole story, which is yet but the common story of witch confessions?

"*Adv.* Then did not he confess this before the Commissioners, at the Time of his Tryal?

"*Clerg.* No, but maintained his Innocence stoutly, and challenged them to make Proof of such Things as they laid to his Charge. I had this from a Person of Credit, who was then in Court, and heard his Tryal. I may add, that tho' his Case is remembered better than others that suffered, yet I never heard any one speak of him, but with great Compassion, because of his Age and Character, and their Belief of his Innocence: And when he came to his Execution, because he would have Christian Burial, he read the Office himself, and that way committed his own Body to the Ground, in sure and certain Hope of the Resurrection to eternal Life.

"In the Notes upon those Verses that I quoted out of Hudibras, it is said, that he had been a painful Preacher for many Years, I may add for Fifty, for so long he had been Vicar of Brandeston in the County of Suffolk, as appears by the Time of his Institution. That I might know the present Sense of the Chief Inhabitants of that Place, I wrote to Mr. Wilson, the Incumbent of that Town, and by his Means received the following Letter from Mr. Rivett, a worthy

After the lapse of another half century, and at the very period when the persecution against witches waxed hotter, and the public prejudice had become only more inveterate, from the ingredient of fanaticism having been largely thrown in as a stimulant, another ally to the cause of compassion and common sense started up, in the person of one whose name has rounded many a period and given point to many an invective. To find the proscribed author of the *Patriarcha* purging with "euphrasy and rue" the eyes of the dispensers of justice, and shouldering the crowd to obtain for reason a fair and impartial hearing, is indeed like meeting with Saul among the prophets. If there be one name which has been doomed to run the gauntlet, and against which every pert and insolent political declaimer has had his fling, it is that of this unfortunate writer; yet in his short but masterly and unanswerable "Advertisement to the Jurymen of England, touching Witches, together with a difference between an English and Hebrew Witch," first published in 1653, 4to., he has addressed himself so cogently and decisively to the main fallacy of the arguments in favour of witchcraft which rested their force on Scripture misunderstood, and has so pertinently and popularly urged the points to be considered, that his tract

---

Gentleman who lived lately in the same Place, and whose Father lived there before him.

"'SIR,

"'In Answer to your Request concerning Mr. Lowes, my Father was always of the opinion, that Mr. Lowes suffered wrongfully, and hath often said, that he did believe, he was no more a Wizzard than he was. I have heard it from them that watched with him, that *they kept him awake several Nights together, and run him backwards and forwards about the Room, until he was out of Breath: Then they rested him a little, and then ran him again: And thus they did for several Days and Nights together, till he was weary of his Life, and was scarce sensible of what he said or did.* They swam him at Framlingham, but that was no true Rule to try him by; for they put in honest People at the same Time, and they swam as well as he."

must have had the greatest weight on the class to whom his reasoning was principally addressed, and on whose fiat the fates of his unhappy clients may be said to have hung. For this good service, reason and common sense owe Sir Robert Filmer a debt which does not yet appear to have been paid. The verdict of proscription against him was pronounced by the most incompetent and superficial æra of our literature, and no friendly appellant has yet moved the court of posterity for its reversal. Yet without entering upon the theory of the patriarchal scheme, which after all, perhaps, was not so irrational as may be supposed, or discussing on an occasion like the present the conflicting theories of government, it may be allowable to express a doubt whether even the famous author of the "Essay on the Human Understanding," to whose culminating star the decadence of the rival intelligence is attributable, can be shewn to have been as much in advance of his generation in the time of king William, as from the tract on witchcraft, and another written on a different subject, but with equally enlightened views,[20] Sir Robert Filmer manifestly appears to have outrun his at the period of the usurpation.[21]

---

[20] I allude to his little tract on Usury.

[21] Between the period of the publication of Filmer's Advertisement and the appearance of Wagstaffe's work, a tract was published too important in this controversy to be passed over without notice. It is entitled *A Candle in the Dark, or a Treatise concerning the Nature of Witches and Witchcraft; being Advice to Judges, Sheriffs, Justices of the Peace, and Grand Jurymen, what to do before they passe sentence on such as are arraigned for their lives as Witches. By Thomas Ady, M.A. London, printed for R.J., to be sold by Thomas Newberry, at the Three Lions in Cornhill, by the Exchange, 1656,* 4to. Ady, of whom, unfortunately, nothing is known, presses the arguments against the witchmongers and witchfinders with unanswerable force. In fact, this tract comprises the quintessence of all that had been urged against the popular system, and his "Candle" was truly a burning and a shining light. His Dedication is too curious to be omitted:—

"To the Prince of the Kings of the Earth. It is the manner of men, O heavenly King, to dedicate their books to some great men, thereby to have their works

The next champion in this unpopular cause, John Wagstaffe, who published "The Question of Witchcraft Debated," 1669, 12mo,[22] was, as A. à Wood informs us, "the son of John Wagstaffe, citizen of London, descended from those of his name of Hasland Hall, in Derbyshire, was born in Cheapside, within the city of London, became a commoner of Oriel College in the latter end of 1649, took the degrees in Arts, and applied himself to the study of politics and other learning. At length, being raised from an academical life to the inheritance of Hasland, by the death of an uncle, who died without male issue, he spent his life afterwards in single estate." His death took place in 1677. The Oxford historian, who had little reverence for new lights, and never loses an opportunity of girding at those whose weights and measures were not according to the current and only authentic standard, has left no very flattering account of his person. "He was a little crooked

---

protected and countenanced among them; but thou only art able, by thy holy Spirit of Truth, to defend thy Truth, and to make it take impression in the heart and understanding of men. Unto thee alone do I dedicate this work, entreating thy Most High Majesty to grant, that whoever shall open this book, thy holy Spirit may so possess their understanding, as that the Spirit of errour may depart from them, and that they may read and try thy Truth by the touchstone of thy Truth, the holy Scriptures; and finding that Truth, may embrace it and forsake their darksome inventions of Antichrist, that have deluded and defiled the nations now and in former ages. Enlighten the world, thou that art the Light of the World, and let darkness be no more in the world, now or in any future age; but make all people to walk as children of the Light for ever; and destroy Antichrist, that hath deceived the nations, and save us the residue by thyself alone; and let not Satan any more delude us, for the Truth is thine for ever." He then puts his "Dilemma that cannot be answered by Witchmongers." It is too long to quote, but it is a dilemma that would pose the stoutest Coryphæus of the party to whom he addressed himself.

[22] I have not seen his earlier work, "Historical Reflections on the Bishop of Rome, &c." Oxford, 1660, 4to. If it be written with any portion of the power evinced in his "Question of Witchcraft Debated," the ridicule with which Wood says it was received by the wits of the university, and the oblivion into which it subsequently fell, were both equally undeserved.

man, and of a despicable presence. He was laughed at by the boys of this University, because, as they said, he himself looked like a little wizard." Small as might be his stature, and questionable the shape in which he appeared, he might still have taken up the boast of the author of the *Religio Medici*: "Men that look upon my outside do err in my altitude, for I am above Atlas's shoulders." None but a large-souled and kindly-affectioned man, whose intellect was as comprehensive as his feelings were benevolent, could have produced the excellent little treatise which claims him as its author. The following is the lofty and memorable peroration in which he sums up the strength of his cause:—

"I cannot think without trembling and horror on the vast numbers of people that in several ages and several countries have been sacrificed unto this idol, Opinion. Thousands, ten thousands, are upon record to have been slain, and many of them not with simple deaths, but horrid, exquisite tortures. And yet, how many are there more who have undergone the same fate, of whom we have no memorial extant. Since, therefore, the opinion of witchcraft is a mere stranger unto Scripture, and wholly alien from true religion; since it is ridiculous by asserting fables and impossibilities; since it appears, when duly considered, to be all bloody and full of dangerous consequence unto the lives and safety of men; I hope that with this my Discourse, opposing an absurd and pernicious error, I can not at all disoblige any sober, unbiassed person; especially if he be of such ingenuity as to have freed himself from a slavish subjection unto those prejudicial opinions which custom and education do with too much tyranny impose.—If the doctrine of witchcraft should be carried up to a height, and the inquisition after it should be intrusted in the hands of ambitious, covetous and malicious men, it would prove of far more fatal consequence unto the lives and safety of mankind, than that ancient, heathenish custom of sacrificing men unto idol gods; insomuch that we stand in need of another Hercules Liberator, who, as the former freed the world from human sacrifice, should, in like manner, travel from country to country, and by his all-commanding authority, free it from *this euil and base custom of torturing people to confess themselves witches, and burning them after extorted confessions.* Surely the blood of men ought not to be so cheap, nor so easily to be shed by those who, under the name of God, do gratifie exorbitant passions and selfish ends; for without question, under this side heaven, there is nothing so sacred as the life of man; for the preservation whereof all policies and forms of government, all laws and magistrates are most especially ordained. Wherefore I presume that this Discourse of mine, attempting to prove the vanity and impossibility of witchcraft, is so far from any deserved censure and blame, that it rather deserves commendation and praise, if I can the least measure contribute to the saving of the lives of men."

Wagstaffe was answered by Meric Casaubon in his treatise "Of Credulity and Incredulity in Things Divine and Spiritual," 1670, 12mo; and if his reply be altogether inconclusive, it cannot be denied to be, as indeed every thing of Meric Casaubon's writing was, learned, discursive and entertaining. He observes of Wagstaffe:—

"He doth make some show of a scholar and a man of some learning, but whether he doth acquit himself as a gentleman (which I hear he is) in it, I shall leave to others to judge." This is surely the first time that a belief in witchcraft was ever made a test of gentlemanly propriety.

Two years before the trial, which is the subject of the following republication, took place, the hamlet of

Thornton, in the parish of Coxwold, in the adjoining county of York, gave birth to one who was destined so utterly to demolish the unstable and already shaken and tottering structure which Bodin, Delrio, and their followers had set up, as not to leave one stone of that unhallowed edifice remaining upon another. Of the various course of life of John Webster, the author of "The Displaying of supposed Witchcraft," his travels, troubles, and persecutions; of the experience he had had in restless youth and in unsettled manhood of religion under various forms, amongst religionists of almost every denomination; and of those profound and wide-ranging researches in every art and science in which his vigorous intellect delighted, and by which it was in declining age enlightened, sobered and composed; it is much to be regretted that we have not his own narrative, written in the calm evening of his days, when he walked the slopes of Pendle, from where,

"Through shadow dimly seen
Rose Clid'row's castle grey;"[23]

when, to use his own expressions, he lived a "solitary and sedentary life, *mihi et musis*, having more converse with the dead than the living, that is, more with books than with men." The facts for his biography are scanty and meagre, and are rather collected by inference from his works, than from any other source. He was born at Thornton on the 3rd of February, 1610. From a passing notice of A. à Wood, and an incidental allusion in his own works, he may be presumed to have passed some time at Cambridge, though

---

[23] "Poems, by the Rev. R. Parkinson, Canon of Manchester," 1845, 12mo. (Hunter's Song.) A most pleasing volume of a very accomplished author. Long may he survive to add honours to the ancient stock of which he has given so interesting an account, by well-earned trophies gathered from the fair fields of literature and theology, and by a most exemplary discharge of the appropriate duties of his own sacred profession.

with what views, or at what period of his life, is uncertain. He was ordained Presbyter by Dr. Morton, when Bishop of Durham, who was, it will be recollected, the sagacious prelate by whom the frauds of the boy of Bilson were detected. In the year 1634, Webster was curate of Kildwick in Craven, and while in that cure the scene occurred which he has so vividly sketched in the passage after quoted, and which supplied the hint, and laid the foundation, for the work which has perpetuated his fame. How long he continued in this cure we know not: but, if one authority may be relied on, he was Master of the Free Grammar School at Clitheroe in 1643. To this foundation he may be considered as a great benefactor, for, from information supplied from a manuscript source, I find that he recovered for its use, with considerable trouble and no small personal charge, an income of about £60. per annum, which had been given to the school, but was illegally diverted and withheld. From this period there is a blank in his biography for about ten years. Most probably his life was rambling and desultory. He speaks of himself as having been about that time a chaplain in the army. His first two works, published in 1653 and 1654, "The Saints' Guide," and "The Judgment Set and the Books Opened,"[24] show that in the

---

[24] "*The Saints' Guide, or Christ the Rule and Ruler of Saints. Manifested by way of Positions, Consectaries, and Queries. Wherein is contained the Efficacy of Acquired Knowledge; the Rule of Christians; the Mission and Maintenance of Ministers; and the Power of Magistrates in Spiritual Things. By John Webster, late Chaplain in the Army.*" London, 1653, 4to.

"*The Judgement Set, and the Bookes Opened. Religion Tried whether it be of God or of men. The Lord cometh to visit his own, For the time is come that Judgement must begin at the House of God.*

               {  The Sheep from the Goats,

To separate  {  and

               {  The Precious from the Vile.

interval he had deserted the Established Church, and, probably, after some of those restless fluctuations of belief to which men of his ardent temperament are subject, settled at last in a wilder sort of Independency, which he eulogizes as "unmanacling the simple and pure light of the Gospel from the chains and fetters of cold and dead formality, and of restrictive and compulsory power." His language in these two works is more assimilated to that of the Seekers or Quakers, which it resembles in the cloudy mysteriousness of its phraseology, than that of the more rational and sober writers of the Independent school. Amongst the dregs of fanaticism of which they consist, the reader will look in vain for any germ or promise of future excellence or distinction as an author. It would seem that he preached the sermons contained in "The Judgment Set and Books Opened" at the church of All-Hallows, Lombard-street, at which he must have been for some time the officiating minister, and where the amusing incident, in which

---

*And to discover the Blasphemy of those that say,*

|  |  | { *Apostles,* } |  |  | { *Found Lyars,* |
|---|---|---|---|---|---|
|  |  | { *Teachers,* } |  |  | { *Deceivers,* |
| *They are* | { | *Alive,* | } | *but are* { | *Dead,* |
|  |  | { *Rich,* } |  |  | { *Poore, blind, naked,* |
|  |  | { *Jewes,* } |  |  | { *The Synagogue of Satan.* |

*In severall Sermons at Alhallows Lumbard-street, By John Webster, A servant of Christ and his Church. Micah 3. 5. &c. Thus saith the Lord, concerning the Prophets that make my people erre, that bite with their teeth, and cry peace: and he that putteth not into their mouths, they prepare war against him: Therefore night shall be upon them, that they shall not have a vision, &c. The Sun shall goe down over the prophets, and the Day shall be dark. Their seers shall be ashamed, and the Deviners confounded: yea, they shall All cover their lips, for there is no answer of God."* London, 1654. 4to.

Webster was concerned, narrated by Wood, which had many a parallel in those times, no doubt occurred. "On the 12th of Oct., 1653," says the author of the *Athenæ.*,[25] "he (*i.e.* William Erbury) with John Webster, sometimes a Cambridge scholar, endeavoured to knock down learning and the ministry both together, in a disputation that they then had against two ministers in a church in Lombard-street, in London. Erbury then declared that the wisest ministers and purest churches were at that time befool'd, confounded, and defil'd, by reason of learning. Another while he said, that the ministry were monsters, beasts, asses, greedy dogs, false prophets; and that they are the Beast with seven heads and ten horns. The same person also spoke out and said that Babylon is the Church in her ministers, and that the Great Whore is the Church in her worship, &c.; so that with him there was an end of ministers and churches and ordinations altogether. While these things were babbled to and fro, the multitude being of various opinions, began to mutter, and many to cry out, and immediately it came to a meeting or tumult, (call it which you please,) *wherein the women bore away the Bell, but lost some of them their kerchiefs*: and the dispute being hot, there was more danger of pulling down the church than the ministry."[26]

Of Erbury who, being originally in holy orders and a beneficed clergyman, deserted the Established Church and ran into all the excesses of Antinomianism, Webster was a great admirer, and has in a preface, hitherto unnoticed, prefixed to a scarce tract of Erbury's, entitled "The great Earthquake, or Fall of all the Churches," published in 1654, 4to, left a sketch of his opinions and character, in which his defence is undertaken with great zeal and no small

---

[25] *Athen. Oxon.*, Vol. ii., p. 175. Edit. 1721.
[26] Old Anthony chronicles this battle of the kerchiefs with a sly humour very different from his usual solemn matter-of-fact style.

ingenuity. One of his apologist's conclusions most of Erbury's readers will find no difficulty in assenting to, "the world is not ripe for such discoveries as our author held forth." The verses which are appended to this sketch, characterizing Erbury—

"As him
Who did the saintship sever
From the opinion; this fails, that shall never,
Chymist of Truth and Gospel;"—

are, also, evidently Webster's, and their quality is not such as to make us unreasonably impatient for any further manifestations of his poetical skill. In the year 1654 he published another tract of singular interest and curiosity, in which he attacks the Universities and the received system of education there, always with vigour and various learning, and frequently with success. It is entitled "Academiarum Examen, or the Examination of Academies; wherein is discussed and examined the matter, method, and customes of academick and scholastic learning, and the insufficiency thereof discovered and laid open; as also some expedients proposed for the reforming of schools, and the perfecting and promoting of all kind of science; offered to the judgment of all those that love the proficiencie of arts and sciences and the advancement of learning. By Jo. Webster. In moribus et institutis academiarum, collegiorum et similium conventium quo ad doctorum hominum sedes et operas mutuas destinata sunt, omnia progressui scientiarum in ulterius adversa inveniri. Franc. Bacon de Verulamio lib. de cogitat. et vis. pag. mihi. 14. London: Printed for Giles Calvert, and are to be sold at the sign of the Black Spread-Eagle, at the west end of Paul's. 1654." 4to. In this tract, which, like some other attacks upon the seats of learning, displays more power in objection than in substitution, in pulling down than in building up again, he shews the same fondness for the philosophers of the Hermetic school, for Paracelsus, Dee, Fludd and Van Helmont, and the same adhesion to planetary sigils, astrology, and the doctrine of sympathies and primæval signatures, which is perceptible in the deliberate performance of his old age. Of himself he observes: "I owe little to the advantages of those things called the goods of fortune, but most (next under the goodness of God) to industry: however, I am a free born Englishman, a citizen of the world and a seeker of knowledge, and am willing to teach what I know, and learn what I know not." No one can read the *Academiarum Examen* without feeling that it is the production of a vigorous and powerful mind, which had "tasted," and that not scantily, of the "sweet fruit of far fetched and dear bought science." Yet it still remains a literary problem rather difficult of solution, how a performance so clear, well digested, and rational, could proceed, and that contemporaneously, from the same author as the cloudy and fanatical "Judgment Set and Books Opened." On behalf of the Universities, answerers started up in the persons of Ward and Wilkins, both afterwards bishops, and the part taken by the first of them in the controversy was considered of sufficient importance to form matter of commemoration in his monumental inscription. Two opponents so famous, might almost seem to threaten extinction to one, of whom it could only be said, that he had been an obscure country schoolmaster, and whose acquirements, whatever they were, were mainly the result of his own unassisted study. In the joint answer, the title of which is "Vindiciæ Academiarum, containing some briefe animadversions upon Mr. Webster's book entitled the 'Examination of Academies,' together with an appendix concerning what Mr. Hobbes and Mr. Dell have published in this argument, Oxford, 1654," 4to., there is no want of bitterness nor of controversial skill, but though, particularly in the limited arena of the prescribed course of academical study, the knowledge displayed in it is more exact, there is neither visible in it the same power of mind, nor the same breadth of views, nor even the same variety of learning, as is conspicuous in the original tract. This, with the two fanatical pieces which Webster published contemporaneously with it, were entirely unknown to his biographer, Dr. Whitaker, who has ceded him a place amongst the distinguished natives and residents of the parish of Whalley, in the full confidence "that there is no puritanical taint in his writings, and that his taste had evidently been formed upon better models.[27]" Had these early theological and literary delinquencies of the physician of Clitheroe been communicated to his historian, it may be questioned whether the portals of his provincial temple of fame would have opened to receive so heinous a transgressor. But Dr. Whitaker's deduction would have

---

[27] What would Dr. Whitaker have thought of the following explosion, in which Webster sounds the tocsin with a vehemence and vigour which no Macbriar or Kettledrumle of the period could have surpassed. The extract is from his *Judgment Set and Books Opened*:—

"All those that claim an Ordination by Man, or from Man, that speak from the Spirit of the World, from Wit, Learning and Humane Reason, who Preach for Hire, and make Merchandize of the Souls of Men; I witness they are all Baal's Priests and Idol-Shepherds, who destroy the Sheep, and are Theives and Robbers, who came not in by the Door of the Sheep-fold, but climbed up another way, and *are the Magicians, Sorcerers, Inchanters, Soothsayers, Necromancers, and Consulters with Familiar Spirits, which the Lord will cut off out of the Land*, so that his People shall have no more Soothsayers; and as Jannes and Jambres resisted Moses, so do these resist the Truth; Men of corrupt Minds, reprobate concerning the Faith; but they shall proceed no farther, for their Folly shall be manifest to all Men, as theirs also was. Woe unto them, for they have gone in the way of Cain, and ran greedily after the Errors of Balaam, for Reward, and Perished in the Gainsaying of Core. These are Spots in your Feasts of Charity, when they Feast with you, feeding themselves without fear: Clouds they are without Water, carried of Winds; Trees, whose Fruit withered, without Fruit, twice dead, plucked up by the Roots: Raging Waves of the Sea, foaming out their own Shame, wandring Stars, to whom is reserved the blackness of Darkness for ever."

been perhaps perfectly warrantable, had Webster left no remains but his *History of Metals*, and *Displaying of Witchcraft*—so little do an author's latest works afford a clue to the character of his earliest. From 1654 to 1671, when he published his *History of Metals*, little is known of Webster's course of life. He appears to have retired into the country and devoted himself to medical practice and study, and to have taken up his residence in or near Clitheroe. He complains, that in the year 1658 all his books and papers were taken from him, an abstraction which, so far as his manuscripts are concerned, posterity is not called upon to lament, if they all resembled his *Judgment Set and Books Opened*. But his capacious and acute understanding was gradually unfolding new resources, supplying the defects, and overcoming the disadvantages of his imperfect education and desultory and irregular studies, while his matured and enlightened judgment had abandoned and discarded the fanatical pravities and erroneous tenets, which his ardent enthusiasm had too hastily imbibed. When he again became a candidate for the honours of authorship, it was evident that he knew well how to apply those quarries of learning into which, during his long recess, he had been digging so indefatigably, to furnish materials for solid and durable structures, rising in honourable and gratifying contrast to the fabrics which had preceded them. In 1671 came forth his "Metallographia, or History of Metals,"[28] in which all that recondite learning and

---

[28] "*Metallographia: or, An History of Metals. Wherein is declared the signs of Ores and Minerals both before and after digging, the causes and manner of their generations, their kinds, sorts and differences; with the description of sundry new Metals or Semi-Metals, and many other things pertaining to Mineral knowledge. As also, the handling and shewing of their Vegetability, and the discussion of the most difficult Questions belonging to Mystical Chymistry, as of the Philosophers Gold, their Mercury, the Liquor Alkahest, Aurum potabile, and such like. Gathered forth of the most approved Authors that have written in Greek, Latine, or High Dutch; With some Observations and Discoveries of the Author himself. By John Webster, Practitioner in*

extensive observation could bring together, on a subject which experiment had scarcely yet placed upon a rational basis, is collected. He styles himself on the Title page, "Practitioner in Physic and Chirurgery." In 1677, he published his great work. Its Title is "The Displaying of supposed Witchcraft. Wherein is affirmed that there are many sorts of Deceivers and Impostors. And Divers persons under a passive Delusion of Melancholy and Fancy. But that there is a Corporeal League made betwixt the Devil and the Witch, Or that he sucks on the Witches Body, has Carnal Copulation, or that Witches are turned into Cats, Dogs, raise Tempests, or the like, is utterly denied and disproved. Wherein also is handled, the Existence of Angels and Spirits, the truth of Apparitions, the Nature of Astral and Sydereal Spirits, the force of Charms and Philters; with other abstruse matters. By John Webster, Practitioner in Physic. Falsæ etenim opiniones Hominum præoccupantes, non solum surdos, sed et cæcos faciunt, ita ut videre nequeant, quæ aliis perspicua apparent. Galen, lib. 8. de Comp. Med. London, Printed by J.M. and are to be sold by the Booksellers in London. 1677," (fol.) In this memorable book he exhausts the subject, as far as it is possible to do so, by powerful ridicule, cogent arguments, and the most various and well applied learning, leaving to Hutchinson, and others who have since followed in his track, little further necessary than to reproduce his facts and reasonings in a more

---

*Physick and Chirurgery. Qui principia naturalia in seipso ignoraverit, hic jam multum remotus est ab arte nostra, quoniam non habet radicem veram supra quam intentionem suam fundet. Geber. Sum. perfect. l. c. i. p. 21.*
*Sed non ante datur telluris operta subire,*
*Auricomos quam quis discerpserit arbore fœtus.*
*Virg. Æneid. l. 6.*
*London, Printed by A.C. for Walter Kettilby at the Bishops-Head in Duck-lane, 1671, 4to."*

popular, it can scarcely be said, in a more effective, form.[29]
Those who love literary parallels may compare Webster, as

---

[29] Dr. Whitaker's assertion, that Webster was "neglected alike by the wise and unwise," seems to be a mere *gratis dictum*. The age of folios was rapidly passing away; but few folios of the period appear to have been more generally read, if we are to judge at least from its being frequently mentioned and quoted, than Webster's *Displaying of Supposed Witchcraft*. The same able writer's "Doubt whether Sir Matthew Hale ever read Webster's *Discovery of Supposed Witchcraft*," might easily have been satisfied by a reference to any common life of that great judge, which would have shown the historian of Whalley that Hale died before the book was published. Nor is Dr. Whitaker correct in stating that all tradition of Webster is now lost in the neighbourhood where he resided. The following anecdote, which would have delighted him, I had from an old inhabitant of Burnley, to whom it had been handed down by his grandfather:—In the days of Webster's fanaticism, during the usurpation, he is stated, in the zealous crusade then so common against superstitious relics, to have headed a party by whom the three venerable crosses, now set up in the churchyard of Whalley, commonly called the Crosses of Paulinus, and supposed to be coeval with the first preaching of Christianity in the North of England, were removed and taken away from their site and appropriated as a boundary fence for some adjoining fields. After the Restoration, and when his religious views had become sobered and settled, he is said, in an eager desire to atone for the desecration of which he had been guilty, to have purchased the crosses from the person who was then in possession of them, and to have been at the cost of re-erecting them on their present site, from which no sacrilegious hand will, I trust, ever again remove them. It is further said, that Webster's favourite and regular walk, in the latter part of his life, till his infirmities rendered him unable to take exercise of any kind, was to the remains of Whalley Abbey; and that a path along the banks of the stream which glides by those most picturesque and pleasing ruins, was long called "Webster's Walk." If this tradition be founded in fact, and I give it as I received it, John Webster, of Clitheroe, if not identical, as Mr. Collier has contended, with the dramatic poet of that name, must have felt something assimilated in spirit to the fine inspiration of those noble lines of the latter:—
"I do love these ancient ruins.
We never tread upon them but we set
Our foot upon some reverend history;
And, questionless, here in this open court,
Which now lies naked to the injuries
Of stormy weather, some men lie interred that
Lov'd the Church so well and gave so largely to't,
They thought it should have canopied their bones

he appears in this his last and most characteristic performance, with two famous medical contemporaries, Sir Thomas Browne, and Thomas Bartholinus the Dane, whom he strongly resembled in the character of his mind, in the complexion and variety of his studies, in grave simplicity, in exactness of observation, in general philosophical incredulity with some startling reserves, in elaborate and massive ratiocination, and in the enthusiasm, subdued but not extinguished, which gives zest to his speculations and poignancy and colouring to his style. He who seeks to measure great men in their strength and in their weakness, and what operation of literary analysis is more instructive or delightful, will find ample employment for collation and comparison in this extraordinary book, in which, keen as is the penetration displayed on almost every subject of imposition and delusion, he appears still to cling, with the obstinacy of a veteran, to some of the darling Dalilahs of his youth, "to the admirable and soul-ravishing knowledge of the three great Hypostatical principles of nature, salt, sulphur, and mercury," and, *proh pudor!* to alchemy and astrology—and those seraphic doctors and professors, Crollius, Libavius, and Van Helmont. He closed his literary performances with this noble fabric of logic and learning, not the less striking, and scarcely less useful, because it is chequered by some of the mosaic work of human imperfection,—a performance which may be said to have grown up under the umbrage of Pendle, and which he might have bequeathed to its future Demdikes and Chattox's as an amulet of irresistible power.[30]

---

Till doomsday: but all things have their end.
Churches and cities, which have diseases like to men,
Must have like death that we have."

[30] Webster's death took place on the 18th June, 1682. He left an extensive library, composed principally of chemical, hermetical, and philosophical works,

of which the MSS. catalogue is now in the possession of my friend, the Rev. T. Corser. I have two books which appear to have at one time formed part of his collection, from having his favourite signature, Johannes Hyphantes, in his autograph, on the title pages. Before I conclude with Webster, I ought perhaps to observe, that in the valuable edition of the works of Webster, the dramatic poet, published by the Rev. A. Dyce, that most accurate and judicious editor has proved indisputably, by an elaborate argument, that the John Webster, the writer of the *Examen Academiarum*, and John Webster, the author of the *Displaying of Supposed Witchcraft*, were one and the same person, who was not identical with the dramatic writer of the same name. Mr. Dyce does not, however, appear to have been aware, that the identity of the author of the *Examen Academiarum* and the writer on witchcraft is distinctly stated by Dr. Henry More, in his *Præfatio Generalissima*, to the Latin edition of his works, whose testimony being that of a contemporary, who was, like Webster, "a Cambridge scholar," may perhaps be considered sufficient, without resorting to internal and circumstantial evidence. The inscription on Webster's monument in the chapel of St. Mary Magdalen, at Clitheroe, is too characteristic and curious to be omitted. I give it entire:—

"*Qui hanc figuram intelligunt*
*Me etiam intellexisse, intelligent.*

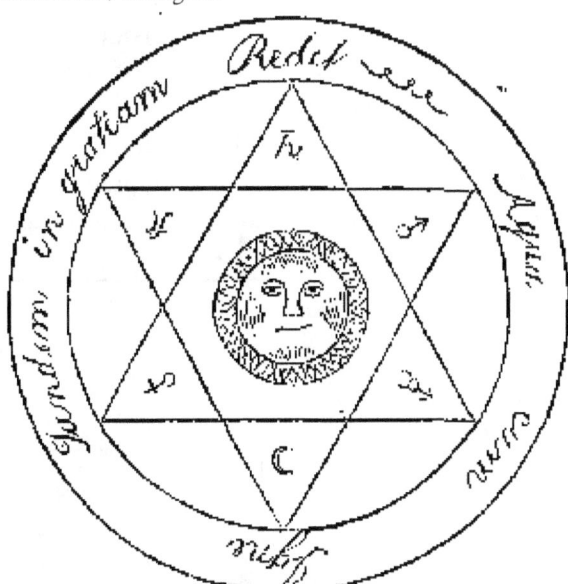

*Hic jacet ignotus mundo, mersusque tumultu*
*Invidiæ, semper mens tamen æqua fuit,*

But it is necessary to proceed from the authors on witchcraft to that extraordinary case which forms the subject of the present republication, and which first gave to Pendle its title to be considered as the Hartz Forest of England.

The Forest of Pendle is a portion of the greater one of Blackburnshire, and is so called from the celebrated mountain of that name, over the declivity of which it extends and stretches in a long but interrupted descent of five miles, to the water of Pendle, a barren and dreary tract. Dr. Whitaker observes of this and the neighbouring forests, and the remark even yet holds good, "that they still bear the marks of original barrenness, and recent cultivation; that they are still distinguished from the ancient freehold tracts around them, by want of old houses, old woods, high fences; (for these were forbidden by the forest laws;) by peculiarities of dialect and manners in their inhabitants; and lastly, by a general air of poverty which all the opulence of manufactures cannot remove." He considers that "at an uncertain period during the occupancy of the Lacies, the first principle of population" (in these forests) commenced; it was found that these wilds, bleak and barren as they were, might be occupied to some advantage in breeding young and depasturing lean "cattle, which were afterwards

---

*Multa tulit veterum ut sciret secreta sophorum*
*Ac tandem vires noverit ignis aquæ.*

*Johannes Hyphantes sive Webster,*
*In villa Spinosa supermontana, in*
*Parochia silvæ cuculatæ, in agro*
*Eboracensi, natus 1610 Feb. 3,*
*Ergastulum animæ deposuit 1682, Junii 18,*
*Annoq. ætatis suæ 72 currente.*
*Sicq. peroravit moriens mundo huic valedicens,*
*Aurea pax vivis, requies æterna sepultis."*

fattened in the lower domains. *Vaccaries*, or great upland pastures, were laid out for this purpose; *booths* or mansions erected upon them for the residence of herdsmen; and at the same time that herds of deer were permitted to range at large as heretofore, *lawnds*, by which are meant parks within a forest, were inclosed, in order to chase them with greater facility, or, by confinement, to produce fatter venison. Of these lawnds Pendle had new and old lawnd, with the contiguous park of Ightenhill."

In the early part of the seventeenth century, the inhabitants of this district must have been, with few exceptions, a wretchedly poor and uncultivated race, having little communication with the occupants of the more fertile regions around them, and in whose minds superstition, even yet unextinguished, must have had absolute and uncontrollable domination. Under the disenchanting influence of steam, manufactures, and projected rail-roads, still much of the old character of its population remains. *Hodie manent vestigia ruris.* The "parting genius" of superstition still clings to the hoary hill tops and rugged slopes and mossy water sides, along which the old forest stretched its length, and the voices of ancestral tradition are still heard to speak from the depth of its quiet hollows, and along the course of its gurgling streams. He who visits Pendle[31] will yet find that charms are generally resorted to

---

[31] It was my good fortune to visit this wizard-haunted spot within the last few weeks, in company with the able and zealous Archdeacon [The Venerable the Archdeacon of Manchester, the Rev. John Rushton, who is also the Incumbent of New Church, in Pendle.] within whose ecclesiastical cure it is comprized, and to whose singularly accurate knowledge of this district, and courteous communication of much valuable information regarding it, I hold myself greatly indebted. Following, with unequal steps, such a guide, accompanied, likewise, by an excellent Canon of the Church [The Rev. Canon Parkinson.] with all the "armamentaria cœli" at command against the powers of darkness, and a lay auxiliary [J.B. Wanklyn, Esq.], whose friendly converse would make the roughest journey appear smooth, I need scarcely say, I passed through

amongst the lower classes; that there are hares which, in their persuasion, never can be caught, and which survive only to baffle and confound the huntsman; that each small hamlet has its peculiar and gifted personage, whom it is dangerous to offend; that the wise man and wise woman (the white witches of our ancestors) still continue their investigations of truth, undisturbed by the rural police or the progress of the schoolmaster; that each locality has its haunted house; that apparitions still walk their ghostly rounds—and little would his reputation for piety avail that clergyman in the eyes of his parishioners who should refuse to lay those "extravagant and erring spirits," when requested, by those due liturgic ceremonies which the orthodoxy of tradition requires.

In the early part of the reign of James the first, and at the period when his execrable statute against witchcraft might have been sharpening its appetite by a temporary fast for the full meal of blood by which it was eventually glutted,— for as yet it could count no recorded victims,—two wretched old women with their families resided in the Forest of Pendle. Their names were Elizabeth Southernes and Ann Whittle, better known, perhaps, in the chronicles of witchcraft, by the appellations of Old Demdike and Old Chattox.[32] Both had attained, or had reached the verge of the advanced age of eighty, were evidently in a state of extreme poverty, subsisting with their families by occasional employment, by mendicancy, but principally, perhaps, by the assumption of that unlawful power, which

---

"The forest wyde,
Whose hideous horror and sad trembling sownd
Full griesly seem'd,"
unscathed by the old lords of the soil, and needed not Mengus's Fuga, Fustis et Flagellum Dæmonum, as a triple coat of mail.
[32] The Archdeacon of Manchester suggests that this is merely a corruption of Chadwick or Chadwicks, and not from her chattering as she went along.

commerce with spirits of evil was supposed to procure, and of which their sex, life, appearance, and peculiarities, might seem to the prejudiced neighbourhood in the Forest to render them not unsuitable depositaries. In both, perhaps, some vindictive wish, which appeared to have been gratified nearly as soon as uttered, or some one of those curious coincidences which no individual's life is without, led to an impression which time, habit, and general recognition would gradually deepen into full conviction, that each really possessed the powers which witchcraft was believed to confer. Whether it be with witches as it is said to be with a much maligned branch of a certain profession, that it needs two of its members in a district to make its exercise profitable, it is not for me to say; but it is seldom found that competition is accompanied by any very amicable feeling in the competitors, or by a disposition to underrate the value of the merchandize which each has to offer for sale. Accordingly, great was the rivalry, constant the feuds, and unintermitting the respective criminations of the Erictho and Canidia of Pendle,[33] who had opened shops for the vending of similar contraband commodities, and were called upon to decry each other's stock, as well as to magnify their own. Each "gave her little senate laws," and had her own party (or tail, according to modern phraseology) in the Forest. Some looked up to and patronized one, and some the other. If old Demdike could boast that she had Tibb as a familiar, old Chattox was not without her Fancy. If the former had skill in waxen images, the latter could dig up the scalps of the dead, and make their teeth serviceable to her unhallowed purposes. In the anxiety which each felt to outvie the other, and to secure the greater share of the general custom of a not very

---

[33] These bickerings were no doubt exasperated by the robbery committed upon old Demdike and Alizon Device, which is detailed in the examinations, some of the *opima spolia* abstracted on which occasion she detected on the person of old Chattox's daughter.

extended or very lucrative market, each would wish to be represented as more death-dealing, destructive, and powerful than her neighbour; and she who could number up the most goodly assortment of damage done to man and beast, whether real or not was quite immaterial, as long as the draught was spiced and flavoured to suit the general taste, stood the best chance of obtaining a monopoly. It is a curious fact, that the son-in-law of one of these two individuals, and whose wife was herself executed as a witch, paid to the other a yearly rent,[34] on an express covenant that she should exempt him from her charms and witchcrafts. Where the possession of a commission from the powers of darkness was thus eagerly and ostentatiously paraded, every death, the cause of which was not perfectly obvious, whether it ended in a sudden termination or a slow and gradual decline, would be placed to the general account of one of the two (to use Master Potts's description,) "agents for the devil in those parts," as the party responsible for these unclaimed dividends of mortality. Did a cow go mad, or was a horse unaccountably afflicted with the staggers, the same solution was always at hand to clear negligence and save the trouble of inquiry; and so far from modestly disclaiming these atrocities, the only struggle on the parts of Mothers Demdike and Chattox would be which should first appropriate them. And in all this it must not be forgotten that their own credulity was at least as great as the credulity of their neighbours, and that each had the power in question was so much an admitted point, that she

---

[34] Of an aghendole of meal. I am indebted to Miss Clegg, of Hallfoot, near Clitheroe, for information as to the exact quantity contained in an aghendole, which is eight pounds. This measure, she informs me, is still in use in Little Harwood, in the district of Pendle. The Archdeacon of Manchester considers that an aghendole, or more properly, as generally pronounced, a nackendole, is a kneading-dole, the quantity of meal, &c. usually taken for kneading at one time. There can be no doubt that this is the correct derivation.

had long ceased, in all probability, to entertain any doubts on the subject. With this general conviction on one hand, and a sincere persuasion on the other, it would be surprising if, in the course of a few years, the scandalous chronicle of Pendle had not accumulated a *corpus delicti* against them, which only required that "*one of his Majesties Justices in these parts, a very religious honest gentleman, painful in the service of his country,*" should work the materials into shape, and make "the gruel thick and slab."

Such a man was soon found in the representative of the old family of the Nowels of Read, who, desirous of signalizing himself as an active and stirring justice, took up the case of these self-accusing culprits, for both made confessions when examined before him, with a vigour worthy of a better cause. On the 2nd April, 1612, he committed old Demdike, old Chattox, Alizon Device, and Anne Redfern to Lancaster, to take their trial at the next assizes for various murders and witchcrafts. "Here," says the faithful chronicler, Master Potts, "they had not stayed a weeke, when their children and friendes being abroad at libertie, laboured a speciall meeting at Malking Tower[35] in the

---

[35] Baines confounds Malking-Tower with Hoar-stones, a place rendered famous by the second case of pretended witchcraft in 1633, but at some distance from the first-named spot, the residence of Mother Demdike, which lies in the township of Barrowford. The witch's mansion—
"Where that same wicked wight
Her dwelling had—
Dark, doleful, dreary, like a greedy grave
That still for carrion carcases doth crave,
On top whereof ay dwelt the ghastly owle,
Shrieking his baleful note, which ever drave
Far from that haunt all other cheerful fowl,
And all about it wandering ghosts did wail and howle"—
is now, alas! no more. It stood in a field a little elevated, on a brow above the building at present called Malking-Tower. The site of the house or cottage is still distinctly traceable, and fragments of the plaster are yet to be found

Forrest of Pendle, vpon Good-fryday, within a weeke after they were committed, of all the most dangerous, wicked, and damnable witches in the county farre and neere. Vpon Good-fryday they met, according to solemne appoyntment, solemnized this great festiuall day according to their former order, with great cheare, merry company, and much conference. In the end, in this great assemblie it was decreed that M. Covell, [he was the gaoler of Lancaster Castle,] by reason of his Office, shall be slaine before the next Assises, the Castle at Lancaster to be blown up," &c., &c. This witches' convention, so historically famous, we unquestionably owe to the "painful justice" whose scent after witches and plots entitled him to a promotion which he did not obtain. An overt act so alarming and so indisputable, at once threw the country, far and near, into the greatest ferment—*furiis surrexit Etruria justis*—while it supplied an admirable *locus in quo* for tracing those whose retiring habits had prevented their propensities to witchcraft from being generally known to their intimate friends and connexions. The witness by whose evidence this legend was principally supported, was Jennet Device, a child about nine years old, and grand-daughter of old Demdike. A more dangerous tool in the hands of an unscrupulous evidence-compeller, being at once intelligent, cunning and pliant, than the child proved herself, it would not have been easy

---

imbedded in the boundary wall of the field. The old road to Gisburne ran almost close to it. It commanded a most extensive prospect in front, in the direction of Alkincoates, Colne, and the Yorkshire moors; while in another direction the vast range of Pendle, nearly intercepted, gloomed in sullen majesty. At the period when Mother Demdike was in being, Malking-Tower would be at some distance from any other habitation; its occupier, as the vulgar would opine—
"So choosing solitarie to abide
Far from all neighbours, that her devilish deedes
And hellish arts from people she might hide,
And hurt far off unknown whomever she envide."

to have discovered. A foundation being now laid capable of embracing any body of confederates, the indefatigable justice proceeded in his inquiries, and in the end, Elizabeth Device the daughter of old Demdike, James Device her son, Alice Nutter, Katherine Hewitt, John Bulcock, Jane Bulcock, with some others, were committed for trial at Lancaster. The very curious report of that trial is contained in the work now republished, which was compiled under the superintendence of the judges who presided, by Master Thomas Potts, clerk in court, and present at the trial. His report, notwithstanding its prolixity and its many repetitions, it has been thought advisable to publish entire, and the reprint which follows is as near a fac-simile as possible of the original tract.

It is rather strange that Dr. Whitaker, to whom local superstitions were always matters of the strongest interest, and welcome as manna to the sojourners in the wilderness,[36] should have been ignorant, not merely of Master Potts's discovery, but even of the fact of this trial of the witches in 1612. It is equally singular that Sir Walter Scott should have forgotten, when writing his letters on Demonology and Witchcraft, that he had republished this tract, somewhat inaccurately, but with rather a long introduction and notes, in the third volume of his edition of

---

[36] In a scarce little book, "The Triumph of Sovereign Grace, or a Brand plucked out of the Fire, by David Crosly, Minister, Manchester," 1743, 12mo., which I owe to the kindness of the very able historian of Cheshire, George Ormerod, Esq., Dr. Whitaker, to whom the volume formerly belonged, has been at the pains of chronicling the superstitions connected with a family, ranking amongst the more opulent yeomen of Cliviger, of the name of Briercliffe, on the execution of one of whom for murder the tract was published. The Briercliffe's, from the curious anecdotes which the Doctor gives with great unction, appear to have been one of those gloomy and fated races, dogged by some unassuageable Nemesis, in which crime and horror are transmitted from generation to generation with as much certainty as the family features and name.

the Somers Tracts, which appeared in 1810. He mentions Potts's *Discoverie*, in the amusing but very inaccurate and imperfect historical sketch referred to,[37] as a curious and rare book, which he had then for the first time obtained a sight of. What could have been his meaning in referring his readers, for an account of Mother Demdike and a description of Malking Tower, to "Mr. Roby's Antiquities of Lancaster," that apocryphal historian having given no such account or description, and having published no such work, it is rather difficult to conjecture.

With all his habitual tautology and grave absurdity, Master Potts is, nevertheless, a faithful and accurate chronicler, and we owe his memory somewhat for furnishing us with so elaborate a report of what took place on this trial, and giving us, "in their own country terms," the examinations of the witnesses, which contain much which throws light on the manners and language of the times, and nearly all that is necessary to enable us to form a judgment on the proceedings. It will be observed that he follows with great exactness the course pursued in court, in opening the case and recapitulating the evidence separately against each prisoner, so as most graphically to place before us the whole scene as it occurred. The part in which he is felt to be most deficient, is in the want of some further account of the prisoners convicted, from the trial up to the time of their execution. To Master Potts, a man of legal forms and

---

[37] We yet want a full, elaborate, and satisfactory history of witchcraft. Hutchinson's is the only account we have which enters at all at length into the detail of the various cases; but his materials were generally collected from common sources, and he confines himself principally to English cases. The European history of witchcraft embraces so wide a field, and requires for its just completion a research so various, that there is little probability, I fear, of this *desideratum* being speedily supplied.

ceremonies, the entire interest in the case seems to have come in and gone out with the judge's trumpets.

As most of the points in the trial which appeared to require observation, have been adverted to in the notes which follow the reprint, it is not considered necessary to enter into any analysis or review of the evidence adduced at the trial, which presents such a miserable mockery of justice. Mother Demdike, it will be seen, died in prison before the trial came on. Of the Pendle witches four, namely Old Chattox, Elizabeth Device, James Device, and Alizon Device, had all made confessions, and had little chance, therefore, of escaping condemnation. They were all found guilty; and with them were convicted, Anne Redfern, Alice Nutter, Katherine Hewitt, John Bulcock, and Jane Bulcock, who were all of Pendle or its neighbourhood, and who maintained their innocence and refused to make any confession. They were executed, along with the first-mentioned four and Isabel Robey, who was of Windle, in the parish of Prescot, and had been found guilty of similar practises, the day after the trial, viz. on the 18th of August, 1612, "at the common place of execution near to Lancaster."

The main interest in reviewing this miserable band of victims will be felt to centre in Alice Nutter.[38] Wealthy,

---

[38] The explorer of Pendle will find the mansion of Alice Nutter, Rough Lee, still standing. It is impossible to look at it, recollecting the circumstances of her case, without being strongly interested. It is a very substantial, and rather a fine specimen of the houses of the inferior gentry in the time of James the first, and is now divided into cottages. On one of the side walls is an inscription, almost entirely obliterated, which contained the date of the building and the initials of the name of its first owner. At a little distance from Rough Lee, pursuing the course of the stream, he will find the foundations of an ancient mill, and the millstones still unremoved, though the building itself has been pulled down long ago. This was, doubtless, the mill of Richard Baldwin, the miller, who, as stated in Old Demdike's confession, ejected her and Alizon

well conducted, well connected, and placed probably on an equality with most of the neighbouring families and the magistrate before whom she was brought, and by whom she was committed, she deserves to be distinguished from the companions with whom she suffered, and to attract an attention which has never yet been directed towards her.[39] That Jennet Device, on whose evidence she was convicted, was instructed to accuse her by her own nearest relatives, to whom "superfluous lagged the veteran on the stage," and that the magistrate, Roger Nowell, entered actively as a confederate into the conspiracy from a grudge entertained against her on account of a long disputed boundary, are allegations which tradition has preserved, but the truth or falsehood of which, at this distance of time, it is scarcely

---

Device her daughter, from his land so contumeliously; immediately after which her "Spirit or divell called Tibb appeared, and sayd Revenge thee of him." Greenhead, the residence of Robert Nutter, one of the reputed victims of the prisoners tried on this occasion, is at some distance from Rough Lee, and is yet in good preservation, and occupied as a farmhouse.

[39] The instances are very few in England in which the statute of James the first was brought to bear against any but the lowest classes of the people. Indeed, there are not many attempts reported to attack the rich and powerful with weapons derived from its provisions. One of such attempts, which did not, like that against Alice Nutter, prove successful, is narrated in a curious and scarce pamphlet, which I have now before me, with this title—"Wonderful News from the North, or a true Relation of the sad and grievous Torments inflicted upon the Bodies of three children of Mr. George Muschamp, late of the County of Northumberland, by Witchcraft, and how miraculously it pleased God to strengthen them and to deliver them; as also the prosecution of the say'd Witches, as by Oaths and their own Confessions will appear, and by the Indictment found by the Jury against one of them at the Sessions of the Peace held at Alnwick, the 24th day of April, 1650. London, printed by T.H., and are to be sold by Richard Harper at his Shop in Smithfield. 1650," 4to. This was evidently a diabolical plot, in which these children were made the puppets, and which was got up to accomplish the destruction of a person of condition, Mrs. Dorothy Swinnow, the wife of Colonel Swinnow, of Chatton, in Northumberland, and from which she had great difficulty in escaping.

possible satisfactorily to examine. With such a witness, however, as Jennet Device, and such an admirable engine as the meeting at Malking-Tower, the guests at which she could multiply *ad libitum*, doling out the *plaat*, as Titus Oates would call it, by such instalments, and in such fragmentary portions, as would conduce to an easy digestion of the whole, the wonder seems not to be, that one unfortunate victim of a higher class should have perished in the meshes of artful and complicated villainy, but that its ramifications were not more extensive, and still more fatal and destructive. From one so capable of taking a hint as the little precocious prodigy of wickedness, in whose examination, Potts tells us, "*Mr. Nowell took such great paines*," a very summary deliverance might be expected from troublesome neighbours, or still more troublesome relatives; and if, by a leading question, she could only be induced to marshal them in their allotted places at the witches' imaginary banquet, there was little doubt of their taking their station at a place of meeting where the sad realities of life were only to be encountered, "the common place of execution near to Lancaster."

The trial of the Samlesbury witches, Jennet Bierley, Ellen Bierley, and Jane Southworth, forms a curious episode in Potts's *Discoverie*. A Priest or Jesuit, of the name of Thomson, *alias* Southworth, had tutored the principal evidence, Grace Sowerbuts, a girl of the age of fourteen, but who had not the same instinctive genius for perjury as Jennet Device, to accuse the three persons above mentioned of having bewitched her; "so that," as the indictment runs, "by means thereof her body wasted and consumed." "The chief object," says Sir Walter Scott, "in this imposture, was doubtless the advantage and promotion of the Catholic cause, as the patient would have been in due time exorcised and the fiend dispossessed, by the same priest who had taught her to counterfeit the fits. Revenge against the women, who had become proselytes to the Church of England, was probably an additional motive." But the imposture broke down, from the inability of the principal witness to support the scheme of deception. Unsuccessful, however, as it proved, the time was well chosen, the groundwork excellently laid, the evidence industriously got up, and it must ever deserve a prominent place in the history—a history, how delightful when it shall be written in the spirit of philosophy and with due application of research—of human fraud and imposture.

We can only speculate, of course, on such an occasion, but perhaps no trial is recorded as having taken place, with the results of which every body, the parties convicted only excepted, was, in all probability, better pleased or satisfied, than at this witch trial at Lancaster in 1612. The mob would be delighted with a pageant, always acceptable, in the execution of ten witches; and still more, that one of them was of a rank superior to their own;—the judge had no doubt, in his opinion, avoided each horn of the dilemma—the abomination mentioned in Scripture—punishing the innocent or letting the guilty go free—by tracking guilt with well breathed sagacity, and unravelling imposture with unerring skill;—a Jesuit had been unkennelled, a spectacle as gratifying to a serious Protestant in those days, as running down a fox to a thorough sportsman;—a plot had been discovered which might have made Lancaster Castle "to topple on its warders" and "slope its head to its foundations," and Master Cowell, who had held so many inquests, to vanish without leaving anything in his own person whereon an inquest could be holden;—a pestilent nest of incorrigible witches had been dug out and rooted up, and Pendle Hill placed under sanatory regulations;—and last, and not least, as affording matter of pride and exultation to every loyal subject, a commentary had at last been collected for two texts, which had long called for some such support without finding it, King James's *Demonology*, and his statute against witchcraft. When the *Discoverie* of Master Potts, with its rich treasury of illustrative evidence, came to hand, would not the monarch be the happiest man in his dominions!

Twenty years after the publication of the tract now reprinted, Pendle Forest again became the scene of pretended witchcrafts; and from various circumstances, the trial which took place then (in 1633) has acquired even greater notoriety than the one which preceded it, though no Master Potts could be found to transmit a report of the proceedings in the second case, a deficiency which is greatly to be lamented. The particulars are substantially comprised in the following examination, which is given from the copy in Whitaker's *Whalley*, p. 213, which, on comparison, is unquestionably more accurate than the other two versions, in Webster, p. 347, and Baines's *Lancashire*, vol. i. p. 604:[40]—

"The Examination of Edmund Robinson,

"Son of *Edm. Robinson*, of *Pendle* forest, mason,[41] taken at *Padiham* before *Richard Shuttleworth*[42] and *John Starkie*,[43]

---

[40] The copy in Baines is from the Harl. MSS., cod. 6854, fo. 26 *b*, and though inserted in his history as more correct than that in Whitaker's Whalley, is so disfigured by errors, particularly in the names of persons and places, as to be utterly unintelligible. From what source Whitaker derived his transcript does not appear; for the confession of Margaret Johnson he cites Dodsworth MSS. in Bodleian Lib., vol. 61, p. 47.

[41] "The informer was one Edmund Robinson (yet living at the writing hereof, and commonly known by the name of Ned of Roughs) whose Father was by trade a Waller, and but a poor Man, and they finding that they were believed and had incouragement by the adjoyning Magistrates, and the persons being committed to prison or bound over to the next Assizes, the boy, his Father and some others besides did make a practice to go from Church to Church that the

Esqs. two of his majesty's justices of the peace, within the county of *Lancaster*, 10th of February, A.D. 1633.

"Who informeth upon oath, (beeinge examined concerninge the greate meetings of the witches) and saith, that upon All-saints day last past, hee, this informer, beeinge with one *Henry Parker*, a neare doore neighbor to him in *Wheatley-lane*,[44] desyred the said *Parker* to give him leave to get

---

Boy might reveal and discover Witches, pretending that there was a great number at the pretended meeting whose faces he could know, and by that means they got a good living, that in a short space the Father bought a Cow or two, when he had none before. And it came to pass that this said Boy was brought into the Church of Kildwick a large parish Church, where I (being then Curate there) was preaching in the afternoon, and was set upon a stall (he being but about ten or eleven years old) to look about him, which moved some little disturbance in the Congregation for a while. And after prayers I inquiring what the matter was, the people told me that it was the Boy that discovered Witches, upon which I went to the house where he was to stay all night, where I found him, and two very unlikely persons that did conduct him, and manage the business; I desired to have some discourse with the Boy in private, but that they utterly refused; then in the presence of a great many people, I took the Boy near me, and said: Good Boy tell me truly, and in earnest, did thou see and hear such strange things of the meeting of Witches, as is reported by many that thou dost relate, or did not some person teach thee to say such things of thy self? But the two men not giving the Boy leave to answer, did pluck him from me, and said he had been examined by two able Justices of the Peace, and they did never ask him such a question, to whom I replied, the persons accused had therefore the more wrong."—Webster's *Displaying of Witchcraft*, p. 276.

[42] This was Richard Shuttleworth of Gawthorp, Esq., who married the daughter and heiress of R. Fleetwood, Esq., of Barton, and died June 1669, aged 82.

[43] John Starkie, Esq., of the family of Starkie of Huntroyd, the same probably who was sheriff of Lancashire 9 Charles I, and one of the seven demoniacs at Cleworth in the year 1595, on whose evidence Hartley was hanged for witchcraft. Having commenced so early, he must by this time have qualified himself, if he only improved the advantages of his Cleworth education, to take the chair and proceed as professor, in all matters appertaining to witchcraft.

[44] Wheatley-lane is still a place of note in Pendle.

some bulloes,[45] which hee did. In which tyme of gettinge bulloes, hee sawe two greyhounds, viz. a blacke and a browne one, came runninge over the next field towards him, he verily thinkinge the one of them to bee Mr. *Nutters*,[46] and the other to bee Mr. *Robinsons*,[47] the said Mr. *Nutter* and Mr. *Robinson* havinge then such like. And the said greyhounds came to him and fawned on him, they havinge about theire necks either of them a coller, and to either of which collers was tyed a stringe, which collers as this informer affirmeth did shine like gould, and hee thinkinge that some either of Mr. *Nutter's* or Mr. *Robinson's* family should have followed them: but seeinge noe body to followe them, he tooke the said greyhounds thinkinge to hunt with them, and presently a hare did rise very neare before him, at the sight whereof he cryed, loo, loo, but the dogges would not run. Whereupon beeinge very angry, he tooke them, and with the strings that were at theire collers tyed either of them to a little bush on the next hedge, and with a rod that hee had in his hand, hee bett them. And in stede of the blacke greyhound, one *Dickonson* wife stoode up (a neighb[r].) whom this informer knoweth, and in stede of the browne greyhound a little boy whom this informer knoweth not. At which sight this informer beeinge affraid indevoured to run away: but beeinge stayed by the woman, viz. by *Dickonson's* wife, shee put her hand into her pocket, and pulled out a peace of silver much like

---

[45] Wild plums.

[46] It would seem as if a case of witchcraft in Pendle, without a Nutter in some way connected with it, could not occur.

[47] What Mr. Robinson is intended does not appear. It was a common name in Pendle. It is, however, a curious fact, that a family of this name, *with the alias of Swyer*, (see Potts, confession of Elizabeth Device,) is even now, or very recently was, to be met with in Pendle, of whom the John Robinson, *alias* Swyer, one of the supposed victims of Witchcraft, was probably an ancestor. There are few instances of an *alias* being similarly transmitted in families for upwards of two centuries.

to a faire shillinge, and offered to give him to hould his tongue, and not to tell, whiche hee refused, sayinge, nay thou art a witch; Whereupon shee put her hand into her pocket againe, and pulled out a stringe like unto a bridle[48] that gingled, which shee put upon the litle boyes heade that stood up in the browne greyhounds steade; whereupon the said boy stood up a white horse. Then immediately the said *Dickonson* wife tooke this informer before her upon the said horse, and carried him to a new house called *Hoarestones*,[49] beinge about a quarter of a mile off, whither, when they were comme, there were divers persons about the doore, and hee sawe divers others cominge rideinge upon horses of severall colours towards the said house, which tyed theire horses to a hedge neare to the sed house; and which persons went into the sed house, to the number of threescore or thereabouts, as this informer thinketh, where they had a fyer and meate roastinge, and some other meate stirringe in the house, whereof a yonge woman whom hee this informer knoweth not, gave him flesh and breade upon a trencher, and drinke in a glasse, which, after the first taste, hee refused, and would have noe more, and said it was nought. And presently after, seeinge diverse of the company goinge to a barn neare adioyneinge,[50] hee followed after, and there he sawe sixe of them kneelinge, and pullinge at sixe severall roapes which were fastened or tyed to ye toppe of the house; at or with which pullinge came then in this informers sight flesh smoakeinge, butter in lumps, and milke as it were

---

[48] Mother Dickenson, as Sir Walter Scott remarks, brings to mind the magician Queen in the Arabian Tales.
[49] This house is still standing, and though it has undergone some modernizations, has every appearance of having been built about this period.
[50] The old barn, so famous as the scene of these exploits, is no longer extant. A more modern and very substantial one has now been erected on its site.

syleinge[51] from the said roapes, all which fell into basons whiche were placed under the saide roapes. And after that these sixe had done, there came other sixe which did likewise, and duringe all the tyme of theire so pullinge, they made such foule faces that feared[52] this informer, soe as hee was glad to steale out and run home, whom, when they wanted, some of theire company came runninge after him neare to a place in a high way, called Boggard-hole,[53] where this informer met two horsemen, at the sight whereof the sed persons left followinge him, and the foremost of which persons yt followed him, hee knoweth to bee one *Loynd* wife, which said wife, together with one *Dickonson* wife, and one *Jenet Davies*[54] he hath seene at severall tymes in a croft or close adioninge to his fathers house, whiche put him in a greate feare. And further, this informer saith, upon Thursday after New Yeares day last past, he sawe the sed *Loynd* wife sittinge upon a crosse peece of wood, beeinge within the chimney of his father's dwellinge house, and hee callinge to her, said, come downe thou *Loynd* wife, and immediately the sed *Loynd* wife went up out of his sight. And further, this informer saith, yt after hee was comme from ye company aforesed to his father's house, beeinge towards eveninge, his father bad him goe fetch home two kyne to seale,[55] and in the way, in a field

---

[51] Syleing, from the verb sile or syle, to strain, to pass through a strainer. See Jamieson, under "sile."

[52] Frightened.

[53] Boggard Hole lies in a hollow, near to Hoarstones, and is still known by that name.

[54] "It is the sport to see the engineer hoist with his own petar." Her old occupation as witness having got into other hands, Janet or Jennet Davies, or Device, for the person spoken of appears to be the same with the granddaughter of Old Demdike, on whose evidence three members of her family were executed, has now to take her place amongst the witnesses against.

[55] Seale, from sele, *s.* a yoke for binding cattle in the stall. Sal (A.S.) denotes "a collar or bond." Somner. Sile (Isl.) seems to bear the very same sense with our

called the Ollers, hee chanced to hap upon a boy, who began to quarrell with him, and they fought soe together till this informer had his eares made very bloody by fightinge, and lookinge downe, hee sawe the boy had a cloven foote, at which sight hee was affraid, and ran away from him to seeke the kyne. And in the way hee sawe a light like a lanthorne, towards which he made hast, supposinge it to bee carried by some of Mr. *Robinson's* people: But when hee came to the place, hee onely found a woman standinge on a bridge, whom, when hee sawe her, he knewe to bee *Loynd* wife, and knowinge her, he turned backe againe, and immediatly hee met with ye aforesed boy, from whom he offered to run, which boy gave him a blow on the back which caus'd him to cry. And hee farther saith, yt when hee was in the barne, he sawe three women take three pictures from off the beame, in the which pictures many thornes, or such like things sticked, and yt *Loynd* wife tooke one of the said pictures downe, but thother two women yt tooke thother two pictures downe hee knoweth not.[56] And

---

sele, being exp. a ligament of leather by which cattle and other things are bound. Vide Jamieson, under "sele."

[56] Heywood and Broome, in their play, "The late Lancashire Witches," 1634, 4to, follow the terms of this deposition very closely. It is very probable that they had seen and conversed with the boy, to whom, when taken up to London, there was a great resort of company. The Lancashire dialect, as given in this play, and by no means unfaithfully, was perhaps derived from conversations with some of the actors in this drama of real life, a drama quite as extraordinary as any that Heywood's imagination ever bodied forth from the world of fiction.

"*Enter Boy with a switch.*

*Boy.* Now I have gathered Bullies, and fild my bellie pretty well, i'le goe see some sport. There are gentlemen coursing in the medow hard by; and 'tis a game that I love better than going to Schoole ten to one.

*Enter an invisible spirit. J. Adson [Sic in orig.] with a brace of greyhounds.*
What have we here a brace of Greyhounds broke loose from their masters: it must needs be so, for they have both their Collers and slippes about their neckes. Now I looke better upon them, me thinks I should know them, and so I do: these are Mr. Robinsons dogges, that dwels some two miles off, i'le take them up, and lead them home to their master; it may be something in my way,

for he is as liberall a gentleman, as any is in our countrie, Come Hector, come. Now if I c'ud but start a Hare by the way, kill her, and carry her home to my supper, I should thinke I had made a better afternoones worke of it than gathering of bullies. Come poore curres along with me.
*Exit.*"
✺ ✺ ✺ ✺ ✺ ✺ ✺
✺ ✺ ✺ ✺ ✺ ✺ ✺

"*Enter Boy with the Greyhounds.*
A Hare, a Hare, halloe, halloe, the Divell take these curres, will they not stir, halloe, halloe, there, there, there, what are they growne so lither and so lazie? Are Mr. Robinsons dogges turn'd tykes with a wanion? the Hare is yet in sight, halloe, halloe, mary hang you for a couple of mungrils (if you were worth hanging,) and have you serv'd me thus? nay then ile serve you with the like sauce, you shall to the next bush, there will I tie you, and use you like a couple of curs as you are, and though not lash you, yet lash you whilest my switch will hold, nay since you have left your speed, ile see if I can put spirit into you, and put you in remembrance what halloe, halloe meanes.
*As he beats them, there appeared before him Gooddy Dickison, and the Boy upon the dogs, going in.*
Now blesse me heaven, one of the Greyhounds turn'd into a woman, the other into a boy! The lad I never saw before, but her I know well; it is my gammer *Dickison.*
*G. Dick.* Sirah, you have serv'd me well to swindge me thus. You yong rogue, you have vs'd me like a dog.
*Boy.* When you had put your self into a dogs skin, I pray how c'ud I help it; but gammer are not you a Witch? if you bee, I beg upon my knees you will not hurt me.
*Dickis.* Stand up my boie, for thou shalt have no harme,
Be silent, speake of nothing thou hast seene.
And here's a shilling for thee.
*Boy.* Ile have none of your money, gammer, because you are a Witch; and now she is out of her foure leg'd shape, ile see if with my two legs I can out-run her.
*Dickis.* Nay sirra, though you be yong, and I old, you are not so nimble, nor I so lame, but I can overtake you.
*Boy.* But Gammer what do you meane to do with me
Now you have me?
*Dickis.* To hugge thee, stroke thee, and embrace thee thus,
And teach thee twentie thousand pretty things,
So thou tell no tales; and boy this night
Thou must along with me to a brave feast.
*Boy.* Not I gammer indeed la, I dare not stay out late,
My father is a fell man, and if I bee out long, will both chide and beat me.

*Dickis.* Not sirra, then perforce thou shalt along,
This bridle helps me still at need,
And shall provide us of a steed.
Now sirra, take your shape and be
Prepar'd to hurrie him and me.
*Exit.*
Now looke and tell mee wher's the lad become.
*Boy.* The boy is vanisht, and I can see nothing in his stead
But a white horse readie sadled and bridled.
*Dickis.* And thats the horse we must bestride,
On which both thou and I must ride,
Thou boy before and I behinde,
The earth we tread not, but the winde,
For we must progresse through the aire,
And I will bring thee to such fare
As thou ne're saw'st, up and away,
For now no longer we can stay.
*She catches him up, and turning round.*
*Boy.* Help, help.
*Exit.*"
✵ ✵ ✵ ✵ ✵ ✵
✵ ✵ ✵ ✵ ✵ ✵

"*Rob.* What place is this? it looks like an old barne: ile peep in at some cranny or other, and try if I can see what they are doing. Such a bevy of beldames did I never behold; and cramming like so many Cormorants: Marry choke you with a mischiefe.
*Gooddy Dickison.* Whoope, whurre, heres a sturre,
Never a cat, never a curre,
But that we must have this demurre.
*Mal.* A second course.
*Mrs. Gen.* Pull, and pull hard
For all that hath lately him prepar'd
For the great wedding feast.
*Mall.* As chiefe
Of Doughtyes Surloine of rost Beefe.
*All.* Ha, ha, ha.
*Meg.* 'Tis come, 'tis come.
*Mawd.* Where hath it all this while beene?
*Meg.* Some
Delay hath kept it, now 'tis here,
For bottles next of wine and beere,
The Merchants cellers they shall pay for't.

*Mrs. Gener.* Well,
What sod or rost meat more, pray tell.
*Good. Dick.* Pul for the Poultry, Foule, and Fish,
For emptie shall not be a dish.
*Robin.* A pox take them, must only they feed upon hot meat, and I upon nothing but cold sallads.
*Mrs. Gener.* This meat is tedious, now some Farie,
Fetch what belongs unto the Dairie,
*Mal.* Thats Butter, Milk, Whey, Curds and Cheese,
Wee nothing by the bargaine leese.
*All.* Ha, ha, ha.
*Goody Dickison.* Boy, theres meat for you.
*Boy.* Thanke you.
*Gooddy Dickis.* And drinke too.
*Meg.* What Beast was by thee hither rid?
*Mawd.* A Badger nab.
*Meg.* And I bestrid
A Porcupine that never prickt.
*Mal.* The dull sides of a Beare I kickt.
I know how you rid, Lady Nan.
*Mrs. Gen.* Ha, ha, ha, upon the knave my man.
*Rob.* A murrein take you, I am sure my hoofes payd for't.
*Boy.* Meat lie there, for thou hast no taste, and drinke there, for thou hast no relish, for in neither of them is there either salt or savour.
*All.* Pull for the posset, pull.
*Robin.* The brides posset on my life, nay if they come to their spoone meat once, I hope theil breake up their feast presently.
*Mrs. Gen.* So those that are our waiters nere,
Take hence this Wedding cheere.
We will be lively all,
And make this barn our hall.
*Gooddy Dick.* You our Familiers, come.
In speech let all be dumbe,
And to close up our Feast,
To welcome every gest
A merry round let's daunce.
*Meg.* Some Musicke then ith aire
Whilest thus by paire and paire,
We nimbly foot it; strike.
*Musick.*
*Mal.* We are obeyd.
*Sprite.* And we hels ministers shall lend our aid.
*Dance and Song together. In the time of which the Boy speakes.*

beeinge further asked, what persons were at ye meeteinge aforesed, hee nominated these persons hereafter mentioned, viz. *Dickonson* wife, *Henry Priestley* wife and her sone, *Alice Hargreaves* widdowe, *Jennet Davies*, *Wm.*

---

*Boy.* Now whilest they are in their jollitie, and do not mind me, ile steale away, and shift for my selfe, though I lose my life for't.
*Exit.*"
\* \* \* \* \* \*
\* \* \* \* \* \*
"*Dought.* He came to thee like a Boy thou sayest, about thine own bignesse?
*Boy.* Yes Sir, and he asked me where I dwelt, and what my name was.
*Dough.* Ah Rogue!
*Boy.* But it was in a quarrelsome way; Whereupon I was as stout, and ask'd him who made him an examiner?
*Dough.* Ah good Boy.
*Mil.* In that he was my Sonne.
*Boy.* He told me he would know or beat it out of me,
And I told him he should not, and bid him doe his worst;
And to't we went.
*Dough.* In that he was my sonne againe, ha boy; I see him at it now.
*Boy.* We fought a quarter of an houre, till his sharpe nailes made my eares bleed.
*Dough.* O the grand Divell pare 'em.
*Boy.* I wondred to finde him so strong in my hands, seeming but of mine owne age and bignesse, till I looking downe, perceived he had clubb'd cloven feet like Oxe feet; but his face was as young as mine.
*Dought.* A pox, but by his feet, he may be the Club-footed Horse-coursers father, for all his young lookes.
*Boy.* But I was afraid of his feet, and ran from him towards a light that I saw, and when I came to it, it was one of the Witches in white upon a Bridge, that scar'd me backe againe, and then met me the Boy againe, and he strucke me and layd mee for dead.
*Mil.* Till I wondring at his stay, went out and found him in the Trance; since which time, he has beene haunted and frighted with Goblins, 40 times; and never durst tell any thing (as I sayd) because the Hags had so threatned him till in his sicknes he revealed it to his mother.
*Dough.* And she told no body but folkes on't. Well Gossip Gretty, as thou art a Miller, and a close thiefe, now let us keepe it as close as we may till we take 'hem, and see them handsomly hanged o'the way: Ha my little Cuffe-divell, thou art a made man. Come, away with me.
*Exeunt.*"
Heywood and Broome's *Late Lancashire Witches*, Acts 2 and 3.

*Davies*, uxor. *Hen. Jacks* and her sone *John*, *James Hargreaves* of *Marsden*, *Miles* wife of *Dicks*, *James* wife, *Saunders* sicut credit, *Lawrence* wife of *Saunders*, *Loynd* wife, *Buys* wife of *Barrowford*, one *Holgate* and his wife sicut credit, *Little Robin* wife of *Leonard's*, of the *West Cloase*.[57]

"*Edmund Robinson* of *Pendle*, father of ye sd *Edmunde Robinson*, the aforesaid informer, upon oath saith, that upon *All Saints' Day*, he sent his sone, the aforesed informer, to fetch home two kyne to seale, and saith yt hee thought his sone stayed longer than he should have done,

---

[57] These names are thus given in Baines's Transcript:—
"Dickensons
Henrie Priestleyes wife and his ladd
Alice Hargrave, widdowe
Jane Davies (als. Jennet Device)
William Davies
The wife of Henrie Offep and her sonnes
John and Myles
The wife of Duckers
James Hargrave of Maresden
Loyards wife
James wife
Sanders wife, And as hee beleeveth
Lawnes wife
Sander Pynes wife of Baraford
One Foolegate and his wife
And Leonards of the West Close."
And thus in Webster:—
"Dickensons Wife, Henry Priestleys Wife, and his Lad, Alice Hargreene Widow, Jane Davies, William Davies, and the Wife of Henry Fackes, and her Sons John and Miles, the Wife of —— Denneries, James Hargreene of Marsdead, Loynd's Wife, one James his Wife, Saunders his Wife, and Saunders himself *sicut credit*, one Laurence his Wife, one Saunder Pyn's Wife of Barraford, one Holgate and his Wife of Leonards of the West close."

went to seeke him, and in seekinge him, heard him cry very pittifully, and found him soe afraid and distracted, yt hee neither knew his father, nor did know where he was, and so continued very neare a quarter of an hower before he came to himselfe,[58] and he tould this informer, his father, all the particular passages yt are before declared in the said *Edmund Robinson*, his sone's information."

The name of Margaret Johnson does not appear in Edmund Robinson's examination. Whether accused or not, the opportunity was too alluring to be lost by a personage full of matter, being like old Mause Headrigg, "as a bottle that lacketh vent," and too desirous of notoriety, to let slip such an occasion. She made, on the 2nd of March following, before the same justices who had taken Robinson's examination, the following confession, which must have been considered a most instructive one by those who were in search of some short *vade mecum* of the statistics of witchcraft in Pendle:—

"The Confession of Margaret Johnson.

---

[58] The learned "practitioner in physick," Mr. William Drage, in his "Treatise of Diseases from Witchcraft," published Lond. 1668, 4to. p. 22, recommends "birch" in such cases, "as a specifical medicine, antipathetical to demons." One can only lament that this valuable remedy was not vigorously applied in the present instance, as well as in most others in which these juvenile sufferers appear. I doubt whether, in the whole Materia Medica, a more powerful *Lamia-fuge* could have been discovered, or one which would have been more universally successful, if applied perseveringly, whenever the suspicious symptoms recurred. The following is, however, Drage's great panacea in these cases, a mode of treatment which must have been vastly popular, judging from its extensive adoption in all parts of the country: "*Punish the witch, threaten to hang her if she helps not the sick, scratch her and fetch blood. When she is cast into prison the sick are some time delivered, some time he or she (they are most females, most old women, and most poor,) must transfer the disease to other persons, sometimes to a dog, or horse, or cow, &c. Threaten her and beat her to remove it.*"—Drage, p. 23.

"That betwixt seaven and eight yeares since, shee beeinge in her owne house in *Marsden,* in a greate passion of anger and discontent, and withall pressed with some want, there appeared unto her a spirit or devill in ye proportion or similitude of a man, apparrelled in a suite of blacke, tyed about with silk points, who offered yt if shee would give him her soule hee would supply all her wants, and bringe to her whatsoever shee did neede. And at her appointment would in revenge either kill or hurt whom or what shee desyred, weare it man or beast. And saith, yt after a solicitation or two shee contracted and covenanted with ye said devill for her soule. And yt ye said devill or spirit badde her call him by the name of *Mamilian.* And when shee would have him to doe any thinge for her, call in *Mamilian,* and hee would bee ready to doe her will. And saith, yt in all her talke or conference shee calleth her said devill, *Mamil* my God. Shee further saith, yt ye said *Mamilian,* her devill, (by her consent) did abuse and defile her body by comittinge wicked uncleannesse together. And saith, yt shee was not at the greate meetings at *Hoarestones,* at the forest of *Pendle,* upon All-Saints Day, where ———. But saith yt shee was at a second meetinge ye Sunday next after All-Saints Day, at the place aforesaid; where there was at yt tyme between 30 and 40 witches, who did all ride to the said meetinge, and the end of theire said meeting was to consult for the killinge and hurtinge of men and beasts. And yt besides theire particular familiars or spirits, there was one greate or grand devill or spirit more eminent than the rest. And if any desyre to have a greate and more wonderfull devill, whereby they may have more power to hurt, they may have one such. And sayth, yt such witches as have sharp bones given them by the devill to pricke them, have no pappes or dugges whereon theire devill may sucke, but theire devill receiveth bloud from the place, pricked with the bone. And they are more grand witches than any yt have marks. Shee allsoe saith, yt if a witch have but one marke, shee hath but one spirit, if two then two spirits, if three yet but two spirits. And saith, yt theire spirits usually have knowledge of theire bodies. And being desyred to name such as shee knewe to be witches, shee named, &c.[59] And if they would torment a man, they bid theire spirit goe and tormt. him in any particular place. And yt Good-Friday is one constant day for a yearely generall meetinge of witches. And yt on Good-Friday last, they had a meetinge neare *Pendle* water syde. Shee alsoe saith, that men witches usually have women spirits, and women witches men spirits. And theire devill or spirit gives them notice of theire meetinge, and tells them the place where it must bee. And saith, if they desyre to be in any place upon a sodaine, theire devill or spirit will upon a rodde, dogge, or any thinge els, presently convey them thither: yea, into any roome of a man's house. But shee saith it is not the substance of theire bodies, but theire spirit assumeth such form and shape as goe into such roomes. Shee alsoe saith, yt ye devill (after he begins to sucke) will make a pappe or dugge in a short tyme, and the matter which hee sucks is blood. And saith yt theire devills can cause foule weather and storms, and soe did at theire meetings. Shee alsoe saith yt when her devill did come to sucke her pappe, hee usually came to her in ye liknes of a cat, sometymes of one colour and sometymes of an other. And yt since this trouble befell her, her spirit hath left her, and shee never sawe him since."

---

[59] The omission here is thus supplied in Baines's Transcript; but the actual names are scarcely to be recognised, from the clerical errors of the copy:—
"One Pickerne and his wife both of Wyndwall,
Rawson of Clore and his wife
Duffice wife of Clore by the water side
Cartmell the wife of Clore
And Jane of the hedgend in Maresden."

On the evidence contained in these examinations several persons were committed for trial at Lancaster, and seventeen, on being tried at the ensuing assizes, were found guilty by the jury. The judge before whom the trial took place was, however, more sagacious and enlightened than his predecessors, Bromley and Altham. He respited the execution of the prisoners; and on the case being reported to the king in council, the Bishop of Chester, Dr. Bridgman, was required to investigate the circumstances. The inquiry was instituted at Chester, and four of the convicted witches, namely, Margaret Johnson, Frances Dickonson, Mary Spencer, and the wife of one of the Hargreaves's, were sent to London, and examined, first by the king's physicians and surgeons, and afterwards by Charles the first in person.

"A stranger scene" to quote Dr. Whitaker's concluding paragraph "can scarcely be conceived; and it is not easy to imagine whether the untaught manners, rude dialect, and uncouth appearance of these poor foresters, would more astonish the king; or his dignity of person and manners, together with the splendid scene with which they were surrounded, would overwhelm them. The end, however, of the business was, that strong presumptions appeared of the boy having been suborned to accuse them falsely, and they were accordingly dismissed. The boy afterwards confessed that he was suborned."[60]

---

[60] Webster gives the sequel of this curious case of imposture:—"Four of them, to wit Margaret Johnson, Francis Dicconson, Mary Spenser, and Hargraves Wife, were sent for up to London, and were viewed and examined by his Majesties Physicians and Chirurgeons, and after by his Majesty and the Council, and no cause of guilt appearing but great presumptions of the boys being suborned to accuse them falsely. Therefore it was resolved to separate the boy from his Father, they having both followed the women up to London, they were both taken and put into several prisons asunder. Whereupon shortly after the Boy confessed that he was taught and suborned to devise, and feign those things against them, and had persevered in that wickedness by the counsel of

In Dr. Whitaker's astonishment that Margaret Johnson should make the confession she appears to have done, in a clear case of imposture, few of his readers will be disposed to participate, who are at all conversant with the trials of reputed witches in this country. Confessions were so common on those occasions, that there is, I believe, not a single instance of any great number of persons being convicted of witchcraft at one time, some of whom did not make a confession of guilt. Nor is there anything extraordinary in that circumstance, when it is remembered that many of them sincerely believed in the existence of the powers attributed to them; and others, aged and of weak understanding, were, in a measure, coerced by the strong persuasion of their guilt, which all around them manifested, into an acquiescence in the truth of the accusation. In many cases the confessions were made in the hope, and no doubt with the promise, seldom performed, that a respite from punishment would be eventually granted. In other instances, there is as little doubt, that they were the final results of irritation, agony, and despair.[61] The confessions are generally composed of "such stuff as dreams are made of," and what they report to have occurred, might either proceed, when there was no intention to fabricate, from intertwining the fantastic threads which sometimes stream upon the waking senses from the land of shadows, or be caused by those ocular hallucinations of which medical

---

his Father, and some others, whom envy, revenge and hope of gain had prompted on to that devillish design and villany; and he also confessed, that upon that day when he said that they met at the aforesaid house or barn, he was that very day a mile off, getting Plums in his Neighbours Orchard. And that this is a most certain truth, there are many persons yet living, of sufficient reputation and integrity, that can avouch and testifie the same; and besides, what I write is the most of it true, upon my own knowledge, and the whole I have had from his own mouth."—*Displaying of Witchcraft*, p. 277.

[61] The confession in the "Amber Witch" is a true picture, drawn from the life. What is there, indeed, unlike truth in that wonderful fiction?

science has supplied full and satisfactory solution. There is no argument which so long maintained its ground in support of witchcraft as that which was founded on the confessions referred to. It was the last plank clung to by many a witch-believing lawyer and divine. And yet there is none which will less bear critical scrutiny and examination, or the fallacy of which can more easily be shown, if any particular reported confession is taken as a test and subjected to a searching analysis and inquiry.

It is said that we owe to the grave and saturnine Monarch, who extended his pardon to the seventeen convicted in 1633, that happy generalisation of the term, which appropriates honourably to the sex in Lancashire the designation denoting the fancied crime of a few miserable victims of superstition. That gentle sex will never repudiate a title bestowed by one, little given to the playful sports of fancy, whose sorrows and unhappy fate have never wanted their commiseration, and who distinguished himself on this memorable occasion, at a period when

"'twas the time's plague
That madmen led the blind,"

—in days when philosophy stumbled and murder arrayed itself in the robes of justice—by an enlightened exercise of the kingly prerogative of mercy. Proceeding from such a fountain of honour, and purified by such an appropriation, the title of witch has long lost its original opprobrium in the County Palatine, and survives only to call forth the gayest and most delightful associations. In process of time even the term *witchfinder* may lose the stains which have adhered to it from the atrocities of Hopkins, and may be adopted by general usage, as a sort of companion phrase, to signify the fortunate individual, who, by an union with a

Lancashire witch, has just asserted his indefeasible title to be considered as the happiest of men.

J.C.

# THE WONDERFVLL DISCOVERIE OF WITCHES, &c.

# THE
WONDERFVLL
DISCOVERIE OF
WITCHES IN THE COVNTIE
OF LANCASTER.

With the Arraignement and Triall of **Nineteene notorious Witches, at the Assizes and generall Gaole deliuerie, holden at the Castle of Lancaster,** *vpon Munday, the seuenteenth of August last,* 1612.

Before Sir I a m e s  A l t h a m, and **Sir Edward Bromley, Knights; Barons of his Maiesties Court of Excheqver: And Iustices** *of Assize,* **Oyer** *and* **Terminor,** *and generall* Gaole deliuerie in the circuit of the *North Parts.*

Together with the Arraignement and Triall of Iennet Preston, *at the Assizes holden at the Castle of Yorke, the seuen and twentieth day of Iulie last past,* with her Execution for the murther of Master Lister *by Witchcraft.*

Published and set forth by commandement of his Maiesties Iustices of Assize in the North Parts.

*By* **Thomas Potts** *Esquier.*

# TO THE RIGHT HONORABLE,
## *THOMAS*, LORD KNYVET, BARON OF ESCRICK
### in the Countie of Yorke, my very honorable good Lord and Master.[62]

And

# TO THE RIGHT HONORABLE
## *AND VERTVOVS LADIE, THE*
### *Ladie* Elizabeth Knyvet *his Wife,* my honorable good Ladie and Mistris.

---

Right Honorable,

---

[62] Dedication. "*The Right Honorable Thomas Lord Knyvet.*"] Sir Thomas Knivet, or Knyvet, Gentleman of the Privy Chamber to James the First, was afterwards created Baron of Escricke, in the county of York. He it was who was intrusted to search the vaults under the Parliament House, and who discovered the thirty-six barrels of gunpowder, and apprehended Guido Fawkes, who declared to him, that if he had happened to be within the house when he took him, as he was immediately before, he would not have failed to blow him up, house and all. (Howell's *State Trials*, vol. ii., p. 202.) His courage and conduct on this occasion seem to have recommended him to the especial favour of James. Dying without issue, the title of Lord Howard of Escrick was conferred on Sir Edward Howard, son of Thomas Howard, Earl of Suffolk, who had married the eldest daughter and co-heir of Sir H. Knivet; and, having been enjoyed successively by his two sons, ended in his grandson Charles, in the beginning of the last century. It must be admitted that the writer has chosen his patron very felicitously. Who so fit to have the book dedicated to him as one who had acted so conspicuous a part on the memorable occasion at Westminster? The blowing up of Lancaster Castle and good Mr. Covel, by the conclave of witches at Malkin's Tower, was no discreditable imitation of the grand metropolitan drama on provincial boards.

*LET it stand (I beseech you) with your fauours whom profession of the same true Religion towards God, and so great loue hath vnited together in one, Jointly to accept the Protection and Patronage of these my labours, which not their owne worth hath encouraged, but your Worthinesse hath enforced me to consecrate vnto your Honours.*

*To you (Right Honourable my very good Lord) of Right doe they belong: for to whom shall I rather present their first fruits of my learning then to your Lordship: who nourished then both mee and them, when there was scarce any being to mee or them? And whose iust and vpright carriage of causes, whose zeale to Justice and Honourable curtesie to all men, have purchased you a Reuerend and worthie Respect of all men in all partes of this Kingdome, where you are knowne. And to your good Ladiship they doe of great right belong likewise; Whose Religion, Iustice, and Honourable admittance of my Vnworthie Seruice to your Ladiship do challenge at my handes the vttermost of what euer I may bee able to performe.*

*Here is nothing of my own act worthie to bee commended to your Honours, it is the worke, of those Reuerend Magistrates, His Maiesties Iustices of Assizes in the North partes, and no more then a Particular Declaration of the proceedings of Iustice in those partes. Here shall you behold the Iustice of this Land, truely administred,* Prœmium & Pœnam, *Mercie and Iudgement, freely and indifferently bestowed and inflicted; And aboue all thinges to bee remembred, the excellent care of these Iudges in the Triall of offendors.*

*It hath pleased them out of their respect to mee to impose this worke vpon mee, and according to my vnderstanding, I haue taken paines to finish, and now confirmed by their Iudgement to publish the same, for the benefit of my*

*Countrie. That the example of these conuicted vpon their owne Examinations, Confessions, and Euidence at the Barre, may worke good in others, Rather by with-holding them from, then imboldening them to, the Atchieuing such desperate actes as these or the like.*

*These are some part of the fruits of my time spent in the Seruice of my Countrie, Since by your Graue and Reuerend Counsell (my Good Lord) I reduced my wauering and wandring thoughts to a more quiet harbour of repose.*

*If it please your Honours to giue them your Honourable respect, the world may iudge them the more worthie of acceptance, to whose various censures they are now exposed.*

*God of Heauen whose eies are on them that feare him, to bee their Protector and guide, behold your Honours with the eye of fauor, be euermore your strong hold, and your great reward, and blesse you with blessings in this life, Externall and Internall, Temporall and Spirituall, and with Eternall happines in the World to come: to which I commend your Honours; And rest both now and euer, From my Lodging in Chancerie Lane, the sixteenth of Nouember 1612.*

**Your Honours**

humbly deuoted

Seruant,

*Thomas Potts.*

UPON the Arraignement and triall of these Witches at the last Assizes and Generall Gaole-deliuerie, holden at Lancaster, wee found such apparent matters against them, that we thought it necessarie to publish them to the World, and thereupon imposed the labour of this Worke vpon this Gentleman, by reason of his place, being a Clerke at that time in Court, imploied in the Arraignement and triall of them.

*Ja. Altham.*

*Edw. Bromley.*[63]

---

[63] First Imprimatur. "*Ja. Altham, Edw. Bromley.*"] These two judges were Barons of the Court of Exchequer, but neither of them seems to have left a name extraordinarily distinguished for legal learning. Altham was one of the assistants named in the commission for the trial of the Countess of Somerset for the murder of Sir Thomas Overbury in 1616. Bromley appears, from incidental notices contained in the diary of Nicholas Assheton, (see Whitaker's *Whalley*, third edition, page 300,) and other sources, to have frequently taken the northern circuit. He was not of the family of Lord Chancellor Bromley, but of another stock.

*AFTER he had taken great paines to finish it, I tooke vpon mee to reuise and correct it, that nothing might passe but matter of Fact, apparant against them by record. It is very little he hath inserted, and that necessarie, to shew what their offences were, what people, and of what condition they were: The whole proceedings and Euidence against them, I finde vpon examination carefully set forth, and truely reported, and iudge the worke fit and worthie to be published.*

Edward Bromley.[64]

---

[64] Second Imprimatur: "*Edward Bromley. I took upon mee to reuise and correct it.*"] This revision by the judge who presided at the trial gives a singular and unique value and authority to the work. We have no other report of any witch trial which has an equal stamp of authenticity. How many of the rhetorical flourishes interspersed in the book are the property of Thomas Potts, Esquier, and how many are the interpolation of the "excellent care" of the worthy Baron, it is scarcely worth while to investigate. Certainly never were judge and clerk more admirably paired. The *Shallow* on the bench was well reflected in the *Master Slender* below.

Gentle Reader, although the care of this Gentleman the Author, was great to examine and publish this his worke perfect according to the Honorable testimonie of the Iudges, yet some faults are committed by me in the Printing, and yet not many, being a worke done in such great haste, at the end of a Tearme, which I pray you, with your fauour to excuse.

A particular Declaration of
the most barberous and damnable Practises,
**Murthers, wicked and diuelish Conspiracies,**
**practized**
*and executed by the most dangerous and malitious*
**Witch** *Elizabeth Sowthernes* **alias** *Demdike,*
**of the Forrest of** *Pendle* **in the Countie of**
*Lancaster* **Widdow, who died in the**
**Castle at** *Lancaster* **before she**
**came to receiue her tryall.**

THOUGH publique iustice hath passed at these Assises vpon the Capitall offendours, and after the Arraignement & tryall of them, Iudgement being giuen, due and timely Execution succeeded; which doth import and giue the greatest satisfaction that can be, to all men; yet because vpon the caryage, and euent of this businesse, the Eyes of all the partes of *Lancashire*, and other Counties in the North partes thereunto adioyning were bent: And so infinite a multitude came to the Arraignement & tryall of these Witches at *Lancaster*, the number of them being knowen to exceed all others at any time heretofore, at one time to be indicted, arraigned, and receiue their tryall,[65] especially for so many Murders, Conspiracies, Charmes, Meetinges, hellish and damnable practises, so apparant vpon their owne examinations & confessions. These my honourable & worthy Lords, the Iudges of Assise, vpon great consideration, thought it necessarie & profitable, to publish to the whole world, their most barbarous and damnable practises, with the direct proceedinges of the Court against them, aswell for that there doe passe diuers vncertaine reportes and relations of such Euidences, as was publiquely giuen against them at their Arraignement. As for that diuers came to prosecute against many of them that were not found guiltie, and so rest very discontented, and not satisfied. As also for that it is necessary for men to know and vnderstande the meanes whereby they worke their mischiefe, the hidden misteries of their diuelish and wicked Inchauntmentes, Charmes, and Sorceries, the better to

---

[65] "*The number of them being knowen to exceed all others at any time heretofore at one time to be indicted, arraigned, and receiue their tryall.*"] Probably this was the case, at least in England; but a greater number had been convicted before, even in this country, at one time, than were found guilty on this occasion, as it appears from Scot, (*Discovery of Witchcraft*, page 543, edition 1584,) that seventeen or eighteen witches were condemned at once, at St. Osith, in Essex, in 1576, of whom an account was written by Brian Darcy, with the names and colours of their spirits.

preuent and auoyde the danger that may ensue. And lastly, who were the principall authors and actors in this late woefull and lamentable *Tragedie*, wherein so much Blood was spilt.

Therefore I pray you giue me leaue, (with your patience and fauour,) before I proceed to the Indictment, Arraignement, and Tryall of such as were prisoners in the Castle, to lay open the life and death of this damnable and malicious Witch, of so long continuance (old *Demdike*) of whom our whole businesse hath such dependence, that without the particular Declaration and Record of her Euidence, with the circumstaunces, wee shall neuer bring any thing to good perfection: for from this Sincke of villanie and mischiefe, haue all the rest proceeded; as you shall haue them in order.

She was a very old woman, about the age of Fourescore[66] yeares, and had been a Witch for fiftie yeares. Shee dwelt in the Forrest of *Pendle*, a vaste place, fitte for her profession: What shee committed in her time, no man knowes.

Thus liued shee securely for many yeares, brought vp her owne Children, instructed her Graund-children, and tooke great care and paines to bring them to be Witches. Shee

---

[66] "*She was a very old woman, about the age of fourescore.*"] Dr. Henry More would have styled old Demdike "An eximious example of Moses, his Mecassephah, the word which he uses in that law,—Thou shalt not suffer a witch to live." Margaret Agar and Julian Cox, (see Glanvill's *Collection of Relations*, p. 135, edition 1682,) on whom he dwells with such delighted interest, were very inferior subjects to what, in his hands, Elizabeth Sothernes would have made. They had neither of them the finishing attribute of blindness, so fearful in a witch, to complete the sketch; nor such a fine foreground for the painting as the forest of Pendle presented; nor the advantage, for grouping, of a family of descendants in which witchcraft might be transmitted to the third generation.

was a generall agent for the Deuill in all these partes: no man escaped her, or her Furies, that euer gaue them any occasion of offence, or denyed them any thing they stood need of: And certaine it is, no man neere them, was secure or free from danger.

But God, who had in his diuine prouidence prouided to cut them off, and roote them out of the Commonwealth, so disposed aboue, that the Iustices of those partes, vnderstanding by a generall charme and muttering, the great and vniuersall resort to *Maulking Tower*, the common opinion, with the report of these suspected people, the complaint of the Kinges subiectes for the losse of their Children, Friendes, Goodes, and Cattle, (as there could not be so great Fire without some Smoake,) sent for some of the Countrey, and tooke great paynes to enquire after their proceedinges, and courses of life.

In the end, *Roger Nowell* Esquire,[67] one of his Maiesties Iustices in these partes, a very religious honest Gentleman, painefull in the seruice of his Countrey: whose fame for this great seruice to his Countrey, shall liue after him, tooke vpon him to enter into the particular examination of these suspected persons: And to the honour of God, and the great

---

[67] "*Roger Nowell, Esquire.*"] This busy and mischievous personage who resided at Read Hall, in the immediate neighbourhood of Pendle, was sheriff of Lancashire in 1610. He married Katherine, daughter of John Murton, of Murton, and was buried at Whalley, January 31st, 1623. He was of the same family as Alexander Nowell, the Dean of St. Paul's, and Lawrence Nowell, the restorer of Saxon literature in England; and tarnished a name which they had rendered memorable, by becoming, apparently, an eager and willing instrument in that wicked persecution which resulted in the present trial. His ill-directed activity seems to have fanned the dormant embers into a blaze, and to have given aim and consistency to the whole scheme of oppression. From this man was descended, in the female line, one whose merits might atone for a whole generation of Roger Nowells, the truly noble-minded and evangelical Reginald Heber.

comfort of all his Countrey, made such a discouery of them in order, as the like hath not been heard of: which for your better satisfaction, I haue heere placed in order against her, as they are vpon Record, amongst the Recordes of the *Crowne* at *Lancaster*, certified by M. *Nowell*, and others.

## The voluntarie Confession and Examination of *Elizabeth Sowtherns* alias *Demdike*, taken at the Fence in the Forrest of *Pendle* in the Countie of *Lancaster*.

### The second day of Aprill, *Annoq; Regni Regis Iacobi Anggliæ, &c. Decimo, et Scotiæ, Quadragesimo quinto;* Before *Roger Nowell* of *Reade* Esquire, one of his Maiesties Iustices of the peace within the sayd Countie, *Viz.*

THE said *Elizabeth Sowtherns* confesseth, and sayth; That about twentie yeares past, as she was comming homeward from begging, there met her this Examinate neere vnto a Stonepit in *Gouldshey*,[68] in the sayd Forrest of *Pendle*, a Spirit or Deuill in the shape of a Boy, the one halfe of his Coate blacke, and the other browne, who bade this Examinate stay, saying to her, that if she would giue him her Soule, she should haue any thing that she would request. Wherevpon this Examinat demaunded his name? and the Spirit answered, his name was *Tibb*:[69] and so this

---

[68] "*Gouldshey*,"] so commonly pronounced, but more properly Goldshaw, or Goldshaw Booth.

[69] "*The spirit answered, his name was Tibb.*"] Bernard, who is learned in the nomenclature of familiar spirits, gives, in his *Guide to Grand Jurymen*, 1630, 12mo, the following list of the names of the more celebrated familiars of English witches. "Such as I have read of are these: Mephistophiles, Lucifer, Little Lord, Fimodes, David, Jude, Little Robin, Smacke, Litefoote, Nonsuch, Lunch, Makeshift, Swash, Pluck, Blue, Catch, White, Callico, Hardname, Tibb, Hiff, Ball, Puss, Rutterkin, Dicke, Prettie, Grissil, and Jacke." In the confession of Isabel Gowdie, a famous Scotch witch, (in *Pitcairne's Trials*, vol. iii. page 614,) we have the following catalogue of attendant spirits, rather, it must be confessed, a formidable band. "The names of our Divellis, that waited

Examinate in hope of such gaine as was promised by the sayd Deuill or *Tibb*, was contented to giue her Soule to the said Spirit: And for the space of fiue or sixe yeares next after, the sayd Spirit or Deuill appeared at sundry times vnto her this Examinate about *Day-light* Gate,[70] alwayes bidding her stay, and asking her this Examinate what she would haue or doe? To whom this Examinate replyed, Nay nothing: for she this Examinate said, she wanted nothing yet. And so about the end of the said sixe yeares, vpon a Sabboth day in the morning, this Examinate hauing a litle Child vpon her knee, and she being in a slumber, the sayd Spirit appeared vnto her in the likenes of a browne Dogg, forcing himselfe to her knee, to get blood vnder her left Arme: and she being without any apparrell sauing her Smocke, the said Deuill did get blood vnder her left arme.[71]

---

upon us, ar thes: first, Robert the Jakis; Sanderis, the Read Roaver; Thomas the Fearie; Swain, the Roaring Lion; Thieffe of Hell; Wait upon Hirself; Mak Hectour; Robert the Rule; Hendrie Laing; and Rorie. We would ken them all, on by on, from utheris. Some of theim apeirit in sadd dunn, som in grasse-grein, som in sea-grein, and some in yallow." Archbishop Harsnet, in his admirable *Declaration of Popish Impostures, under the pretence of casting out Devils*, 1605, 4to, a work unsurpassed for rich humour and caustic wit, clothed in good old idiomatic English, has a chapter "on the strange names of these devils," in which he observes, (p. 46,) "It is not amiss that you be acquainted with these extravagant names of devils, least meeting them otherwise by chance you mistake them for the names of tapsters, or juglers." Certainly, some of the names he marshalls in array smell strongly of the tavern. These are some of them: Pippin, Philpot, Modu, Soforce, Hilco, Smolkin, Hillio, Hiaclito, Lustie Huffe-cap, Killico, Hob, Frateretto, Fliberdigibbet, Hoberdidance, Tocobatto, and Lustie Jollie Jenkin.

[70] "*About Day-light Gate.*"] Day-light Gate, i.e. Evening, the down gate of daylight. See *Promptuarium Parvulorum*, (edited by Way for the Camden Society,) page 188, "Gate down, or downe gate of the Sunne or any other planet."—Occasus. Palgrave gives, "At the sonne gate downe; sur le soleil couchant."

[71] "*The said Deuill did get blood vnder her left arme.*"] It would seem (see Elizabeth Device's Examination afterwards) as if some preliminary search were made, in the case of this poor old woman, for the marks which were supposed to come by the sucking or drawing of the Spirit or Familiar. Most probably her

confession was the result of this and other means of annoyance and torture employed in the usual unscrupulous manner, upon a blind woman of eighty. Of those marks supposed to be produced by the sucking of the Spirit or Familiar, the most curious and scientific (if the word may be applied to such a subject) account will be found in a very scarce tract, which seems to have been unknown to the writers on witchcraft. Its title is "A Confirmation and Discovery of Witchcraft, containing these several particulars; That there are Witches called bad Witches, and Witches untruly called good or white Witches, and what manner of people they be, and how they may be knowne, with many particulars thereunto tending. Together with the Confessions of many of those executed since May, 1645, in the several Counties hereafter mentioned. As also some objections Answered. By John Stearne, now of Lawshall, neere Burie Saint Edmunds in Suffolke, sometimes of Manningtree in Essex. Prov. xvii. 15, He that justifieth the wicked, and he that condemneth the just, even they both are an abomination to the Lord. Deut. xiii. 14, Thou shall therefore enquire, and make search, and ask diligently whether it be truth and the thing certaine. London, Printed by William Wilson, dwelling in Little Saint Bartholomews, neere Smithfield, 1648, pages 61, besides preface." Stearne, in whom Remigius and De Lancre would have recognized a congenial soul, had a sort of joint commission with Hopkins, as Witch-finder, and tells us (see address to Reader) that he had been in part an agent in finding out or discovering about 200 witches in Essex, Suffolk, Northamptonshire, Huntingtonshire, Bedfordshire, Norfolk, Cambridgeshire, and the Isle of Ely. He deals with the subject undoubtedly like a man whose extensive experience and practice had enabled him to reduce the matter to a complete system. (See his account of their marks, pp. 43 to 50.) He might, like John Kincaid in Tranent, (see Pitcairne's *Criminal Trials*, vol. iii. p. 599,) have assumed the right of Common Pricker, i.e. Searcher for the devil's marks, and had his own tests, which were infallible. He complains, good man, "that in many places I never received penny as yet, nor any am like, notwithstanding I have hands for satisfaction, except I should sue; [he should have sued by all means, we might then have had his bill of particulars, which would have been curious;] but many rather fall upon me for what hath been received, but I hope such suits will be disannulled, and that where I have been out of moneys for Towns in charges and otherwise such course will be taken that I may be satisfied and paid with reason." He was doubtless well deserving of a recompense, and his neighbours were much to blame if he did not receive a full and ample one. Of the latter end of his coadjutor, Hopkins, whom Sir Walter Scott (see Somers's Tracts, vol. iii. p. 97, edit. 1810,) and several other writers represent as ultimately executed himself for witchcraft, he gives a very different, and no doubt more correct account; which, singularly enough, has hitherto remained entirely unnoticed. "He died peaceably at Manningtree, after a long sicknesse of a consumption, as many of his generation had done before him, without any

And this Examinate awaking, sayd, *Iesus saue my Child*; but had no power, nor could not say, *Iesus saue her selfe*: wherevpon the Browne Dogge vanished out of this Examinats sight: after which, this Examinate was almost starke madd for the space of eight weekes.

And vpon her examination, she further confesseth, and saith. That a little before Christmas last, this Examinates Daughter hauing been to helpe *Richard Baldwyns* Folkes at the Mill: This Examinates Daughter did bid her this Examinate goe to the sayd *Baldwyns* house, and aske him some thing for her helping of his Folkes at the Mill, (as aforesaid:) and in this Examinates going to the said *Baldwyns* house, and neere to the sayd house, she mette with the said *Richard Baldwyn*; Which *Baldwyn* sayd to this Examinate, and the said *Alizon Deuice*[72] (who at that time ledde this Examinate, being blinde) get out of my ground Whores and Witches, I will burne the one of you, and hang the other.[73] To whom this Examinate answered: I

---

trouble of conscience for what he had done, as was falsely reported of him. He was the son of a godly minister, and therefore, without doubt, within the Covenant." Were not the interests of truth too sacred to be compromised, it might seem almost a pity to demolish that merited and delightful retribution which Butler's lines have immortalized.

[72] "*Alizon Device.*"] Device is merely the common name Davies spelled as pronounced in the neighbourhood of Pendle.

[73] "*I will burne the one of you and hang the other.*"] The following extracts from that fine old play, "The Witch of Edmonton," bear a strong resemblance to the scene described in the text. Mother Sawyer, in whom the milk of human kindness is turned to gall by destitution, imbittered by relentless outrage and insult, and who, driven out of the pale of human fellowship, is thrown upon strange and fearful allies, would almost appear to be the counterpart of Mother Demdike. The weird sisters of our transcendant bard are wild and wonderful creations, but have no close relationship to the plain old traditional witch of our ancestors, which is nowhere represented by our dramatic writers with faithfulness and truth except in the Witch of Edmonton:—

*Enter* Elizabeth Sawyer, *gathering sticks.*

*Saw.* And why on me? why should the envious world
Throw all their scandalous malice upon me?
'Cause I am poor, deform'd, and ignorant,
And like a bow buckled and bent together,
By some more strong in mischiefs than myself,
Must I for that be made a common sink,
For all the filth and rubbish of men's tongues
To fall and run into? Some call me Witch,
And being ignorant of myself, they go
About to teach me how to be one; urging,
That my bad tongue (by their bad usage made so)
Forespeaks their cattle, doth bewitch their corn,
Themselves, their servants, and their babes at nurse.
This they enforce upon me; and in part
Make me to credit it; and here comes one
Of my chief adversaries.
*Enter* Old Banks.
*Banks.* Out, out upon thee, witch!
*Saw.* Dost call me witch?
*Banks.* I do, witch, I do; and worse I would, knew I a name more hateful. What makest thou upon my ground?
*Saw.* Gather a few rotten sticks to warm me.
*Banks.* Down with them when I bid thee, quickly; I'll make thy bones rattle in thy skin else.
*Saw.* You won't, churl, cut-throat, miser!—there they be; [*Throws them down.*] would they stuck across thy throat, thy bowels, thy maw, thy midriff.
*Banks.* Say'st thou me so, hag? Out of my ground!
[*Beats her.*
*Saw.* Dost strike me, slave, curmudgeon! Now thy bones aches, thy joints cramps, and convulsions stretch and crack thy sinews!
*Banks.* Cursing, thou hag! take that, and that.
[*Beats her, and exit.*
*Saw.* Strike, do!—and wither'd may that hand and arm
Whose blows have lamed me, drop from the rotten trunk!
Abuse me! beat me! call me hag and witch!
What is the name? where, and by what art learn'd,
What spells, what charms or invocations?
May the thing call'd Familiar be purchased?
* * * * * * *

*Saw.* Still vex'd! still tortured! that curmudgeon Banks
Is ground of all my scandal; I am shunn'd
And hated like a sickness; made a scorn
To all degrees and sexes. I have heard old beldams

Talk of familiars in the shape of mice,
Rats, ferrets, weasels, and I wot not what,
That have appear'd, and suck'd, some say, their blood;
But by what means they came acquainted with them,
I am now ignorant. Would some power, good or bad,
Instruct me which way I might be revenged
Upon this churl, I'd go out of myself,
And give this fury leave to dwell within
This ruin'd cottage, ready to fall with age!
Abjure all goodness, be at hate with prayer,
And study curses, imprecations,
Blasphemous speeches, oaths, detested oaths,
Or anything that's ill; so I might work
Revenge upon this miser, this black cur,
That barks and bites, and sucks the very blood
Of me, and of my credit. 'Tis all one,
To be a witch, as to be counted one:
Vengeance, shame, ruin light upon that canker!
*Enter a* Black Dog.
*Dog.* Ho! have I found thee cursing? now thou art
Mine own.
*Saw.* Thine! what art thou?
*Dog.* He thou hast so often
Importuned to appear to thee, the devil.
*Saw.* Bless me! the devil!
*Dog.* Come, do not fear; I love thee much too well
To hurt or fright thee; if I seem terrible,
It is to such as hate me. I have found
Thy love unfeign'd; have seen and pitied
Thy open wrongs, and come, out of my love,
To give thee just revenge against thy foes.
*Saw.* May I believe thee?
*Dog.* To confirm't, command me
Do any mischief unto man or beast.
And I'll effect it, on condition
That, uncompell'd, thou make a deed of gift
Of soul and body to me.

*Saw.* Out, alas!
 My soul and body?

*Dog.* And that instantly,
And seal it with thy blood: if thou deniest,

I'll tear thy body in a thousand pieces.

*Saw.* I know not where to seek relief: but shall I,
After such covenants seal'd, see full revenge
On all that wrong me?

*Dog.* Ha, ha! silly woman!
The devil is no liar to such as he loves—
Didst ever know or hear the devil a liar
To such as he affects?

*Saw.* Then I am thine; at least so much of me
As I can call mine own—

*Dog.* Equivocations?
Art mine or no? speak, or I'll tear—
*Saw.* All thine.
*Dog.* Seal't with thy blood.
[*She pricks her arm, which he sucks.—Thunder and lightning.*
See! now I dare call thee mine!
For proof, command me: instantly I'll run
To any mischief; goodness can I none.

*Saw.* And I desire as little. There's an old churl,
One Banks—
*Dog.* That wrong'd thee: he lamed thee, call'd thee witch.
*Saw.* The same; first upon him I'd be revenged.
*Dog.* Thou shalt; do but name how?
*Saw.* Go, touch his life.
*Dog.* I cannot.
*Saw.* Hast thou not vow'd? Go, kill the slave!
*Dog.* I will not.
*Saw.* I'll cancel then my gift.
*Dog.* Ha, ha!
*Saw.* Dost laugh!
Why wilt not kill him?

*Dog.* Fool, because I cannot.
Though we have power, know, it is circumscribed,
And tied in limits: though he be curst to thee,
Yet of himself, he is loving to the world,
And charitable to the poor; now men, that,
As he, love goodness, though in smallest measure,

care not for thee, hang thy selfe: Presently wherevpon, at this Examinates going ouer the next hedge, the said Spirit or Diuell called *Tibb*, appeared vnto this Examinat, and sayd, *Reuenge thee of him*. To whom, this Examinate sayd againe to the said Spirit. *Revenge thee eyther of him, or his*. And so the said Spirit vanished out of her sight, and she neuer saw him since.

And further this Examinate confesseth, and sayth, that the speediest way to take a mans life away by Witchcraft, is to make a Picture of Clay\*, like vnto the shape of the person whom they meane to kill, & dry it thorowly: and when they would haue them to be ill in any one place more then an other; then take a Thorne or Pinne, and pricke it in that part of the Picture you would so haue to be ill: and when you would haue any part of the Body to consume away, then take that part of the Picture, and burne it. And when they would haue the whole body to consume away, then take the remnant of the sayd Picture, and burne it: and so therevpon by that meanes, the body shall die.

---

\*"*Is to make a picture of clay.*"]

*Hecate.* What death is't you desire for Almachildes?

---

Live without compass of our reach: his cattle
And corn I'll kill and mildew; but his life
(Until I take him, as I late found thee,
Cursing and swearing) I have no power to touch.

*Saw.* Work on his corn and cattle then.
*Dog.* I shall.
The Witch of Edmonton shall see his fall.
*Ford's Plays*, edit. 1839, p. 190.

*Duchess.* A sudden and a subtle.

*Hecate.* Then I've fitted you.
Here be the gifts of both; sudden and subtle:
His picture made in wax and gently molten
By a blue fire kindled with dead men's eyes
Will waste him by degrees.

*Duchess.* In what time, prithee?

*Hecate.* Perhaps in a moon's progress.

*Middleton's Witch*, edit. 1778, p. 100.

None of the offices in the Witches rubric had higher classical warrant than this method, a favourite one, it appears, of Mother Demdike, but in which Anne Redfern had the greatest skill of any of these Pendle witches, of victimizing by moulding and afterwards pricking or burning figures of clay representing the individual whose life was aimed at. Horace, Lib. i. Sat. 8, mentions both waxen and woollen images—

Lanea et effigies erat altera cerea, &c.

And it appears from Tacitus, that the death of Germanicus was supposed to have been sought by similar practices. By such a Simulachrum, or image, the person was supposed to be devoted to the infernal deities. According to the Platonists, the effect produced arose from the operation of the sympathy and synergy of the Spiritus Mundanus, (which Plotinus calls τον μεγαν γοητα, the grand magician,) such as they resolve the effect of the weaponsalve and other magnetic cures into. The following is the Note in Brand on this part of witchcraft:—

King James, in his "Dæmonology," book ii., chap. 5, tells us, that "the Devil teacheth how to make pictures of wax or clay, that, by roasting thereof, the persons that they bear the name of may be continually melted or dried away by continual sickness."

See Servius on the 8th Eclogue of Virgil; Theocritus, Idyll, ii., 22; Hudibras, part II., canto ii., l. 351.

Ovid says:

"Devovet absentes, simulachraque cerea figit
Et miserum tenues in jecur urget acus."
*Heroid.* Ep. vi., l. 91.

See also "Grafton's Chronicle," p. 587, where it is laid to the charge (among others) of Roger Bolinbrook, a cunning necromancer, and Margery Jordane, the cunning Witch of Eye, that they, at the request of Eleanor, Duchess of Gloucester, had devised an image of wax, representing the king, (Henry the Sixth,) which by their sorcery a little and a little consumed; intending thereby in conclusion to waste and destroy the king's person. Shakspeare mentions this, Henry VI., P. II., act i., sc. 4.

It appears, from Strype's "Annals of the Reformation,", vol. i., p. 8, under anno 1558, that Bishop Jewel, preaching before the queen, said, "It may please your grace to understand that witches and sorcerers within these few last years are marvellously increased within your grace's realm. Your grace's subjects pine away, even unto the death; their colour fadeth, their flesh rotteth, their speech is benumbed, their senses are bereft. I pray God they never practise *further than upon the subject.*" "This," Strype adds, "I make no doubt was the occasion of bringing in a bill, the next parliament, for making enchantments and witchcraft felony." One of the bishop's strong expressions is, "*These eyes have seen* most evident and manifest marks of their wickedness."

It appears from the same work, vol. iv., p. 6, sub anno 1589, that "one Mrs. Dier had practised conjuration against the queen, to work some mischief to her majesty; for which she was brought into question: and accordingly her words and doings were sent to Popham, the queen's attorney, and Egerton, her solicitor, by Walsingham, the secretary, and Sir Thomas Heneage, her vice-chamberlain, for their judgment, whose opinion was that Mrs. Dier was not within the compass of the statute touching witchcraft, for that she did no act, and spake certain lewd speeches tending to that purpose, but neither set figure nor made pictures." *Ibid.,* vol. ii., p. 545, sub anno 1578, Strype says: "Whether it were the effect of magic, or proceeded from some natural cause, but the queen was in some part of this year under excessive anguish *by pains of her teeth*, insomuch that she took no rest for divers nights, and endured very great torment night and day."

Andrews, in his "Continuation of Henry's History of Great Britain," 4to, p. 93, tells us, speaking of Ferdinand, Earl of Derby, who in the reign of Queen Elizabeth died by poison, "The credulity of the age attributed his death to witchcraft. The disease was odd, and operated as a perpetual emetic; and a *waxen image, with hair like that of the unfortunate earl*, found in his chamber, reduced every suspicion to certainty."

"The wife of Marshal d'Ancre was apprehended, imprisoned, and beheaded for a witch, upon a surmise that she had inchanted the queen to dote upon her husband; and they say the young king's picture was found in her closet, in virgin wax, with one leg melted away. When asked by her judges what spells she had made use of to gain so powerful an ascendancy over the queen, she replied, 'that ascendancy only which strong minds ever gain over weak ones.'" Seward's "Anecdotes of some Distinguished Persons," &c., vol. ii., p. 215.

Blagrave, in his "Astrological Practice of Physick," p. 89, observes that "the way which the witches usually take for to afflict man or beast in this kind is, as I conceive, done by image or model, made in the likeness of that man or beast they intend to work mischief upon, and by the subtlety of the devil made at such hours and times when it shall work most powerfully upon them, by thorn, pin, or needle, pricked into that limb or member of the body afflicted."

This is farther illustrated by a passage in one of Daniel's Sonnets:

"The slie inchanter, when to work his will
And secret wrong on some forspoken wight,
Frames waxe, in forme to represent aright
The poore unwitting wretch he meanes to kill,
And prickes the image, framed by magick's skill,
Whereby to vex the partie day and night."
*Son. 10; from Poems and Sonnets annexed to "Astrophil and Stella,"* 4to, 1591.

Again, in "Diaria, or the Excellent Conceitful Sonnets of H.C.," (Henry Constable,) 1594:

"Witches, which some murther do intend,
Doe make a picture, and doe shoote at it;
And in that part where they the picture hit,
The parties self doth languish to his end."
*Decad. II., Son. ii.*

Coles, in his "Art of Simpling," &c., p. 66, says that witches "take likewise the roots of mandrake, according to some, or, as I rather suppose, the *roots of briony*, which simple folke take for the true mandrake, and make thereof an ugly image, by which they represent the person on whom they intend to exercise their witchcraft." He tells us, *ibid.*, p. 26, "Some plants have roots with a number of threads, like beards, as mandrakes, whereof witches and impostors make an ugly image, giving it the form of the face at the top of the root, and leave those strings to make a broad beard down to the feet."—*Brand's Antiquities*, vol. iii. p. 9.

Ben Johnson has not forgotten this superstition in his learned and fanciful *Masque of Queens*, in which so much of the lore of witchcraft is embodied. There are few finer things in English poetry than his 3rd Charm:—

The owl is abroad, the bat, and the toad,
And so is the cat-a-mountain,
The ant and the mole sit both in a hole,
And the frog peeps out o' the fountain;
The dogs they do bay, and the timbrels play,
The spindle is now a turning;
The moon it is red, and the stars are fled,
But all the sky is a burning:
The ditch is made, and our nails the spade,
*With pictures full, of wax and of wool;*
*Their livers I stick, with needles quick;*
There lacks but the blood, to make up the flood.
Quickly, dame, then bring your part in,
Spur, spur upon little Martin,
Merrily, merrily, make him sail,
A worm in his mouth, and a thorn in his tail,
Fire above, and fire below,
With a whip in your hand, to make him go.
*Ben Johnson's Works, by Gifford*, vol. vii. p. 121.

Meric Casaubon, who is always an amusing writer, and whose works, notwithstanding his appetite for the wonderful, do not merit the total oblivion into which they have fallen, is very angry with Jerome Cardan, an author not generally given to scepticism, for the hesitation he displays on the subject of these waxen images:—

I know some who question not the power of devils or witches; yet in this particular are not satisfied how such a thing can be. For there is no relation or sympathy in nature, (saith one, who hath written not many years ago,) between a man and his effigies, that upon the pricking of the one the other should grow sick. It is upon another occasion that he speaks it; but his exception reacheth this example equally. A wonder to me he should so argue, who in many things hath very well confuted the incredulity of others, though in some things too credulous himself. If we must believe nothing but what we can reduce to natural, or, to speak more properly, (for I myself believe the devil doth very little, but by nature, though to us unknown,) manifest causes, he doth overthrow his own grounds, and leaves us but very little of magical operations to believe. But of all men, Cardan had least reason to except against this kind of magick as ridiculous or incredible, who himself is so full of incredible stories in that kind, upon his own credit alone, that they had need to be of very easie belief that believe him, especially when they know (whereof more afterwards) what manner of man he was. But I dare say, that from Plato's time, who, among other appurtenances of magic, doth mention these, κηρινα μιμηματα that is, as Ovid doth call them, *Simulachra cerea,* or as Horace, *cereas imagines,* (who also in another place more particularly describes them,) there is not any particular rite belonging to that art more fully attested by histories of all ages than this is. Besides, who doth not know that it is the devil's fashion (we shall meet with it afterwards again) to amuse his servants and vassals with many rites and ceremonies, which have certainly no ground in nature, no relation or sympathy to the thing, as for other reasons, so to make them believe, they have a great hand in the production of such and such effects; when, God knows, many times all that they do, though taught and instructed by him, is nothing at all to the purpose, and he, in very deed, is the only agent, by means which he doth give them no account of. Bodinus, in his preface to his "Dæmonology," relateth, that three waxen images, whereof one of Queen Elizabeth's, of glorious memory, and two other, *Reginæ proximorum,* of two courtiers, of greatest authority under the queen, were found in the house of a priest at Islington, a magician, or so reputed, to take away their lives. This he doth repeat again in his second book, chap. 8, but more particularly that it was in the year of the Lord 1578, and that Legatus Angliæ and many Frenchmen did divulge it so; but withal, in both places he doth add, that the business was then under trial, and not yet perfectly known. I do not trust my memory: I know my age and my infirmities. Cambden, I am sure, I have read; and read again; but neither in him, nor in Bishop Carleton's "Thankful Remembrancer," do I remember any such thing. Others may, perchance. Yet, in the year 1576, I read in both of some pictures, representing some that would have kill'd that glorious queen with a motto, *Quorsum hæc, alio properantibus!* which pictures were made by some of the conspiracy for their incouragement; but intercepted, and showed, they say, to the queen. Did the time agree, it is possible these pictures might be the ground of those mistaken, if mistaken, waxen images, which I desire to be taught by others who can give a better account.— *Casaubon's (M.) Treatise, proving Spirits, Witches, and Supernatural Operations,* 1672. 12mo., p. 92.

In Scotland this practice was in high favour with witches, both in ancient and modern times. The lamentable story of poor King Duff, as related by Hector Boethius, a story which has blanched the cheek and spoiled the rest of many a youthful reader, is too well known to need extracting. Even so late as 1676, Sir George Maxwell, of Pollock, (See Scott's *Letters on Demonology and*

*Witchcraft*, p. 323,) apparently a man of melancholy and valetudinarian habits, believed himself bewitched to death by six witches, one man and five women, who were leagued for the purpose of tormenting a clay image in his likeness. Five of the accused were executed, and the sixth only escaped on account of extreme youth.

Isabel Gowdie, the famous Scotch witch before referred to, in her confessions gives a very particular account of the mode in which these images were manufactured. It is curious, and worth quoting:—

*Johne Taylor* and *Janet Breadhead*, his wyff, in Bellnakeith, *Bessie Wilsone*, in Aulderne, and *Margret Wilsone*, spows to *Donald Callam* in Aulderne, and I, maid an pictur of clay, to destroy *the Laird of Parkis* meall[74] children. *Johne Taylor* browght hom the clay, in his plaid newk;[75] his wyff brak it verie small, lyk meall,[76] and sifted it with a siew,[77] and powred in water among it, in *the Divellis* nam, and vrought it werie sore, lyk rye-bowt;[78] and maid of it a pictur of *the Lairdis* sones. It haid all the pairtis and merkis of a child, such as heid, eyes, nose, handis, foot, mowth, and little lippes. It wanted no mark of a child; and the handis of it folded down by its sydes. It was lyk a pow,[79] or a flain gryce.[80] We laid the face of it to the fyre, till it strakned;[81] and a cleir fyre round abowt it, till it ves read lyk a cole.[82] After that, we wold rest it now and then; each other day[83] ther wold be an piece of it weill rosten. *The Laird of Parkis* heall maill children by it ar to suffer, if it be not gotten and brokin, als weill as thes that ar borne and dead alreadie. It ves still putt in and taken out of the fyre, in *the Divellis* name. It wes hung wp wpon an knag. It is yet in *Johne Taylor's* hows, and it hes a cradle of clay abowt it. Onlie *Johne Taylor* and his wyff, *Janet Breadhead*, *Bessie* and *Margret Wilsones* in Aulderne, and *Margret Brodie*, thair, and I, were onlie at the making of it. All the multitud of our

---

[74] Male.
[75] In the nook, or corner, of his plaid.
[76] Pounded, or powdered it, like meal.
[77] To make the plaster fine, and free from earthy particles.
[78] Probably a sort of stir-about, or hasty-pudding, made of rye-flour.
[79] In another deposition it is thus expressed, 'lyk a *pow or feadge*.' A *feadge* was a sort of *scone*, or roll, of a pretty large size. Perhaps this term signifies, as large as the quantity of dough or paste necessary for making this kind of bread.
[80] A flayed sucking pig, after being scalded and scraped.
[81] Shrivelled with the heat.
[82] Red like a coal.
[83] Each alternate day.

number of Witches, of all the Coevens, kent[84] all of it, at owr nixt meitting after it was maid.

The wordis which we spak, quhan we maid the pictur, for distroyeing of *the Laird of Parkis* meall-children, wer thus:

'In the Divellis nam, we powr in this water among this mowld (meall,)[85]
For lang duyning and ill heall;
We putt it into the fyre,
That it mey be brunt both stik and stowre.
It salbe brunt, with owr will,
As any stikle[86] wpon a kill.'

The Divell taught ws the wordis; and quhan ve haid learned them, we all fell downe wpon owr bare kneyis, and owr hair abowt owr eyes, and owr handis lifted wp, looking steadfast wpon the Divell, still saying the wordis thryse ower, till it wes maid. And then, in the Divellis nam, we did put it in, in the midst of the fyre. Efter it had skrukned[87] a little before the fyre, and quhan it ves read lyk a coale, we took it owt in the Divellis nam. Till it be broken, it will be the deathe of all the meall children that *the Laird of Park* will ewer get. Cast it ower an Kirk, it will not brak quhill[88] it be broken with an aix, or som such lyk thing, be a man's handis. If it be not broken, it will last an hundreth yeir. It hes ane cradle about it of clay, to preserue it from skaith;[89] and it wes rosten each vther day, at the fyr; som tymes on pairt of it, som tymes an vther pairt of it; it vold be a litle wat with water, and then rosten. The bairn vold be brunt and rosten, ewin as it ves by ws.—*Pitcairne's Criminal Trials*, Vol. iii. pp. 605 and 612.

---

[84] Knew.
[85] It is written *meall* in the other Confession; and the metre (such as it is) requires this liberty. *Mowld* signifies 'earth' or 'dust.'
[86] Stubble.
[87] Parched; shrivelled.
[88] Until.
[89] Harm; injury.

The Confession and Examination
of Anne Whittle *alias* Chattox, being
**Prisoner at *Lancaster*; taken the 19 day of May,**
*Annoq; Regni Regis Iacobi Angliæ, Decimo:
ac Scotie Quadragesimo quinto*; **Before
William Sandes Maior of the Borrough
towne of *Lancaster*.**

*Iames Anderton* **of *Clayton*, one of his Maiesties Iustices
of Peace within the same County, and *Thomas
Cowell* one of his Maiesties Coroners in
the sayd Countie of Lancaster,**
*Viz.*

FIRST, the sayd *Anne Whittle*, alias *Chattox*, sayth, that about foureteene yeares past she entered, through the wicked perswasions and counsell of *Elizabeth Southerns*, alias *Demdike*, and was seduced to condescend & agree to become subiect vnto that diuelish abhominable profession of Witchcraft: Soone after which, the Deuill appeared vnto her in the liknes of a Man, about midnight, at the house of the sayd *Demdike*: and therevpon the sayd *Demdike* and shee, went foorth of the said house vnto him; wherevpon the said wicked Spirit mooued this Examinate, that she would become his Subiect, and giue her Soule vnto him: the which at first, she refused to assent vnto; but after, by the great perswasions made by the sayd *Demdike*, shee yeelded to be at his commaundement and appoyntment: wherevpon the sayd wicked Spirit then sayd vnto her, that hee must haue one part of her body for him to sucke vpon; the which shee denyed then to graunt vnto him; and withall asked him, what part of her body hee would haue for that vse; who said, hee would haue a place of her right side neere to her ribbes, for him to sucke vpon: whereunto shee assented.

And she further sayth, that at the same time, there was a thing in the likenes of a spotted Bitch, that came with the sayd Spirit vnto the sayd *Demdike*, which then did speake vnto her in this Examinates hearing, and sayd, that she should haue Gould, Siluer, and worldly Wealth, at her will.[90] And at the same time she saith, there was victuals, *viz.* Flesh, Butter, Cheese, Bread, and Drinke, and bidde them eate enough. And after their eating, the Deuill called *Fancie*, and the other Spirit calling himselfe *Tibbe*, carried the remnant away: And she sayeth, that although they did eate, they were neuer the fuller, nor better for the same; and that at their said Banquet, the said Spirits gaue them light to see what they did, although they neyther had fire nor Candle light; and that they were both shee Spirites, and Diuels.

---

[90] "*And sayd that she should haue gould, siluer, and worldly wealth at her will.*"] These familiars, to use Warburton's expression, always promised with the lavishness of a young courtier, and performed with the indifference of an old one. Nothing seems to puzzle Dr. Dee more, in the long and confidential intercourse he carried on so many years with his spirits, than to account for the great scarcity of specie they seemed to be afflicted with, and the unsatisfactory and unfurnished state of their exchequer. Bills, to be sure, they gave at long dates; but these constantly required renewing, and were never honoured at last. Any application for present relief, in good current coin of the realm, was invariably followed by what Meric Casaubon very significantly calls "sermonlike stuff." The learned professor in witchery, John Stearne, seems to fix six shillings as the maximum of money payment at one time which in all his experience he had detected between witches and their familiars. He was examining Joan Ruccalver, of Powstead, in Suffolk, who had been promised by her spirit that she should never want meat, drink, clothes, or money. "Then I asked her whether they brought her any money or no; and she said sometimes four shillings at a time, and sometimes six shillings at a time; but that is but seldom, *for I never knew any that had any money before,* except of Clarke's wife, of Manningtree, who confessed the same, and showed some, which, she said, her impe brought her, which was proper money." Confirmation, page 27. Judging from the anxiety which this worthy displays to be "satisfied and paid with reason" for his itinerant labours, such a scanty and penurious supply would soon have disgusted him, if he had been witch, instead of witch-finder.

And being further examined how many sundry Person haue been bewitched to death, and by whom they were so bewitched: She sayth, that one *Robert Nuter*, late of the *Greene-head* in *Pendle*, was bewitched by this Examinate, the said *Demdike*, and Widdow *Lomshawe*, (late of *Burneley*) now deceased.

And she further sayth, that the said *Demdike* shewed her, that she had bewitched to death, *Richard Ashton*, Sonne of *Richard Ashton* of *Downeham* Esquire.[91]

---

[91] "*She had bewitched to death Richard Ashton, sonne of Richard Ashton, of Downeham, Esquire.*"] Richard Assheton, (as the name is more properly spelled,) thus done to death by witchcraft, was the son of Richard Assheton, of Downham, an old manor house, the scite of which is now supplied by a modern structure, which Dr. Whitaker thinks, in point of situation, has no equal in the parish of Whalley. Richard, the son, married Isabel, daughter and heiress of Mr. Hancock, of Pendleton Hall, and died without offspring. The family estate accordingly descended to the younger brother, Nicholas Assheton, whose diary for part of the year 1617 and part of the year following is given, page 303 of Whitaker's *History of Whalley*, edition 1818, and is a most valuable record of the habits, pursuits, and course of life of a Lancashire country gentleman of that period. It well deserves detaching in a separate publication, and illustrating with a more expanded commentary.

The Examination of Alizon
Deuice, of the Forrest of Pendle, in the County
**of *Lancaster* Spinster, taken at *Reade* in the said
Countie of *Lancaster*, the xiij. day of March,
*Anno Regni Jacobi Angliæ, &c.
Nono: et Scotiæ xlv.***

**Before *Roger Nowell* of *Reade* aforesayd Esquire, one of
his Maiesties Iustices of the Peace within the sayd
Countie, against *Elizabeth Sowtherns*, alias
*Demdike* her Graund-mother.
*Viz.***

THe sayd *Alizon Deuice* sayth, that about two yeares agon, her Graund-mother (called *Elizabeth Sowtherns*, alias old *Demdike*) did sundry times in going or walking togeather as they went begging, perswade and aduise this Examinate to let a Deuill or Familiar appeare vnto her; and that shee this Examinate, would let him sucke at some part of her, and shee might haue, and doe what shee would.

And she further sayth, that one *Iohn Nutter* of the *Bulhole* in *Pendle* aforesaid, had a Cow which was sicke, & requested this examinats Grand-mother to amend the said Cow; and her said Graund-mother said she would, and so her said Graund-mother about ten of the clocke in the night, desired this examinate to lead her foorth; which this Examinate did, being then blind: and her Graund-mother did remaine about halfe an houre foorth: and this Examinates sister did fetch her in againe; but what she did when she was so foorth, this Examinate cannot tell. But the next morning this Examinate heard that the sayd Cow was dead. And this Examinate verily thinketh, that her sayd Graund-mother did bewitch the sayd Cow to death.

And further, this Examinate sayth, that about two yeares agon, this Examinate hauing gotten a Piggin full[92] of blew Milke by begging, brought it into the house of her Graundmother, where (this Examinate going foorth presently, and staying about halfe an houre) there was Butter to the quantity of a quarterne of a pound in the said milke, and the quantitie of the said milke still remayning; and her Graundmother had no Butter in the house when this Examinate went foorth: duering which time, this Examinates Graundmother still lay in her bed.

And further this Examinate sayth, that *Richard Baldwin* of *Weethead* within the Forrest of *Pendle*, about 2. yeeres agoe, fell out with this Examinates Graund-mother, & so would not let her come vpon his Land: and about foure or fiue dayes then next after, her said Graund-mother did request this Examinate to lead her foorth about ten of the clocke in the night: which this Examinate accordingly did, and she stayed foorth then about an houre, and this Examinates sister fetched her in againe. And this Examinate heard the next morning, that a woman Child of the sayd *Richard Baldwins* was fallen sicke; and as this Examinate did then heare, the sayd Child did languish afterwards by the space of a yeare, or thereaboutes, and dyed: And this Examinate verily thinketh, that her said Graund-mother did bewitch the sayd Child to death.

And further, this Examinate sayth, that she heard her sayd Graund-mother say presently after her falling out with the sayd *Baldwin*, shee would pray for the sayd *Baldwin* both still and loude: and this Examinate heard her cursse the sayd *Baldwin* sundry times.

---

[92] "*Piggin full.*"] Piggin is properly a sort of bowl, or pail, with one of the staves much longer than the rest, made for a handle, to lade water by, and used especially in brewhouses to measure out the liquor with.

The Examination of *Iames Deuice* of the Forrest of *Pendle*, in the Countie of *Lancaster* Labourer, taken the **27. day of April,** *Annoq; Regni Regis Iacobi, Angliæ, &c.* **Decimo: ac Scotie Quadragesimo quinto: Before Roger Nowell and Nicholas Banister, Esq. two of his Maiesties Iustices of Peace within the sayd Countie.**[93]

THE sayd Examinate *Iames Deuice* sayth, that about a month agoe, as this Examinate was comming towards his Mothers house, and at day-gate of the same night, *Euening*. this Examinate mette a browne Dogge comming from his Graund-mothers house, about tenne Roodes distant from the same house: and about two or three nights after, that this Examinate heard a voyce of a great number of Children screiking and crying pittifully, about day-light gate; and likewise, about ten Roodes distant of this Examinates sayd Graund-mothers house. And about fiue nights then next following, presently after daylight, within 20. Roodes of the sayd *Elizabeth Sowtherns* house, he heard a foule yelling like vnto a great number of Cattes: but what they were, this Examinate cannot tell. And he further sayth, that

---

[93] "*Nicholas Banister.*"] Dr. Whitaker, in the pedigree of the Banisters, of Altham, (genealogy was, it is well known, one of the vulnerable parts of this Achilles of topography,) erroneously states this Nicholas Banister to have been buried at Altham, December 7, 1611. It appears, however, from a deed, an inspection of which I owe to the kindness of my friend, Dr. Fleming, that his will was dated the 15th August, 1612. In all probability he did not die for some years after that date. He married, first, Elizabeth, daughter and heiress of Richard Elston, of Brockall, Esq.; and, second, Catherine, daughter of Edmund Ashton, of Chaderton, Esq. The manor house of Altham, for more than five centuries the residence of this ancient family, stands, to use Dr. Whitaker's words, upon a gentle elevation on the western side of the river Calder, commanding a low and fertile domain. It has been surrounded, according to the prudence or jealousy of the feudal times, with a very deep quadrangular moat, which must have included all the apparatus of the farm.

about three nights after that, about midnight of the same, there came a thing, and lay vpon him very heauily about an houre, and went then from him out of his Chamber window, coloured blacke, and about the bignesse of a Hare or Catte. And he further sayth, that about *S. Peter's* day last, one *Henry Bullocke* came to the sayd *Elizabeth Sowtherns* house, and sayd, that her Graund-child *Alizon Deuice*, had bewitched a Child of his, and desired her that she would goe with him to his house; which accordingly she did: And therevpon she the said *Alizon* fell downe on her knees, & asked the said *Bullocke* forgiuenes, and confessed to him, that she had bewitched the said child, as this Examinate heard his said sister confesse vnto him this Examinate.

The Examination of Elizabeth
Deuice, Daughter of old Demdike, taken
**at *Read* before *Roger Nowell* Esquire, one of
his Maiesties Iustices of Peace within the
Countie of *Lancaster* the xxx. day
of March, *Annoq; Regni Jacobi
Decimo, ac Scotie xlv.***

THe sayd *Elizabeth Deuice* the Examinate, sayth, that the sayd *Elizabeth Sowtherns*, alias *Demdike*, hath had a place on her left side by the space of fourty yeares, in such sort, as was to be seene at this Examinates Examination taking, at this present time.

Heere this worthy Iustice M. *Nowell*, out of these particular Examinations, or rather Accusations, finding matter to proceed; and hauing now before him old *Demdike*, old *Chattox*, *Alizon Deuice*, and *Redferne* both old and young, *Reos confitentes, et Accusantes Inuicem*. About the second of Aprill last past, committed and sent them away to the Castle at *Lancaster*, there to remaine vntill the comming of the Kinges Maiesties Iustices of Assise, then to receiue their tryall.

But heere they had not stayed a weeke, when their Children and Friendes being abroad at libertie, laboured a speciall meeting at *Malking Tower* in the Forrest of *Pendle*,[94] vpon

---

[94] "*At Malking Tower, in the forrest of Pendle.*"] Malkin Tower was the habitation of Mother Demdike, the situation of which is preserved, for the structure no longer exists, by local tradition. Malkin is the Scotch or north country word for hare, as this animal was one into which witches were supposed to be fond of transforming themselves. Malkin Tower is, in fact, the Witches' Tower. The term is used in the following passage in Morison's *Poems*, p. 7, which bears upon the above explanation:—

Good-fryday, within a weeke after they were committed, of all the most dangerous, wicked, and damnable Witches in the County farre and neere. Vpon Good-fryday they met, according to solemne appoyntment, solemnized this great Feastiuall day according to their former order, with great cheare, merry company, and much conference.

In the end, in this great Assemblie, it was decreed M. *Couell* by reason of his Office, shall be slaine before the next Assises: The Castle of *Lancaster* to be blowen vp, and ayde and assistance to be sent to kill M. *Lister*, with his old Enemie and wicked Neighbour *Iennet Preston*; with some other such like practices: as vpon their Arraignement and Tryall, are particularly set foorth, and giuen in euidence against them.

This was not so secret, but some notice of it came to M. *Nowell*, and by his great paines taken in the Examination of *Iennet Deuice*, al their practises are now made knowen. Their purpose to kill M. *Couell*, and blow vp the Castle, is preuented. All their Murders, Witchcraftes, Inchauntments, Charmes, & Sorceries, are discouered; and euen in the middest of their consultations, they are all confounded, and arrested by Gods Iustice: brought before M. *Nowell*, and M. *Bannester*, vpon their voluntary confessions, Examinations, and other Euidence accused, and so by them committed to the Castle: So as now both old and young, haue taken vp their lodgings with M. *Couell*, vntill the next Assises,

---

"Or tell the pranks o' winter's nights,
How Satan blazes uncouth lights;
Or how he does a core convene
Upon a witch-frequented green,
Wi' spells and cauntrips hellish rantin',
Like mawkins thro' the fields they're janting."

expecting their Tryall and deliuerance, according to the Lawes prouided for such like.

In the meane time, M. *Nowell* hauing knowledge by this discouery of their meeting at *Malkeing Tower*, and their resolution to execute mischiefe, takes great paines to apprehend such as were at libertie, and prepared Euidence against all such as were in question for Witches.

Afterwardes sendes some of these Examinations, to the Assises at Yorke, to be giuen in Evidence against *Iennet Preston*, who for the murder of M. *Lister*, is condemned and executed.

The Circuite of the North partes being now almost ended.

The 16. of August.

Vpon Sunday in the after noone, my honorable Lords the Iudges of Assise, came from *Kendall* to *Lancaster*.

Wherevpon M. *Couell*, presented vnto their Lordships a Calender, conteyning the Names of the Prisoners committed to his charge, which were to receiue their Tryall at the Assises: Out of which, we are onely to deale with the proceedings against Witches, which were as followeth.

*Viz.*

The Names of the
### Witches committed to the Castle of *Lancaster*.

*Elizabeth Sowtherns.* } Who dyed before
alias } shee
*Old Demdike.* } came to her tryall.

*Anne Whittle*, alias *Chattox*.
*Elizabeth Deuice*, Daughter of old *Demdike*.
*Iames Deuice*, Sonne of *Elizabeth Deuice*.
*Anne Readfearne*, Daughter of *Anne Chattox*.
*Alice Nutter.*
*Katherine Hewytte.*
*Iohn Bulcocke.*
*Iane Bulcocke.*
*Alizon Deuice*, Daughter of *Elizabeth Deuice*.
*Isabell Robey.*
*Margaret Pearson.*

### The Witches of Salmesbury.

*Iennet Bierley.* } { *Elizabeth Astley.*
*Elen Bierley.* } { *Alice Gray.*
*Iane Southworth.* } { *Isabell Sidegraues.*
*Iohn Ramesden.* } { *Lawrence Haye.*

The next day, being Monday, the 17. of August, were the Assises holden in the Castle of *Lancaster*, as followeth.

# Placita Coronæ.

*DLanc. fss.Eliberatio Gaolæ Domini Regis Castri fui Lancasstr. ac Prisonarioru̅ in eadem existent. Tenta apud Lancastr. in com. Lancastr. Die Lunæ, Decimo septimo die Augusti, Anno Regni Domini nostri Iacobi dei gratia Anglicæ, Franciæ, et Hiberniæ, Regis fidei defensoris; Decimo: et Scotiæ Quadragesimo sexto; Coram Iacobo Altham Milit. vno Baronum Scaccarij Domini Regis, et Edwardo Bromley Milit. altero Baronum eiusdem Scaccarij Domini Regis: ac Iustic. dicti Domini Regis apud Lancastr.*

VPon the Tewesday in the after noone, the Iudges according to the course and order, deuided them selues, where vpon my Lord *Bromley*, one of his Maiesties Iudges of Assise comming into the Hall to proceede with the Pleaes of the Crowne, & the Arraignement and Tryall of Prisoners, commaunded a generall Proclamation, that all Iustices of Peace that had taken any Recognisaunces, or Examinations of Prisoners, should make Returne of them: And all such as were bound to prosecute Indictmentes, and giue Euidence against Witches, should proceede, and giue attendance: For hee now intended to proceede to the Arraignement and Tryall of Witches.

After which, the Court being set, M. Sherieffe was commaunded to present his Prisoners before his Lordship, and prepare a sufficient Iurie of Gentlemen for life and death. But heere we want old *Demdike*, who dyed in the Castle before she came to her tryall.[95]

---

[95] "*We want old Demdike, who dyed in the castle before she came to her tryall.*"] Worn out most probably with her imprisonment, she having been committed in April, and the cruelties she had undergone, both before and after her commitment. Master Nowell and Master Potts both *wanted* her, we may readily conceive, to fill up the miserable pageant; but she was gone where the wicked cease from troubling, and the weary are at rest. With the exception of Alice Nutter, in whom interest is excited from very different grounds, Mother Demdike attracts attention in a higher degree than any other of these Pendle witches. She was, beyond dispute, the Erictho of Pendle. Mother Chattox was but second in rank. There is something fearfully intense in the expression of the former,—blind, on the last verge of the extreme limit of human existence, and mother of a line of witches,—"that she would pray for the said Baldwin, both still and loud." She is introduced in Shadwell's play, the *Lancashire Witches*, 1682, as a *persona dramatis*, along with Mother Dickinson and Mother Hargrave, two of the witches convicted in 1633, but without any regard to the characteristic circumstances under which she appears in the present narrative. The following invocation, which is put into her mouth, is rather a favourable specimen of that play, certainly not one of the worst of Shadwell's, in which there are many vigorous strokes, with an alloy of coarseness not unusual in his works, and some powerful conceptions of character:
Come, sisters, come, why do you stay?
Our business will not brook delay;
The owl is flown from the hollow oak,
From lakes and bogs the toads do croak;
The foxes bark, the screech-owl screams,
Wolves howl, bats fly, and the faint beams
Of glow-worms light grows bright a-pace;
The stars are fled, the moon hides her face.
The spindle now is turning round,
Mandrakes are groaning under ground:
I'th' hole i'th' ditch (our nails have made)
Now all our images are laid,
Of wax and wooll, which we must prick,
With needles urging to the quick.
Into the hole I'le poure a flood
Of black lambs bloud, to make all good.
The lamb with nails and teeth wee'l tear.
Come, where's the sacrifice? appear.

* * * *

Oyntment for flying here I have,
Of childrens fat, stoln from the grave:
The juice of smallage, and night-shade,
Of poplar leaves, and aconite, made
With these.
The aromatic reed I boyl,
With water-parsnip and cinquefoil;
With store of soot, and add to that
The reeking blood of many a bat.
*Lancashire Witches*, pp. 10, 41.

One of the peculiarities of Shadwell's play is the introduction of the Lancashire dialect, which he makes his clown Clod speak. The subjoined extract may perhaps amuse my readers. Collier would have enjoyed it:

*Clod.* An yeow been a mon Ay'st talk wy ye a bit, yeow mun tack a care o your sells, the plecs haunted with Buggarts, and Witches, one of 'em took my Condle and Lanthorn out of my hont, and flew along wy it; and another Set me o top o'th tree, where I feel dawn now, Ay ha well neegh brocken my theegh.

*Doubt.* The fellows mad, I neither understand his words, nor his Sence, prethee how far is it to Whalley?

*Clod.* Why yeow are quite besaid th' road mon, yeow Shoulden a gon dawn th' bonk by *Thomas* o *Georges*, and then ee'n at yate, and turn'd dawn th' Lone, and left the Steepo o'th reeght hont.

*Bell.* Prithee don't tell us what we should have done, but how far is it to Whalley?

*Clod.* Why marry four mail and a bit.

*Doubt.* Wee'l give thee an Angel and show us the way thither.

*Clod.* Marry thats Whaint. I canno see my hont, haw con Ay show yeow to Whalley to neeght.

*Bell.* Canst thou show us to any house where we may have Shelter and Lodging to night? we are Gentlemen and strangers, and will pay you well for't.

*Clod.* Ay byr Lady con I, th' best ludging and diet too in aw Lancashire. Yonder at th' hough where yeow seen th' leeghts there.

*Doubt.* Whose house is that?

*Clod.* Why what a pox, where han yeow lived? why yeow are Strongers indeed! why, 'tis Sir *Yedard Harfourts*, he Keeps oppen hawse to all Gentry, yeou'st be welcome to him by day and by neeght he's Lord of aw here abauts.

*Bell.* My Mistresses Father, Luck if it be thy will, have at my *Isabella*, Canst thou guide us thither?

*Clod.* Ay, Ay, there's a pawer of Company there naw, Sir *Jeffery Shaklehead*, and the Knight his Son, and Doughter.

Heere you may not expect the exact order of the Assises, with the Proclamations, and other solemnities belonging to so great a Court of Iustice; but the proceedinges against the Witches, who are now vpon their deliuerance here in order as they came to the Barre, with the particular poyntes of Euidence against them: which is the labour and worke we now intend (by Gods grace) to performe as we may, to your generall contentment.

Wherevpon, the first of all these, *Anne Whittle*, alias *Chattox*,[96] was brought to the Barre: against whom wee are now ready to proceed.

---

*Doubt.* Lucky above my wishes, O my dear *Theodosia*, how my heart leaps at her! prethee guide us thither, wee'l pay thee well.
*Clod.* Come on, I am e'n breed aut o my sences, I was ne'er so freeghtened sin I was born, give me your hont.—*Lancashire Witches*, p. 14.

[96] "*Ann Whittle, alias Chattox.*"] Chattox, from her continually chattering.

### The Arraignement and Tryall of Anne Whittle, *alias* Chattox, **of the Forrest of *Pendle*, in the Countie of *Lancaster*, Widdow;** **about the age of** Fourescore yeares, or thereaboutes.

## *Anne Whittle*, **alias** *Chattox.*

IF in this damnable course of life, and offences, more horrible and odious, then any man is able to expresse: any man lyuing could lament the estate of any such like vpon earth: The example of this poore creature, would haue moued pittie, in respect of her great contrition and repentance, after she was committed to the Castle at *Lancaster*, vntill the comming of his Maiesties Iudges of Assise. But such was the nature of her offences, & the multitude of her crying sinnes, as it tooke away all sense of humanity. And the repetition of her hellish practises, and Reuenge; being the chiefest thinges wherein she always tooke great delight, togeather with a particular declaration of the Murders shee had committed, layde open to the world, and giuen in Euidence against her at the time of her Arraignement and Tryall; as certainely it did beget contempt in the Audience, and such as she neuer offended.

This *Anne Whittle*, alias *Chattox*, was a very old withered spent and decreped creature, her sight almost gone: A dangerous Witch, of very long continuance; always opposite to old *Demdike*: For whom the one fauoured, the other hated deadly: *Her owne examination* and how they enuie and accuse one an other, in their Examinations, may appeare.

In her Witchcraft, alwayes more ready to doe mischiefe to mens goods, then themselues. Her lippes euer chattering and walking:[97] but no man knew what. She liued in the Forrest of *Pendle*, amongst this wicked company of dangerous Witches. Yet in her Examination and

---

[97] "*Her lippes euer chattering and walking.*"] Walking, *i.e.*, working. Old Chattox might have sat to Archbishop Harsnet for her portrait. What can exceed the force and graphic truth, the searching wit and sarcasm, of the picture he sketches in 1605?

Out of these is shaped vs the true *Idœa* of a Witch, an old weather-beaten Croane, hauing her chinne, & her knees meeting for age, walking like a bow leaning on a shaft, hollow eyed, vntoothed, furrowed on her face, hauing her lips trembling with the palsie, going mumbling in the streetes, one that hath forgottē her *pater noster*, and hath yet a shrewd tongue in her head, to call a drab, a drab. If shee haue learned of an olde wife in a chimnies end: *Pax, max, fax,* for a spel: or can say Sir *Iohn of Grantams* curse, for the Millers Eeles, that were stolne: All you that haue stolne the Millers Eeles, *Laudate dominum de cœlis*. And all they that haue consented thereto, *benedicamus domino*. Why then ho, beware, looke about you my neighbours; if any of you haue a sheepe sicke of the giddies, or an hogge of the mumps, or an horse of the staggers, or a knauish boy of the schoole, or an idle girle of the wheele, or a young drab of the sullens, and hath not fat enough for her porredge, nor her father, and mother, butter enough for their bread; and she haue a little helpe of the *Mother, Epilepsie,* or *Cramp,* to teach her role her eyes, wrie her mouth, gnash her teeth, startle with her body, holde her armes and hands stiffe, make anticke faces, grine, mow, and mop like an Ape, tumble like a Hedge-hogge, and can mutter out two or three words of gibridg, as *obus, bobus*: and then with-all old mother *Nobs* hath called her by chaunce, idle young huswife, or bid the deuill scratch her, then no doubt but mother *Nobs* is the Witch: the young girle is Owle-blasted, and possessed: and it goes hard but ye shall haue some idle adle, giddie, lymphaticall, illuminate dotrel, who being out of credite, learning, sobriety, honesty, and wit, will take this holy aduantage, to raise the ruines of his desperate decayed name, and for his better glory wil be-pray the iugling drab, and cast out *Mopp* the deuil.

They that haue their braines baited, and their fancies distempered with the imaginations, and apprehensions of Witches, Coniurers, and Fayries, and all that Lymphatical *Chimæra*: I finde to be marshalled in one of these fiue rankes, children, fooles, women, cowards, sick, or blacke, melancholicke, discomposed wits. The Scythians being a warlike Nation (as *Plutarch* reports) neuer saw any visions.—*Harsnet's Declaration*, p. 136.

Confession, she dealt always very plainely and truely: for vpon a speciall occasion being oftentimes examined in open Court, shee was neuer found to vary, but always to agree in one, and the selfe same thing.

I place her in order, next to that wicked fire-brand of mischiefe, old *Demdike*, because from these two, sprung all the rest in order:[98] and were the Children and Friendes, of these two notorious Witches.

Many things in the discouery of them, shall be very worthy your obseruation. As the times and occasions to execute their mischiefe. And this in generall: the Spirit could neuer hurt, till they gaue consent.

---

[98] "*From these two sprung all the rest in order.*"] The descent from these two rival witch stocks, between which a deadly feud and animosity prevailed, which led to the destruction of both families, is shewn as follows:

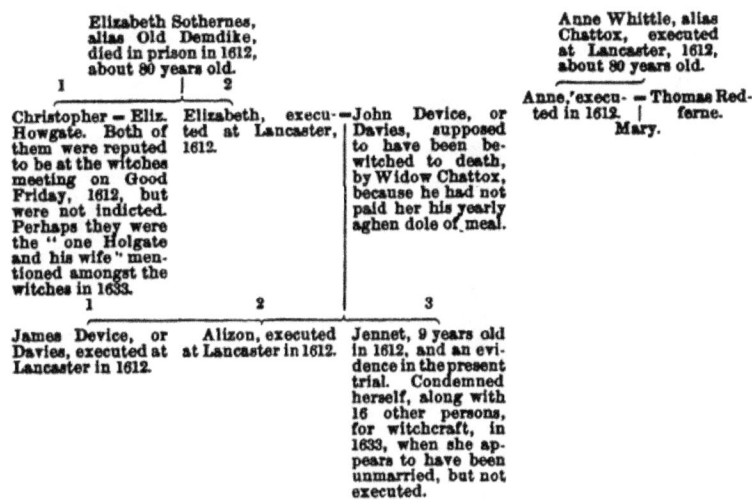

And, but that it is my charge, to set foorth a particular Declaration of the Euidence against them, vpon their Arraignement and Tryall; with their Diuelish practises, consultations, meetings, and murders committed by them, in such sort, as they were giuen in Euidence against them; for the which, I shall haue matter vpon Record. I could make a large Comentarie of them: But it is my humble duety, to obserue the Charge and Commaundement of these my Honorable good Lordes the Iudges of Assise, and not to exceed the limits of my Commission. Wherefore I shall now bring this auncient Witch, to the due course of her Tryall, in order. *viz.*

# Indictment.

THis *Anne Whittle*, alias *Chattox*, of the Forrest of *Pendle* in the Countie of *Lancaster* Widdow, being Indicted, for that shee feloniously had practised, vsed, and exercised diuers wicked and diuelish Artes called Witchcraftes, Inchauntmentes, Charmes, and Sorceries, in and vpon one *Robert Nutter* of *Greenehead*, in the Forrest of *Pendle*, in the Countie of *Lanc*: and by force of the same Witchcraft, feloniously the sayd *Robert Nutter* had killed, *Contra Pacem, &c.* Being at the Barre, was arraigned.

To this Indictment, vpon her Arraignement, shee pleaded, Not guiltie: and for the tryall of her life, put her selfe vpon God and her Country.

Wherevpon my Lord *Bromley* commaunded M. Sheriffe of the County of *Lancaster* in open Court, to returne a Iurie of worthy sufficient Gentlemen of vnderstanding, to passe betweene our soueraigne Lord the Kinges Maiestie, and her, and others the Prisoners, vpon their liues and deathes; as hereafter follow in order: who were afterwardes sworne, according to the forme and order of the Court, the Prisoners being admitted to their lawfull challenges.

Which being done, and the Prisoner at the Barre readie to receiue her Tryall: M. *Nowell*, being the best instructed of any man, of all the particular poyntes of Euidence against her, and her fellowes, hauing taken great paynes in the proceedinges against her and her fellowes; Humbly prayed, her owne voluntary Confession and Examination taken before him, when she was apprehended and committed to the Castle of *Lancaster* for Witchcraft; might openly be published against her: which hereafter followeth. *Viz.*

The voluntary Confession and Examination of
*Anne Whittle*, alias *Chattox*, taken at the *Fence* in the
Forrest of *Pendle*, in the Countie of *Lancaster*;
Before *Roger Nowell Esq*, one of the
Kinges Maiesties Iustices of Peace
in the Countie of Lancaster.
**Viz.**

THE sayd *Anne Whittle*, alias *Chattox*, vpon her Examination, voluntarily confesseth, and sayth, That about foureteene or fifteene yeares agoe, a thing like a Christian man for foure yeares togeather, did sundry times come to this Examinate, and requested this Examinate to giue him her Soule: And in the end, this Examinate was contented to giue him her sayd Soule, shee being then in her owne house, in the Forrest of *Pendle*; wherevpon the Deuill then in the shape of a Man, sayd to this Examinate: Thou shalt want nothing; and be reuenged of whom thou list. And the Deuill then further commaunded this Examinate, to call him by the name of *Fancie*;[99] and when she wanted any thing, or would be reuenged of any, call on *Fancie*, and he would be ready. And the sayd Spirit or Deuill, did appeare vnto her not long after, in mans likenesse, and would haue had this Examinate to haue consented, that he might hurt the wife of *Richard Baldwin* of *Pendle*;[100] But this Examinate would not then consent vnto him: For which

---

[99] "*Commaunded this examinate to call him by the name of Fancie.*"] The fittest name for a familiar she could possibly have chosen. Sir Walter Scott (*Letters on Demonology*, p. 242) unaccountably speaks of Fancie as a female devil. Master Potts would have told him, "that Fancie had a very good face, and was a very proper man."

[100] "*The wife of Richard Baldwin, of Pendle.*"] Richard Baldwin was the miller who accosted Old Dembdike so unceremoniously.

cause, the sayd *Deuill* would then haue bitten her by the arme; and so vanished away, for that time.

And this Examinate further sayth, that *Robert Nutter*[101] did desire her Daughter one *Redfearns* wife, to haue his pleasure of her, being then in *Redfearns* house: but the sayd *Redfearns* wife denyed the sayd *Robert*; wherevpon the sayd *Robert* seeming to be greatly displeased therewith, in a great anger tooke his Horse, and went away, saying in a great rage, that if euer the Ground came to him, shee should neuer dwell vpon his Land. Wherevpon this Examinate called *Fancie* to her; who came to her in the likenesse of a Man in a parcell of Ground called, *The Laund*; asking this Examinate, what shee would haue him to doe? And this Examinate bade him goe reuenge her of the sayd *Robert Nutter*. After which time, the sayd *Robert Nutter* liued about a quarter of a yeare, and then dyed.

---

[101] "*Robert Nutter.*"] The family of the Nutters, of Pendle, bore a great share in the proceedings referred to in this trial. It seems to have been a family of note amongst the inferior gentry or yeomanry of the forest. A Nutter held courts for many years about this period, as deputy steward at Clitheroe. (See Whitaker's *Whalley*, p. 307.) Three of the name are stated in the evidence to have been killed by witchcraft, Christopher Nutter, Robert Nutter, and Anne, the daughter of Anthony Nutter; and one of the unfortunate persons convicted is Alice Nutter. The branch to which Robert belonged is shewn in the following table:

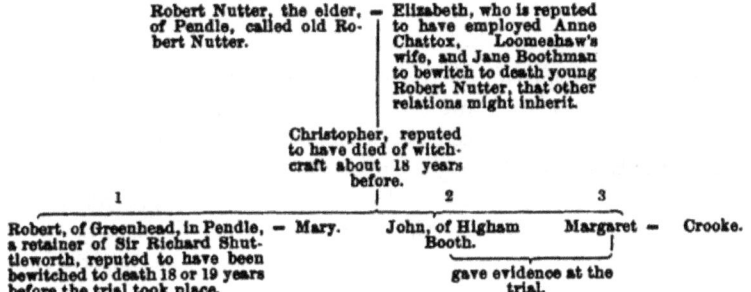

And this Examinate further sayth, that *Elizabeth Nutter*, wife to old *Robert Nutter*, did request this Examinate, and *Loomeshaws* wife of *Burley*, and one *Iane Boothman*, of the same, who are now both dead, (which time of request, was before that *Robert Nutter* desired the company of *Redfearns* wife) to get young *Robert Nutter* his death, if they could; all being togeather then at that time, to that end, that if *Robert* were dead, then the Women their Coosens might haue the Land: By whose perswasion, they all consented vnto it. After which time, this Examinates Sonne in law *Thomas Redfearne*, did perswade this Examinate, not to kill or hurt the sayd *Robert Nutter*; for which perswasion, the sayd *Loomeshaws* Wife, had like to haue killed the sayd *Redfearne*, but that one M. *Baldwyn* (the late Schoole-maister at *Coulne*) did by his learning, stay the sayd *Loomeshaws* wife, and therefore had a Capon from *Redfearne*.[102]

And this Examinate further sayth, that she thinketh the sayd *Loomeshaws* wife, and *Iane Boothman*, did what they could to kill the sayd *Robert Nutter*, as well as this Examinate did.

---

[102] "*One Mr. Baldwyn (the late Schoole-maister at Coulne) did by his learning, stay the sayd Loomeshaws wife, and therefore had a Capon from Redfearne.*"] I regret that I can give no account of this learned Theban, who appears to have stayed the plague, and who taught at the school at which Archbishop Tillotson was afterwards educated. He well deserved his capon. Had he continued at Colne up to the time of this trial, he might perhaps, on the same easy terms, have kept the powers of darkness in check, and prevented some imputed crimes which cost ten unfortunates their lives.

*The Examination of* Elizabeth
**Sothernes, alias Old Dembdike:** *taken at the Fence in the Forrest of Pendle in the Countie of Lancaster, the day and yeare aforesaid.*

**Before,**

**Roger Nowel** *Esquire, one of the Kings Maiesties Iustices of Peace in the said Countie, against* **Anne Whittle, alias Chattox.**

THe said *Elizabeth Southernes* saith vpon her Examination, that about halfe a yeare before *Robert Nutter* died, as this Examinate thinketh, this Examinate went to the house of *Thomas Redfearne*, which was about Mid-sommer, as this Examinate remembreth it. And there within three yards of the East end of the said house, shee saw the said *Anne Whittle*, alias *Chattox*, and *Anne Redferne* wife of the said *Thomas Redferne*, and Daughter of the said *Anne Whittle*, alias *Chattox*: the one on the one side of the Ditch, and the other on the other: and two Pictures of Clay or Marle lying by them: and the third Picture the said *Anne Whittle*, alias *Chattox*, was making: and the said *Anne Redferne* her said Daughter, wrought her Clay or Marle to make the third picture withall. And this Examinate passing by them, the said Spirit, called *Tibb*, in the shape of a black Cat, appeared vnto her this Examinate, and said, turne back againe, and doe as they doe: To whom this Examinate said, what are they doing? whereunto the said Spirit said; they are making three Pictures: whereupon she asked whose pictures they were? whereunto the said Spirit said; they are the pictures of *Christopher Nutter*, *Robert Nutter*, and *Marie*, wife of the said *Robert Nutter*: But this Examinate denying to goe back to helpe them to make the Pictures aforesaid; the said Spirit seeming to be angrie, therefore shoue or pushed this Examinate into the ditch, and so shed the Milke which this Examinate had in a Can or Kit: and so thereupon the Spirit at that time vanished out of this Examinates sight: But presently after that, the said Spirit appeared to this Examinate againe in the shape of a Hare, and so went with her about a quarter of a mile, but said nothing to this Examinate, nor shee to it.

*The Examination and euidence of* Iames **Robinson,**[103] *taken the day and yeare aforesaid.*

**Before**

**Roger Nowel** *Esquire aforesaid, against* **Anne Whittle, alias Chattox,** *Prisoner at the Barre as followeth.* **viz.**

THe said Examinate saith, that about sixe yeares agoe, *Anne Whittle,* alias *Chattox,* was hired by this Examinates wife to card wooll;[104] and so vpon a Friday and Saturday, shee came and carded wooll with this Examinates wife, and so the Munday then next after shee came likewise to card: and this Examinates wife hauing newly tunned drinke into Stands, which stood by the said *Anne Whittle,* alias *Chattox*: and the said *Ann Whittle* taking a Dish or Cup, and drawing drinke seuerall times: and so neuer after that time, for some eight or nine weekes, they could haue any drinke, but spoiled, and as this Examinate thinketh was by the meanes of the said *Chattox.* And further he saith, that the said *Anne Whittle,* alias *Chattox,* and *Anne Redferne* her said Daughter, are commonly reputed and reported to bee Witches. And hee also saith, that about some eighteene yeares agoe, he dwelled with one *Robert Nutter* the elder, of Pendle aforesaid. And that yong *Robert Nutter,* who

---

[103] "*Iames Robinson.*"] Baines, in his *History of Lancashire,* vol. i. p. 605, speaks of Edmund Robinson, the father of the boy on whose evidence the witches were convicted in 1633, as if he had been a witness at the present trial; which is probably a mistake for this James Robinson, as no Edmund Robinson appears amongst the witnessses whose depositions are given.

[104] "*Anne Whittle alias Chattox was hired by this examinates wife to card wooll.*"] She seems to have been by occupation a carder of wool, and to have filled up the intervals, when she had no employment, by mendicancy.

dwelled with his Grand-father, in the Sommer time, he fell sicke, and in his said sicknesse hee did seuerall times complaine, that hee had harme by them: and this Examinate asking him what hee meant by that word *Them*, He said, that he verily thought that the said *Anne Whittle*, alias *Chattox*, and the said *Redfernes* wife, had bewitched him: and the said *Robert Nutter* shortly after, being to goe with his then Master, called Sir *Richard Shattleworth*,[105] into Wales, this Examinate heard him say before his then going, vnto the said *Thomas Redferne*, that if euer he came againe he would get his Father to put the said *Redferne* out of his house, or he himselfe would pull it downe; to whom the said *Redferne* replyed, saying; when you come back againe you will be in a better minde: but he neuer came back againe, but died before Candlemas in Cheshire, as he was comming homeward.

Since the voluntarie confession and examination of a Witch, doth exceede all other euidence, I spare to trouble you with a multitude of Examinations, or Depositions of any other witnesses, by reason this bloudie fact, for the Murder of *Robert Nutter*, vpon so small an occasion, as to threaten to take away his owne land from such as were not worthie to inhabite or dwell vpon it, is now made by that which you haue alreadie heard, so apparant, as no indifferent man will question it, or rest vnsatisfied: I shall now proceede to set forth vnto you the rest of her actions, remaining vpon Record. And how dangerous it was for any man to liue neere these people, to giue them any occasion of offence, I leaue it to your good consideration.

---

[105] "*Sir Richard Shuttleworth.*"} Of the family of the Shuttleworths of Gawthorp, "where they resided" Whitaker observes, "in the condition of inferior gentry till the lucrative profession of the law raised them, in the reign of Elizabeth, to the rank of knighthood and an estate proportioned to its demands." Sir Richard was Sergeant-at-law, and Chief Justice of Chester, 31st Elizabeth, and died without issue about 1600.

*The Examination and voluntarie Confession*
*of* **Anne Whittle, alias Chattox,** *taken*
*at the Fence in the Forrest of Pendle, in the Countie*
*of Lancaster, the second day of Aprill,* **Anno Regni**
**Regis Iacobi Angliæ, Franciæ, & Hiberniæ, decimo**
**& Scotiæ xlv.**

**Before**

**Roger Nowel,** *Esquire, one of his Maiesties*
*Iustices of Peace within the Countie of Lancaster.*

SHe the said Examinate saith, That shee was sent for by the wife of *Iohn Moore*, to helpe drinke that was forspoken or bewitched: at which time shee vsed this Prayer for the amending of it, *viz.*

*A Charme*[106]
*Three Biters hast thou bitten,*
*The Hart, ill Eye, ill Tonge:*
*Three bitter shall be thy Boote,*
*Father, Sonne, and Holy Ghost*
*a Gods name,*
*Fiue Pater-nosters, fiue Auies,*
*and a Creede,*
*In worship of fiue wounds*
*of our Lord.*

After which time that this Examinate had vsed these prayers, and amended her drinke, the said *Moores* wife did chide this Examinate, and was grieued at her.

---

[106] "*A Charme.*"] Evidently in so corrupted a state as to bid defiance to any attempt at elucidation.

And thereupon this Examinate called for her Deuill *Fancie*, and bad him goe bite a browne Cow of the said *Moores* by the head, and make the Cow goe madde: and the Deuill then, in the likenesse of a browne Dogge, went to the said Cow, and bit her: which Cow went madde accordingly, and died within six weekes next after, or thereabouts.

Also this Examinate saith, That she perceiuing *Anthonie Nutter* of Pendle to fauour *Elizabeth Sothernes*, alias *Dembdike*,[107] she, this Examinate, called *Fancie* to her, (who appeared like a man) and bad him goe kill a Cow of the said *Anthonies*; which the said Deuill did, and that Cow died also.

And further this Examinate saith, That the Deuill, or *Fancie*, hath taken most of her sight away from her. And further this Examinate saith, That in Summer last, saue one, the said Deuill, or *Fancie*, came vpon this Examinate in the night time: and at diuerse and sundry times in the likenesse of a Beare, gaping as though he would haue wearied this Examinate.[108] And the last time of all shee, this Examinate, saw him, was vpon Thursday last yeare but one, next before Midsummer day, in the euening, like a Beare, and this Examinate would not then speake vnto him, for the which the said Deuill pulled this Examinate downe.

---

[107] "*Perceiuing Anthonie Nutter of Pendle to fauour Elizabeth Sothernes alias Dembdike.*"] The Sothernes and Davies's and the Whittles and Redfernes were the Montagus and Capulets of Pendle. The poor cottager whose drink was forsepoken or bewitched, or whose cow went mad, and who in his attempt to propitiate one of the rival powers offended the other, would naturally exclaim from the innermost recesses of his heart, "A plague on both your houses."

[108] "*Gaping as though he would haue wearied this Examinate.*"] Wearied for worried.

*The Examination of* Iames Device,[109]
*sonne of* **Elizabeth Device,** *taken the seuen and twentieth day of Aprill,* **Annoq; Reg. Regis Iacobi Angliæ, &c. Decimo ac Scotiæ xlv.**

**Before**

**Roger Nowel and Nicholas Banister,**
*Esquires, two of his Maiesties Iustices of the Peace within the said Countie.* **viz.**

ANd further saith, That twelue yeares agoe, the said *Anne Chattox* at a Buriall at the new Church in Pendle, did take three scalpes of people, which had been buried, and then cast out of a graue, as she the said *Chattox* told this Examinate; and tooke eight teeth out of the said Scalpes, whereof she kept foure to her selfe, and gaue other foure to the said *Demdike*, this Examinates Grand-mother: which foure teeth now shewed to this Examinate, are the foure teeth that the said *Chattox* gaue to his said Grand-mother, as aforesaid; which said teeth haue euer since beene kept, vntill now found by the said *Henry Hargreiues* & this Examinate, at the West-end of this Examinates Grand-mothers house, and there buried in the earth, and a Picture of Clay there likewise found by them, about halfe a yard ouer in the earth, where the said teeth lay, which said

---

[109] "*Examination of Iames Device.*"] This is a very curious examination. The production of the four teeth and figure of clay dug up at the west-end of Malkin Tower would look like a "damning witness" to the two horror-struck justices and the assembled concourse at Read, who did not perhaps consider how easily such evidences may be furnished, and how readily they who hide may find. The incident deposed to at the burial at the New Church in Pendle is a wild and striking one.

picture so found was almost withered away, and was the Picture of *Anne, Anthony Nutters* daughter; as this Examinates Grand-mother told him.

*The Examination of* Allizon Device
*daughter of* **Elizabeth Device:** *Taken at Reade, in the Countie of Lancaster, the thirtieth day of March,* **Annoq; Reg. Regis Iacobi nunc Angliæ, &c. Decimo, & Scotiæ Quadragesimo quinto.**

**Before**

**Roger Nowel** *of Reade aforesaid, Esquire, one of his Maiesties Iustices of the Peace, within the said Countie.*

THis Examinate saith, that about eleuen yeares agoe, this Examinate and her mother had their firehouse broken,[110] and all, or the most part of their linnen clothes, & halfe a peck of cut oat-meale, and a quantitie of meale gone, all which was worth twentie shillings, or aboue: and vpon a Sunday then next after, this Examinate did take a band and a coife, parcell of the goods aforesaid, vpon the daughter of *Anne Whittle, alias Chattox,* and claimed them to be parcell of the goods stolne, as aforesaid.

And this Examinate further saith, That her father, called *Iohn Deuice,* being afraid, that the said *Anne Chattox* should doe him or his goods any hurt by Witchcraft; did couenant with the said *Anne,* that if she would hurt neither of them, she should yearely haue one Aghen-dole of

---

[110] "*About eleuen yeares agoe, this Examinate and her mother had their firehouse broken.*"] The inference intended is, that Whittle's family committed the robbery from Old Demdike's house. This was, in all probability, the origin of their feuds. The abstraction of the coif and band, tempting articles to the young daughter of Old Chattox, not destitute, if we may judge from one occurrence deposed to, of personal attractions, may be said to have convulsed Lancashire from the Leven to the Mersey,—to have caused a sensation, the shock of which, after more than two centuries, has scarcely yet subsided, and to have actually given a new name to the fair sex.

meale;[111] which meale was yearely paid, vntill the yeare which her father died in, which was about eleuen yeares since: Her father vpon his then-death-bed, taking it that the said *Anne Whittle*, alias *Chattox*, did bewitch him to death, because the said meale was not paid the last yeare.

And she also saith, That about two yeares agone, this Examinate being in the house of *Anthony Nutter* of Pendle aforesaid, and being then in company with *Anne Nutter*, daughter of the said *Anthony*: the said *Anne Whittle*, alias *Chattox*, came into the said *Anthony Nutters* house, and seeing this Examinate, and the said *Anne Nutter* laughing, and saying, that they laughed at her the said *Chattox*: well said then (sayes *Anne Chattox*) I will be meet with the one of you. And vpon the next day after, she the said *Anne Nutter* fell sicke, and within three weekes after died. And further, this Examinate saith, That about two yeares agoe, she, this Examinate, hath heard, That the said *Anne Whittle*, alias *Chattox*, was suspected for bewitching the drinke of *Iohn Moore* of Higham Gentleman:[112] and not long after, shee this Examinate heard the said *Chattox* say, that she would meet with the said *Iohn Moore*, or his.[113] Whereupon a child of the said *Iohn Moores*, called *Iohn*,

---

[111] "*One Aghen-dole of meale.*"] This Aghen-dole, a word still, I believe, in use for a particular measure of any article, was, I presume, a kind of witches' black mail. My friend, the Rev. Canon Parkinson, informs me that Aghen-dole, sometimes pronounced Acken-dole, signifies an half-measure of anything, from half-hand-dole. Mr. Halliwell has omitted it in his Glossary, now in progress.

[112] "*Iohn Moore of Higham, Gentleman.*"] Sir Jonas Moore, of whom an account is contained in Whitaker's *Whalley*, p. 479, and whom he characterizes as a sanguine projector, was born in Pendle Forest, and was probably of this family.

[113] "*She would meet with the said Iohn Moore, or his.*"] i.e. She would be equal with him.

fell sick, and languished about halfe a yeare, and then died: during which languishing, this Examinate saw the said *Chattox* sitting in her owne garden, and a picture of Clay like vnto a child in her Apron; which this Examinate espying, the said *Anne Chattox* would haue hidde with her Apron: and this Examinate declaring the same to her mother, her mother thought it was the picture of the said *Iohn Moores* childe.

And she this Examinate further saith, That about sixe or seuen yeares agoe, the said *Chattox* did fall out with one *Hugh Moore* of Pendle, as aforesaid, about certaine cattell of the said *Moores*, which the said *Moore* did charge the said *Chattox* to haue bewitched: for which the said *Chattox* did curse and worry the said *Moore*, and said she would be Reuenged of the said *Moore*: whereupon the said *Moore* presently fell sicke, and languished about halfe a yeare, and then died. Which *Moore* vpon his death-bed said, that the said *Chattox* had bewitched him to death. And she further saith, That about sixe yeares agoe, a daughter of the said *Anne Chattox*, called *Elizabeth*, hauing been at the house of *Iohn Nutter* of the Bull-hole, to begge or get a dish full of milke, which she had, and brought to her mother, who was about a fields breadth of the said *Nutters* house, which her said mother *Anne Chattox* tooke and put into a Kan, and did charne[114] the same with two stickes acrosse in the same field: whereupon the said *Iohn Nutters* sonne came vnto her, the said *Chattox*, and misliking her doings, put the said Kan and milke ouer with his foot; and the morning next after, a Cow of the said *Iohn Nutters* fell sicke, and so languished three or foure dayes, and then died.

---

[114] "*Charne.*"] i.e. Charm.

In the end being openly charged with all this in open Court; with weeping teares she humbly acknowledged them to be true, [115]and cried out vnto God for Mercy and forgiuenesse of her sinnes, and humbly prayed my Lord to be mercifull vnto *Anne Redfearne* her daughter, of whose life and condition you shall heare more vpon her Arraignement and Triall: whereupon shee being taken away, *Elizabeth Deuice* comes now to receiue her Triall being the next in order, of whom you shall heare at large.

---

[115] "*With weeping teares she humbly acknowledged them to be true.*"] She seems to have confessed in the hope of saving her daughter, Anne Redfern. But from such a judge as Sir Edward Bromley, mercy was as little to be expected as common sense from his "faithful chronicler," Thomas Potts.

THE ARRAIGNMENT
*and Triall of* Elizabeth Device
**(*Daughter of* Elizabeth Sothernes,
alias Old Dembdike)** *late wife of* **Io. Device,**
*of the Forrest of Pendle, in the Countie of Lancaster,
widow,
for Witchcraft; Vpon Tuesday the eighteenth of August,
at the Assises and generall Gaole-Deliuerie holden at
Lancaster*

Before

*Sir* **Edward Bromley** *Knight, one of his Maiesties
Iustices of Assise at Lancaster.*

## *Elizabeth Deuice.*

O Barbarous and inhumane Monster, beyond example; so farre from sensible vnderstanding of thy owne miserie, as to bring thy owne naturall children into mischiefe and bondage; and thy selfe to be a witnesse vpon the Gallowes, to see thy owne children, by thy deuillish instructions hatcht vp in Villanie and Witchcraft, to suffer with thee, euen in the beginning of their time, a shamefull and vntimely Death. Too much (so it be true) cannot be said or written of her. Such was her life and condition: that euen at the Barre, when shee came to receiue her Triall (where the least sparke of Grace or modestie would haue procured fauour, or moued pitie) she was not able to containe her selfe within the limits of any order or gouernment: but exclaiming, in very outragious manner crying out against her owne children, and such as came to prosecute Indictments & Euidence for the Kings Maiestie against her, for the death of their Children, Friends, and Kinsfolkes, whome cruelly and bloudily, by her Enchauntments, Charmes, and Sorceries she had murthered and cut off; sparing no man with fearefull execrable curses and banning:[116] Such in generall was the common opinion of the Countrey where she dwelt, in the Forrest of Pendle (a place fit for people of such condition) that no man neere her, neither his wife, children, goods, or cattell should be secure or free from danger.

This *Elizabeth Deuice* was the daughter of *Elizabeth Sothernes*, old *Dembdike*, a malicious, wicked, and dangerous Witch for fiftie yeares, as appeareth by Record: and how much longer, the Deuill and shee knew best with whome shee made her couenant.

It is very certaine, that amongst all these Witches there was not a more dangerous and deuillish Witch to execute mischiefe, hauing old *Dembdike*, her mother, to assist her; *Iames Deuice* and *Alizon Deuice*, her owne naturall children, all prouided with Spirits, vpon any occasion of offence readie to assist her.

Vpon her Examination, although Master *Nowel* was very circumspect, and exceeding carefull in dealing with her, yet she would confesse nothing, vntill it pleased God to raise vp a yong maid, *Iennet Deuice*, her owne daughter, about the age of nine yeares (a witnesse vnexpected) to discouer

---

[116] "*Sparing no man with fearefull execrable curses and banning.*"] Nothing seems to shock the nerves of these witch historiographers so much as the utter want of decorum and propriety exhibited by these unhappy creatures in giving vent to these indignant outbreaks, which a sense of the wicked injustice of their fate, and seeing their own offspring brought up in evidence against them, through the most detestable acts, and by the basest subornation, would naturally extort from minds even of iron mould. If ever Lear's or Timon's power of malediction could be justifiably called into exercise, it would be against such a tribunal and such witnesses as they had generally to encounter.

all their Practises, Meetings, Consultations, Murthers, Charmes, and Villanies: such, and in such sort, as I may iustly say of them, as a reuerend and learned Iudge of this Kingdome speaketh of the greatest Treason that euer was in this Kingdome, *Quis hæc posteris sic narrare poterit, vt facta non ficta esse videantur?* That when these things shall be related to Posteritie, they will be reputed matters fained, not done.

And then knowing, that both *Iennet Deuice*, her daughter, *Iames Deuice*, her sonne, and *Alizon Deuice*, with others, had accused her and layed open all things, in their Examinations taken before Master *Nowel*, and although she were their owne naturall mother, yet they did not spare to accuse her of euery particular fact, which in her time she had committed, to their knowledge; she made a very liberall and voluntarie Confession, as hereafter shall be giuen in euidence against her, vpon her Arraignment and Triall.

This *Elizabeth Deuice* being at libertie, after Old *Dembdike* her mother, *Alizon Deuice*, her daughter, and old *Chattocks* were committed to the Castle of Lancaster for Witchcraft; laboured not a little to procure a solemne meeting at Malkyn-Tower of the Graund Witches of the Counties of Lancaster and Yorke, being yet vnsuspected and vntaken, to consult of some speedie course for the deliuerance of their friends, the Witches at Lancaster, and for the putting in execution of some other deuillish practises of Murther and Mischiefe: as vpon the Arraignement and Triall of *Iames Deuice*, her sonne, shall hereafter in euery particular point appeare at large against her.

## The first Indictment.

THis *Elizabeth Deuice*, late the wife of *Iohn Deuice*, of the Forrest of Pendle in the Countie of Lancaster Widdow, being indicted, for that shee felloniously had practized, vsed, and exercised diuers wicked and deuillish Arts, called *Witch-crafts, Inchantments, Charmes*, and *Sorceries*, in, and vpon one *Iohn Robinson*, alias *Swyer*: and by force of the same felloniously, the said *Iohn Robinson*, alias *Swyer*, had killed. *Contra pacem, &c.* being at the Barre was arraigned.

## 2. Indictment.

The said *Elizabeth Deuice* was the second time indicted in the same manner and forme, for the death of *Iames Robinson*, by Witch-craft. *Contra pacem, &c.*

## 3. Indictment.

The said *Elizabeth Deuice*, was the third time with others, *viz. Alice Nutter*, and *Elizabeth Sothernes*, alias *Old-Dembdike*, her Grand-mother, Indicted in the same manner and forme, for the death of *Henrie Mytton. Contra pacem, &c.*

To these three seuerall Indictments vpon her Arraignement, shee pleaded not guiltie; and for the tryall of her life, put her selfe vpon God and her Countrie.

So as now the Gentlemen of the Iurie of life and death, stand charged to finde, whether shee bee guiltie of them, or any of them.

Whereupon there was openly read, and giuen in euidence against her, for the Kings Majestie, her owne voluntarie Confession and Examination, when shee was apprehended, taken, and committed to the Castle of Lancaster by M.

*Nowel*, and M. *Bannester*, two of his Maiesties Iustices of Peace in the same Countie. *viz.*

*The Examination and voluntarie Confession of* **Elizabeth Device,** *taken at the house of* **Iames Wilsey** *of the Forrest of Pendle, in the Countie of Lancaster, the seuen and twentieth day of Aprill: Anno Reg.* **Iacobi,** *Angl. &c. decimo, &* Scotiæ *xlv.*

**Before**

**Roger Nowel,** *and* **Nicholas Bannester,** *Esquires; two of his Maiesties Iustices of the Peace within the same Countie.* viz.

The said *Elizabeth Deuice*, Mother of the said *Iames*, being examined, confesseth and saith.

THat at the third time her Spirit,[117] the Spirit *Ball*, appeared to her in the shape of a browne Dogge, at, or in her Mothers house in Pendle Forrest aforesaid: about foure yeares agoe the said Spirit bidde this Examinate make a picture of Clay after the said *Iohn Robinson*, alias *Swyer*, which this Examinate did make accordingly at the West end of her said Mothers house, and dryed the same picture with the fire and crumbled all the same picture away within a weeke or thereabouts, and about a weeke after the Picture was crumbled or mulled away; the said *Robinson* dyed.

The reason wherefore shee this Examinate did so bewitch the said *Robinson* to death, was: for that the said *Robinson*

---

[117] "*That at the third time her Spirit.*"] Something seems to be wanting here, as she does not state what occurred at the two previous interviews. The learned judge may have exercised a sound discretion in this omission, as the particulars might be of a nature unfit for publication. The present tract is, undoubtedly, remarkably free from those disgusting details of which similar reports are generally full to overflowing.

had chidden and becalled this Examinate, for hauing a Bastard-child with one *Seller*.

And this Examinate further saith and confesseth, that shee did bewitch the said *Iames Robinson* to death, as in the said *Iennet Deuice* her examination is confessed.

And further shee saith, and confesseth, that shee with the wife of *Richard Nutter*, and this Examinates said Mother, ioyned altogether, and did bewitch the said *Henrie Mytton* to death.

*The Examination and Euidence of* Iennet
Device, *Daughter of the said* Elizabeth
Device, *late Wife of* Iohn Device, *of the
Forrest of Pendle, in the Countie of Lancaster.*

Against

Elizabeth Device *her Mother, Prisoner at the
Barre vpon her Arraignement and Triall.* viz.

THe said *Iennet Deuice*, being a yong Maide, about the age of nine yeares,[118] and commanded to stand vp to giue

---

[118] "*The said Iennet Deuice, being a yong Maide, about the age of nine yeares.*"] This child must have been admirably trained, (some Master Thomson might have been near at hand to instruct her,) or must have had great natural capacity for deception. She made an excellent witness on this occasion. What became of her after the wholesale extinction of her family, to which she was so mainly instrumental, is not now known. In all likelihood she dragged on a miserable existence, a forlorn outcast, pointed at by the hand of scorn, or avoided with looks of horror in the wilds of Pendle. As if some retributive punishment awaited her, she is reported to have been the Jennet Davies who was condemned in 1633, on the evidence of Edmund Robinson the younger, with Mother Dickenson and others, but not executed. Her confession, if she made one at the second trial, might not have been unsimilar to that of Alexander Sussums, of Melford in Suffolk, who, Hearne tells us, confessed "that he had things which did draw those marks I found upon him, but said he could not help it, for that all his kinred were naught. Then I asked him how it was possible they could suck without his consent. He said he did consent to that. Then I asked him again why he should do it when as God was so merciful towards him, as I then told him of, being a man whom I had been formerly acquainted withal, as having lived in town. He answered again, he could not help it, for that all his generation was naught; and so told me *his mother and aunt were hanged, his grandmother burnt for witchcraft, and ten others of them questioned and hanged.* This man is yet living, notwithstanding he confessed the sucking of such things above sixteen years together."— *Confirmation*, p. 36.

euidence against her Mother, Prisoner at the Barre: Her Mother, according to her accustomed manner, outragiously cursing, cryed out against the child in such fearefull manner, as all the Court did not a little wonder at her, and so amazed the child, as with weeping teares shee cryed out vnto my Lord the Iudge, and told him, shee was not able to speake in the presence of her Mother.

This odious Witch was branded with a preposterous marke in Nature, euen from her birth, which was her left eye, standing lower then the other; the one looking downe, the other looking vp, so strangely deformed, as the best that were present in that Honorable assembly, and great Audience, did affirme, they had not often seene the like.

No intreatie, promise of fauour, or other respect, could put her to silence, thinking by this her outragious cursing and threatning of the child, to inforce her to denie that which she had formerly confessed against her Mother, before M. *Nowel*: Forswearing and denying her owne voluntarie confession, which you haue heard, giuen in euidence against her at large, and so for want of further euidence to escape that, which the Iustice of the Law had prouided as a condigne punishment for the innocent bloud shee had spilt, and her wicked and deuillish course of life.

In the end, when no meanes would serue, his Lordship commanded the Prisoner to be taken away, and the Maide to bee set vpon the Table in the presence of the whole Court, who deliuered her euidence in that Honorable assembly, to the Gentlemen of the Iurie of life and death, as followeth. *viz.*

*Iennet Deuice*, Daughter of *Elizabeth Deuice*, late Wife of *Iohn Deuice*, of the Forrest of Pendle aforesaid Widdow, confesseth and saith, that her said Mother is a Witch, and that this shee knoweth to be true; for, that shee had seene her Spirit sundrie times come vnto her said Mother in her owne house, called *Malking-Tower*, in the likenesse of a browne Dogge, which shee called *Ball*; and at one time amongst others, the said *Ball* did aske this Examinates Mother what she would haue him to doe: and this Examinates Mother answered, that she would haue the said *Ball* to helpe her to kill *Iohn Robinson* of *Barley*, alias *Swyer*: by helpe of which said *Ball*, the said *Swyer* was killed by witch-craft accordingly; and that this Examinates Mother hath continued a Witch for these three or foure yeares last past. And further, this Examinate confesseth, that about a yeare after, this Examinates Mother called for the said *Ball*, who appeared as aforesaid, asking this Examinates Mother what shee would haue done, who said, that shee would haue him to kill *Iames Robinson*, alias *Swyer*, of Barlow aforesaid, Brother to the said *Iohn*: whereunto *Ball* answered, hee would doe it; and about three weekes after, the said *Iames* dyed.

And this Examinate also saith, that one other time shee was present, when her said Mother did call for the *Ball*, Her Spirit.who appeared in manner as aforesaid, and asked this Examinates Mother what shee would haue him to doe, whereunto this Examinates Mother then said shee would haue him to kill one *Mitton* of the Rough-Lee, whereupon the said *Ball* said, he would doe it, and so vanished away, and about three weekes after, the said *Mitton* likewise dyed.

*The Examination of* Iames Device,
*sonne of the said* **Elizabeth Device:** *Taken the seuen and twentieth day of Aprill*, **Annoq; Reg. Regis Iacobi Angliæ, &c. Decimo ac Scociæ, xlv.**

**Before**

**Roger Nowel** *and* **Nicholas Banester,** *Esquires, two of his Maiesties Iustices of the Peace, within the said Countie.* **viz.**

THe said *Iames Deuice* being examined, saith, That he heard his Grand-mother say, about a yeare agoe, That his mother called *Elizabeth Deuice*, and others, had killed one *Henry Mitton* of the Rough-Lee aforesaid, by Witchcraft. The reason wherefore he was so killed, was for that this Examinates said Grand-mother *Old Demdike*, had asked the said *Mitton* a penny; and he denying her thereof, thereupon she procured his death, as aforesaid.

And he, this Examinate also saith, That about three yeares agoe, this Examinate being in his Grand-mothers house, with his said mother; there came a thing in shape of a browne dogge, which his mother called *Ball*, who spake to this Examinates mother, in the sight and hearing of this Examinate, and bad her make a Picture of Clay like vnto *Iohn Robinson*, alias *Swyer*, and drie it hard, and then crumble it by little and little; and as the said Picture should crumble or mull away, so should the said *Io. Robinson* alias *Swyer* his body decay and weare away. And within two or three dayes after, the Picture shall so all be wasted, and mulled away; so then the said *Iohn Robinson* should die presently. Vpon the agreement betwixt the said dogge and this Examinates mother; the said dogge suddenly vanished out of this Examinates sight. And the next day, this Examinate saw his said mother take Clay at the West end of her said house, and make a Picture of it after the said *Robinson*, and brought into her house, and dried it some two dayes: and about two dayes after the drying thereof, this Examinates said mother fell on crumbling the said Picture of Clay, euery day some, for some three weekes together; and within two dayes after all was crumbled or mulled away, the said *Iohn Robinson* died.

Being demanded by the Court, what answere shee could giue to the particular points of the Euidence against her, for the death of these seuerall persons; Impudently shee denied them, crying out against her children, and the rest of the Witnesses against her.

But because I haue charged her to be the principall Agent, to procure a solemne meeting at *Malking-Tower* of the Grand-witches, to consult of some speedy course for the deliuerance of her mother, *Old Demdike*, her daughter, and other Witches at Lancaster: the speedie Execution of Master *Couell*, who little suspected or deserued any such practise or villany against him: The blowing up of the Castle, with diuers other wicked and diuellish practises and murthers; I shall make it apparant vnto you, by the particular Examinations and Euidence of her owne children, such as were present at the time of their Consultation, together with her owne Examination and Confession, amongst the Records of the Crowne at Lancaster, as hereafter followeth.

*The voluntary Confession and Examination of* **Elizabeth Device,** *taken at the house of* **Iames Wilsey,** *of the Forrest of Pendle, in the Countie of Lancaster, the seuen and twentieth day of Aprill,* **Annoq: Reg. Regis Iacobi Angliæ, &c. Decimo, & Scotiæ Quadragesimo quinto.**

Before

**Roger Nowel and Nicholas Banister,** *Esquires, two of his Maiesties Iustices of the Peace within the same Countie.* **viz.**

THe said *Elizabeth Deuice* being further Examined, confesseth that vpon Good-Friday last, there dined at this Examinates house, called *Malking-Tower*, those which she hath said are Witches, and doth verily think them to be Witches: and their names are those whom *Iames Deuice* hath formerly spoken of to be there. And she further saith, that there was also at her said mothers house, at the day and time aforesaid, two women of Burneley Parish, whose names the wife of *Richard Nutter* doth know. And there was likewise there one *Anne Crouckshey*[119] of Marsden: And shee also confesseth, in all things touching the Christening of the Spirit, and the killing of Master *Lister* of Westbie, as the said *Iames Deuice* hath before confessed; but denieth of any talke was amongst them the said Witches, to her now remembrance, at the said meeting together, touching the killing of the Gaoler, or the blowing vp of Lancaster Castle.

---

[119] "*Anne Crouckshey.*"] Anne Cronkshaw.

*The Examination and Euidence of* Iennet **Device,** *Daughter of the said* **Elizabeth Device,** *late Wife of* **Iohn Device,** *of the Forrest of Pendle, in the Countie of Lancaster.*

Against

**Elizabeth Device,** *her Mother, Prisoner at the Barre, vpon her Arraignement and Triall,* viz.

THe said *Iennet Deuice* saith, That vpon Good Friday last there was about twentie persons* (whereof onely two were men, to this Examinates remembrance)

---

*" *Vpon Good Friday last there was about twentie persons.*"] This meeting, if not a witches' Sabbath, was a close approximation to one. On the subject of the Sabbath, or periodical meeting of witches, De Lancre is the leading authority. He who is curious cannot do better than consult this great hierophant, (his work is entitled Tableau de l'Inconstance des mauvais Anges et Demons. Paris, 1613, 4to.) whose knowledge and experience well qualified him to have been constituted the Itinerant Master of Ceremonies, an officer who, he assures us, was never wanting on such occasions. In that singular book, *The History of Monsieur Oufle*, p. 288, (English Translation, 1711, 8vo.) are collected from various sources all the ceremonies and circumstances attending the holding the Sabbath. It appears that non-attendance invariably incurred a penalty, which is computed upon the average at the eighth part of a crown, or in French currency at ten sous—that, though the contrary has been maintained by many grave authors, egress and ingress by the chimney (De Lancre had depositions without number, he tells us, *vide* p. 114, on this important head,) was not a matter of solemn obligation, but was an open question—that no grass ever grows upon the place where the Sabbath is kept; which is accounted for by the circumstance of its being trodden by so many of those whose feet are constitutionally hot, and therefore being burnt up and consequently very barren—that two devils of note preside on the occasion, the great negro, who is called Master Leonard, and a little devil, whom Master Leonard sometimes substitutes in his place as temporary vice-president; his name is Master John

Mullin. (De Lancre, p. 126.) With regard to a very important point, the bill of fare, great difference of opinion exists: some maintaining that every delicacy of the season, to use the newspaper phrase, is provided; others stoutly asserting that nothing is served up but toads, the flesh of hanged criminals, dead carcases fresh buried taken out of Churchyards, flesh of unbaptized infants, or beasts which died of themselves—that they never eat with salt, and that their bread is of black millet. (De Lancre, pp. 104, 105.) In this diversity of opinion I can only suggest, that difference of climate, habit, and fashion, might possibly have its weight, and render a very different larder necessary for the witches of Pendle and those of Gascony or Lorrain. The fare of the former on this occasion appears to have been of a very substantial and satisfactory kind, "beef, bacon, and roasted mutton:" the old saying so often quoted by the discontented masters of households applying emphatically in this case:—

"God sends us good meat, but the devil sends cooks."

We find in the present report no mention made of the

"Dance and provencal song"

which formed one great accompaniment of the orgies of the southern witches. Bodin's authority is express, that each, the oldest not excused, was expected to perform a coranto, and great attention was paid to the regularity of the steps. We owe to him the discovery, which is not recorded in any annals of dancing I have met with, that the lavolta, a dance not dissimilar, according to his description, to the polka of the present day, was brought out of Italy into France by the witches at their festive meetings. Of the language spoken at these meetings, De Lancre favours us with a specimen, valuable, like the Punic fragment in the Pœnolus, for its being the only one of the kind. *In nomine patrica araguenco petrica agora, agora, Valentia jouando goure gaiti goustia.* As it passes my skill, I can only commend it to the especial notice of Mr. Borrow against his next journey into Spain. What was spoken at Malkin Tower was, doubtless, a dialect not yet obsolete, and which Tummus and Meary would have had no difficulty in comprehending. On the subject of these witches' Sabbaths, Dr. Ferriar remarks, in his curious and agreeable *Essay on Popular Illusions,* (see *Memoirs of the Manchester Literary and Philosophical Society,* vol. iii., p. 68,) a sketch which it is much to be regretted that he did not subsequently expand and revise, and publish in a separate form:—

The solemn meetings of witches are supposed to be put beyond all doubt by the numerous confessions of criminals, who have described their ceremonies, named the times and places of meeting, and the persons present, and who have agreed in their relations, though separately delivered.[120] But I would observe, first, that the circumstances told of those festivals are ridiculous and incredible in themselves; for they are represented as gloomy and horrible, yet with a mixture of childish and extravagant fancies, more likely to disgust and alienate than to conciliate the minds of the guests. They have every appearance of uneasy dreams; sometimes the devil and his subjects *say mass*, sometimes he *preaches* to them, more commonly he was seen in the form of a black goat, surrounded by imps in a thousand frightful shapes; but none of these forms are *new*, they all resemble known quadrupeds or reptiles. Secondly, I observe, that there is direct proof furnished even by demonologists, that all these supposed journies and entertainments are nothing more than dreams. Persons accused of witchcraft have been repeatedly watched, about the time which they had fixed for the meeting; they have been seen to anoint themselves with soporific compositions, after which they fell into profound sleep, and on awaking, several hours afterwards, they have related their journey through the air, their amusement at the festival, and have named the persons whom they saw there. In the instance told by Hoffman, the dreamer was chained to the floor. Common sense would rest satisfied here, but the enthusiasm of demonology has invented more than one theory to get rid of these untoward facts. Dr. Henry More, as was formerly mentioned, believed that the astral spirit only was carried away: other demonologists imagined that the witch was really removed to the place of meeting, but that a cacodemon was left in her room, as an εἰδωλον, to delude the spectators. Thirdly, some stories of the festivals are evidently tricks. Such is that related by Bodinus, with much gravity: a man is found in a gentleman's cellar, and apprehended as a thief; he declares his wife had brought him thither to a witch-meeting, and on his pronouncing the name of God, she and all her companions had vanished, and left him inclosed. His wife is immediately seized, on this righteous evidence, and hanged, with several other persons, named as present at the meeting.

---

[120] There is a grave relation, in Delrio, of a witch being shot flying, by a Spanish centinel, at the bridge of Nieulet, near Calais, after that place was taken by the Spaniards. The soldier saw a black cloud advancing rapidly, from which voices issued: when it came near, he fired into it; immediately a witch dropped. This is *undoubted proof* of the meetings!—*Disq. Mag.*, p. 708.

at her said Grandmothers house, called Malking-Tower aforesaid, about twelue of the clocke: all which persons this Examinates said mother told her, were Witches, and that they came to giue a name to *Alizon Deuice* Spirit, or Familiar, sister to this Examinate, and now prisoner at Lancaster. And also this Examinate saith, That the persons aforesaid had to their dinners Beefe, Bacon, and roasted Mutton; which Mutton (as this Examinates said brother said) was of a Wether of *Christopher Swyers* of Barley: which Wether was brought in the night before into this Examinates mothers house by the said *Iames Deuice*, this Examinates said brother: and in this Examinates sight killed and eaten, as aforesaid. And shee further saith, That shee knoweth the names of sixe of the said Witches, *viz.* the wife of *Hugh Hargraues* vnder Pendle, *Christopher Howgate* of Pendle, vnckle to this Examinate, and *Elizabeth* his wife, and *Dicke Miles* his wife of the Rough-Lee; *Christopher Iackes* of Thorny-holme, and his wife:[121] and the names of the residue shee this Examinate doth not know, sauing that this Examinates mother and brother were both there. And lastly, she this Examinate confesseth and saith, That her mother hath taught her two prayers: the one to cure the bewitched, and the other to get drinke; both which particularly appeare.

---

[121] "*Christopher Iackes, of Thorny-holme, and his wife.*"] This would appear to be Christopher Hargreaves, called here Christopher Jackes, for o' or of Jack, according to the Lancashire mode of forming patronymics.

*The Examination and Euidence of* Iames
**Device,** *sonne of the said* **Elizabeth Device,**
*late wife of* **Iohn Device,** *of the Forrest of*
*Pendle, in the Countie of Lancaster.*

**Against**

**Elizabeth Device,** *his Mother, prisoner at the*
**Barre,** *vpon her Arraignement and Triall,* **viz.**

THe said *Iames Deuice* saith, That on Good-Friday last, about twelue of the clocke in the day time, there dined in this Examinates said mothers house, at Malking-Tower, a number of persons, whereof three were men, with this Examinate, and the rest women; and that they met there for three causes following (as this Examinates said mother told this Examinate) The first was, for the naming of the Spirit, which *Alizon Deuice,* now prisoner at Lancaster, had: But did not name him, because shee was not there.[122] The second was, for the deliuerie of his said Grandmother, olde *Dembdike*; this Examinates said sister *Allizon*; the said *Anne Chattox,* and her daughter *Redferne*; killing the Gaoler at Lancaster; and before the next Assises to blow vp the Castle there: and to that end the aforesaid prisoners might by that time make an escape, and get away. All which this Examinate then heard them conferre of.

---

[122] "*The first was, for the naming of the Spirit, which Alizon Deuice, now Prisoner at Lancaster, had: But did not name him, because shee was not there.*"] Gaule says, speaking of the ceremonies at the witches' solemn meetings: "If the witch be outwardly Christian, baptism must be renounced, and the party must be rebaptized in the Devil's name, and a new name is also imposed by him; and here must be godfathers too, for the Devil takes them not to be so adult as to promise and vow for themselves." (*Cases of Conscience touching Witches,* page 59. 1646, 12mo.) But Gaule does not mention any naming or baptism of spirits and familiars on such occasions.

And he also sayth, That the names of the said Witches as were on Good-Friday at this Examinates said Grandmothers house, and now this Examinates owne mothers, for so many of them as hee did know, were these, *viz.* The wife of *Hugh Hargreiues* of Burley; the wife of *Christopher Bulcock*, of the Mosse end, and *Iohn* her sonne; the mother of *Myles Nutter*; *Elizabeth*, the wife of *Christopher Hargreiues*, of Thurniholme; *Christopher Howgate*, and *Elizabeth*, his wife; *Alice Graye* of Coulne, and one *Mould-heeles* wife, of the same: and this Examinate, and his Mother. And this Examinate further sayth, That all the Witches went out of the said House in their owne shapes and likenesses. And they all, by that they were forth of the dores, gotten on Horsebacke, like vnto Foales, some of one colour, some of another; and *Prestons* wife was the last: and when shee got on Horsebacke, they all presently vanished out of this Examinates sight. And before their said parting away, they all appointed to meete at the said *Prestons* wiues *Executed at Yorke the last Assises.*house that day twelue-moneths; at which time the said *Prestons* wife promised to make them a great Feast. And if they had occasion to meete in the meane time, then should warning be giuen, that they all should meete vpon *Romleyes* Moore.[123]

And there they parted, with resolution to execute their
deuillish and bloudie
practises, for the deliuerance of their friends, vntill they
came to
meete here, where their power and strength was gone. And
now finding her Meanes was gone, shee cried out for
Mercie. Whereupon shee being taken away, the
next in order was her sonne *Iames Deuice*,

---

[123] "*Romleyes Moore.*"] Romilly's or Rumbles Moor, a wild and mountainous range in Craven, not unaptly selected for a meeting on a special emergency of a conclave of witches.

whom shee and her Mother, old *Dembdike*, brought to act his part in this wofull Tragedie.

THE ARRAIGNMENT
*and Triall of* Iames Device,
**Sonne of Elizabeth Device,** *of the Forrest of Pendle, within the Countie of Lancaster aforesaid, Laborer, for Witchcraft; Vpon Tuesday the eighteenth of August, at the Assises and generall Gaole-Deliuerie holden at Lancaster*

Before

**Sir Edward Bromley** *Knight, one of his Maiesties Iustices of Assise at Lancaster.*

## *James Deuice.*

THIS wicked and miserable Wretch, whether by practise, or meanes, to bring himselfe to some vntimely death, and thereby to auoide his Tryall by his Countrey, and iust iudgement of the Law; or ashamed to bee openly charged with so many deuillish practises, and so much innocent bloud as hee had spilt; or by reason of his Imprisonment so long time before his Tryall (which was with more fauour, commiseration, and reliefe then hee deserued) I know not: But being brought forth to the Barre, to receiue his Triall before this worthie Iudge, and so Honourable and Worshipfull an Assembly of Iustices for this seruice, was so insensible, weake, and vnable in all thinges, as he could neither speake, heare, or stand, but was holden vp[124] when

---

[124] "*Was so insensible, weake, and vnable in all thinges, as he could neither speake, heare, or stand, but was holden vp.*"] Pitiable, truly, was the situation of this vnhappy wretch. Brought out from the restraint of a long imprisonment, before and during which he had, as we may conjecture, been subjected to every inhumanity, in a state more dead than alive, into a court

hee was brought to the place of his Arraignement, to receiue his triall.

This *Iames Deuice* of the Forrest of Pendle, being brought to the Barre, was there according to the forme, order, and course, Indicted and Arraigned; for that hee Felloniously had practised, vsed, and exercised diuers wicked and deuillish Arts, called *Witch-crafts, Inchauntments, Charmes,* and *Sorceries,* in, and vpon one *Anne Towneley,* wife of *Henrie Towneley* of the Carre,[125] in the Countie of Lancaster Gentleman, and her by force of the same, felloniously had killed. *Contra pacem, &c.*

The said *Iames Deuice* was the second time Indicted and Arraigned in the same manner and forme, for the death of *Iohn Duckworth,* by witch-craft. *Contra pacem, &c.*

To these two seuerall Indictments vpon his Arraignment, he pleaded not guiltie, and for the triall of his life put himselfe vpon God and his Countrie.

So as now the Gentlemen of the Iurie of life and death stand charged to finde, whether he be guiltie of these, or either of them.

---

which must have looked like one living mass, with every eye lit up with horror, and curses, not loud but deep, muttered with harmonious concord from the mouths of every spectator.

[125] "*Anne Towneley, wife of Henrie Townely, of the Carre.*"] Would this be Anne, the daughter and co-heiress of Thomas Catterall, of Catterall and Little Mitton, Esq., who married Henry Townley, the son of Lawrence Townley? (See Whitaker's *Whalley,* p. 396.) The Townleys of Barnside and Carr were a branch of the Townleys, of Townley. Barnside, or Barnsete, is an ancient mansion in the township of Colne, which, Whitaker observes, was abandoned by the family, for the warmer situation of Carr, about the middle of the last century.

Whereupon Master *Nowel* humbly prayed Master *Towneley* might be called,[126] who attended to prosecute and giue euidence against him for the King's Majestie, and that the particular Examinations taken before him and others, might be openly published & read in Court,[127] in the hearing of the Prisoner.

But because it were infinite to bring him to his particular
Triall for euery offence, which hee hath committed in his
time, and euery practice wherein he hath had his hand: I
shall proceede in order with the Euidence remayning
vpon Record against him, amongst the Records of the
Crowne; both how, and in what sort hee came to
be a witch: and shew you what apparant proofe there is to
charge him with the death of these two
seuerall persons, for the which hee now standeth vpon his
triall for al the rest of his deuillish
practises, incantantions, murders, charmes, sorceries,
meetings to consult with Witches,
to execute mischiefe (take them as they are against him
vpon Record:) Enough, I
doubt not. For these with the course of his life will serue
his turne to deliuer
you from the danger of him that neuer tooke felicitie in any
things,

---

[126] "*Master Nowel humbly prayed Master Towneley might be called.*"] It is to be regretted we have no copy of the *viva voce* examination of Mr. Townley, the husband of the lady whose life was said to have been taken away by witchcraft. The examinations given in this tract are altogether those of persons in a humble rank of life. The contrast between their evidence and that of an individual occupying the position of the descendant of one of the oldest families in the neighbourhood, with considerable landed possessions, might have been amusing and instructive.

[127] "*Master Nowell humbly prayed, that the particular examinations taken before him and others might be openly published and read in court.*"] This kind of evidence, the witnesses being in court, and capable of being examined, would not be received at the present day. At that time a greater laxity prevailed.

but in reuenge, bloud, & mischiefe with crying out vnto
God
for vengeance; which hath now at the length brought him
to the place where hee standes to receiue his Triall
with more honor, fauour, and respect, then
such a Monster in Nature doth deserue;
And I doubt not, but in due time
by the Iustice of the Law,
to an vntimely and
shamefull
death.

*The Examination of* Iames Device,
**sonne of Elizabeth Device, *of the Forrest of*
*Pendle, in the Countie of Lancaster, Labourer. Taken the*
*seuen and twentieth day of Aprill, Annoq; Reg. Regis*
Iacobi, *Angliæ, &c.* x⁰. *& Scotiæ Quadragesimo quinto.*

**Before**

**Roger Nowel, *and* Nicholas Bannester,**
*Esquires: two of his Maiesties Iustices of Peace*
*within the said Countie.*

HE saith, that vpon Sheare Thursday[128] was two yeares, his Grand-Mother *Elizabeth Sothernes*, alias *Dembdike*, did bid him this Examinate goe to the Church to receiue the Communion (the next day after being Good Friday) and then not to eate the Bread the Minister gaue him, but to bring it and deliuer it to such a thing as should meet him in his way homewards: Notwithstanding her perswasions, this Examinate did eate the Bread: and so in his comming homeward some fortie roodes off the said Church, there met him a thing in the shape of a Hare, who spoke vnto this Examinate, and asked him whether hee had brought the Bread that his Grand-mother had bidden him, or no? whereupon this Examinate answered, hee had not: and thereupon the said thing threatned to pull this Examinate in peeces, and so this Examinate thereupon marked himselfe to God, and so the said thing vanished out of this Examinates sight. And within some foure daies after that, there appeared in this Examinates sight, hard by the new

---

[128] "*Sheare Thursday.*"] The Thursday before Easter, and so called, for that, in the old Fathers' days, the people would that day, "shave their hedes, and clypp their berdes, and pool their heedes, and so make them honest against Easter Day."—*Brand's Popular Antiquities*, vol. i., p. 83, edition 1841.

Church in Pendle, a thing like vnto a browne *Dogge*, who asked this Examinate to giue him his Soule, and he should be reuenged of any whom hee would: whereunto this Examinate answered, that his Soule was not his to giue, but was his *Sauiour Iesus Christs*, but as much as was in him this Examinate to giue, he was contented he should haue it.

And within two or three daies after, this Examinate went to the Carre-Hall, and vpon some speeches betwixt Mistris *Towneley* and this Examinate; Shee charging this Examinate and his said mother, to haue stolne some Turues of hers, badde him packe the doores: and withall as he went forth of the doore, the said Mistris *Towneley* gaue him a knock betweene the shoulders: and about a day or two after that, there appeared vnto this Examinate in his way, a thing like vnto a black dog, who put this Examinate in minde of the said Mistris *Towneleyes* falling out with him this Examinate; who bad this Examinate make a Picture of Clay, like vnto the said Mistris *Towneley*: and that this Examinate with the helpe of his Spirit (who then euer after bidde this Examinate to call it *Dandy*) would kill or destroy the said Mistris *Towneley*: and so the said dogge vanished out of this Examinates sight. And the next morning after, this Examinate tooke Clay, and made a Picture of the said Mistris *Towneley*, and dried it the same night by the fire: and within a day after, hee, this Examinate began to crumble the said Picture, euery day some, for the space of a weeke: and within two daies after all was crumbled away; the said Mistris *Towneley* died.

And hee further saith, That in Lent last one *Iohn Duckworth* of the Lawnde, promised this Examinate an old shirt: and within a fortnight after, this Examinate went to the said *Duckworthes* house, and demanded the said old shirt: but the said *Duckworth* denied him thereof. And going out of the said house, the said Spirit *Dandy* appeared vnto this Examinate, and said, Thou didst touch the said *Duckworth*; whereunto this Examinate answered, he did not touch him: yes (said the Spirit againe) thou didst touch him, and therfore I haue power of him: whereupon this Examinate ioyned with the said Spirit, and then wished the said Spirit to kill the said *Duckworth*: and within one weeke, then next after, *Duckworth* died.

This voluntary Confession and Examination of his owne, containing in it selfe matter sufficient in Law to charge him, and to proue his offences, contained in the two seuerall Indictments, was sufficient to satisfie the Gentlemen of the Iurie of Life and Death, that he is guiltie of them, and either of them: yet my Lord *Bromley* commanded, for their better satisfaction, that the Witnesses present in Court against any of the Prisoners, should be examined openly, *viua voce*, that the Prisoner might both heare and answere to euery particular point of their Euidence; notwithstanding any of their Examinations taken before any of his Maiesties Iustices of Peace within the said Countie.

Herein do but obserue the wonderfull work of God; to raise vp a young Infant, the very sister of the Prisoner, *Iennet Deuice*, to discouer, iustifie and proue these things against him, at the time of his Arraignement and Triall, as hereafter followeth. *viz.*

*The Examination and Euidence of* Iennet **Device** *daughter of* **Elizabeth Device,** *late wife of* **Iohn Device** *of the Forrest of Pendle, in the Countie of Lancaster.*

## Against

**Iames Device,** *Prisoner at the Barre, vpon his Arraignement and Triall.* viz.

BEing examined in open Court, she saith, That her brother *Iames Device*, the Prisoner at the Barre, hath beene a Witch for the space of three yeares: about the beginning of which time, there appeared vnto him, in this Examinates mothers house, a Black-Dogge, which *Dandy.*her said brother called *Dandy*. And further, this Examinate confesseth, & saith: That her said brother about a twelue month since, in the presence of this Examinate, and in the house aforesaid, called for the said *Dandy*, who thereupon appeared: asking this Examinates brother what he would haue him to doe. This Examinates brother then said, he would haue him to helpe him to kill old Mistris *Towneley* of the Carre: whereunto the said *Dandy* answered, and said, That her said brother should haue his best helpe for the doing of the same; and that her said brother, and the said *Dandy*, did both in this Examinates hearing, say, they would make away the said Mistris *Towneley*. And about a weeke after, this Examinate comming to the Carre-Hall, saw the said Mistris *Towneley* in the Kitchin there, nothing well: whereupon it came into this Examinates minde, that her said brother, by the help of *Dandy*, had brought the said Mistris *Towneley* into the state she then was in.

Which Examinat, although she were but very yong, yet it was wonderfull to the Court, in so great a Presence and Audience, with what modestie, gouernement, and vnderstanding, shee deliuered this Euidence against the Prisoner at the Barre, being her owne naturall brother, which he himselfe could not deny, but there acknowledged in euery particular to be iust and true.

But behold a little further, for here this bloudy Monster did not stay his hands: for besides his wicked and diuellish Spels, practises, meetings to consult of murder and mischiefe, which (by Gods grace) hereafter shall follow in order against him; there is yet more bloud to be laid vnto his charge. For although he were but yong, and in the beginning of his Time, yet was he carefull to obserue his Instructions from *Old Demdike* his Grand-mother, and *Elizabeth Deuice* his mother, in so much that no time should passe since his first entrance into that damnable Arte and exercise of Witchcrafts, Inchantments, Charmes and Sorceries, without mischiefe or murder. Neither should any man vpon the least occasion of offence giuen vnto him, escape his hands, without some danger. For these particulars were no sooner giuen in Euidence against him, when he was againe Indicted and Arraigned for the murder of these two. *viz.*

*Iames Deuice* of the Forrest of Pendle aforesaid, in the Countie of Lancaster, Labourer, the third time Indicted and Arraigned for the death of *Iohn Hargraues* of Gould-shey-booth, in the Countie of Lancaster, by Witchcraft, as aforesaid. *Contra &c.*

To this Inditement vpon his Arraignement he pleaded thereunto not guiltie: and for his Triall put himselfe vpon God and his Countrey, &c.

*Iames Deuice* of the Forrest of Pendle aforesaid, in the County of Lancaster, Labourer, the fourth time Indicted and Arraigned for the death of *Blaze Hargreues* of Higham, in the Countie of Lancaster, by Witchcraft, as aforesaid. *Contra Pacem*, &c.

To this Indictment vpon his Arraignement, he pleaded thereunto not guiltie; and for the Triall of his life, put himselfe vpon God and the Countrey. &c.

Hereupon *Iennet Deuice* produced, sworne and examined, as a witnesse on his Maiesties behalfe, against the said *Iames Deuice*, was examined in open Court, as followeth. *viz.*

*The Examination and Euidence of* Iennet
**Device** *aforesaid.*

**Against**

**Iames Device,** *her brother, Prisoner at the Barre, vpon his Arraignement and Triall.* **viz.**

BEing sworne and examined in open Court, she saith, That her brother *Iames Deuice* hath beene a Witch for the space of three yeares: about the beginning of which time, there appeared vnto him, in this Examinates mothers house, a Blacke-Dogge, which her said brother called *Dandy*, which *Dandy* did aske her said brother what he would haue him to doe, whereunto he answered, hee would haue him to kill *Iohn Hargreiues*, of Gold-shey-booth: whereunto *Dandy* answered that he would doe it: since which time the said *Iohn* is dead.

And at another time this Examinate confesseth and saith, That her said brother did call the said *Dandy*: who thereupon appeared in the said house, asking this Examinates brother what hee would haue him to doe: whereupon this Examinates said brother said, he would haue him to kill *Blaze Hargreiues* of Higham: whereupon *Dandy* answered, hee should haue his best helpe, and so vanished away: and shee saith, that since that time the said *Hargreiues* is dead; but how long after, this Examinate doth not now remember.

All which things, when he heard his sister vpon her Oath affirme, knowing them in his conscience to bee iust and true, slenderly denyed them, and thereupon insisted.

To this Examination were diuerse witnesses examined in open Court *viua voce*, concerning the death of the parties, in such manner and forme, and at such time as the said *Iennet Deuice* in her Euidence hath formerly declared to the Court.

Which is all, and I doubt not but matter sufficient in Law to charge him with, for the death of these parties.

For the proofe of his Practises, Charmes, Meetings at Malking-Tower, to consult with Witches to execute mischiefe, Master *Nowel* humbly prayed, his owne Examination, taken and certified, might openly be read; and the rest in order, as they remaine vpon Record amongst the Records of the Crowne at Lancaster: as hereafter followeth, *viz.*

*The Examination of* Iames Device,
**Sonne of Elizabeth Device,** *of the Forrest of Pendle: Taken the seuen and twentieth day of Aprill aforesaid,*

**Before**

**Roger Nowel** *and* **Nicholas Banester**
*Esquires, two of his Maiesties Iustices of Peace within the said Countie,* viz.

ANd being examined, he further saith, That vpon Sheare-Thursday last, in the euening, he this Examinate stole a Wether from *Iohn Robinson* of Barley, and brought it to his Grand-mothers house, old *Dembdike*, and there killed it: and that vpon the day following, being Good-Friday, about twelue of the clocke in the day time, there dined in this Examinates mothers house a number of persons, whereof three were men, with this Examinate, and the rest women; and that they met there for three Causes following, as this Examinates said Mother told this Examinate.

1 The first was, for the naming of the Spirit which *Alizon Deuice*, now prisoner at Lancaster, had, but did not name him, because she was not there.

2 The second Cause was, for the deliuerie of his said Grand-mother; this Examinates said sister *Alizon*; the said *Anne Chattox*, and her daughter *Redferne*; killing the Gaoler at Lancaster; and before the next Assises to blow vp the Castle there, to the end the aforesaid persons might by that meanes make an escape & get away; all which this Examinate then heard them conferre of.

3 And the third Cause was, for that there was a woman dwelling in Gisborne Parish, who came into this Examinates said Grandmothers house, who there came and craued assistance of the rest of them that were then there, for the killing of Master *Lister* of Westby, because (as shee then said) he had borne malice vnto her, and had thought to haue put her away at the last Assises at Yorke, but could not: and this Examinate heard the said woman say, That her power was not strong ynough to doe it her selfe, being now lesse then before time it had beene.

And also, that the said *Iennet Preston* had a Spirit with her like vnto a white Foale, with a blacke spot in the forhead.

And he also saith, That the names of the said Witches as were on Good-Friday at this Examinates said Grandmothers house, & now this Examinates owne mothers, for so many of them as he did know, were these, *viz.* the wife of *Hugh Hargreiues* of Barley; the wife of *Christopher Bulcock* of the Mosse end, and *Iohn* her sonne; the mother of *Myles Nutter*; *Elizabeth*, the wife of *Christopher Hargreiues*, of Thurniholme; *Christopher Howgate*, and *Elizabeth*, his wife; *Alice Graye* of Coulne, and one *Mould-heeles* wife, of the same: and this Examinate, and his Mother. And this Examinate further saith, That all the said Witches went out of the said House in their owne shapes and likenesses. And they all, by that they were forth of the dores, were gotten on Horsebacke, like vnto Foales, some of one colour, some of another; and *Prestons* wife was the last: and when shee got on Horsebacke, they all presently vanished out of this Examinates sight. And before their said parting away, they all appointed to meete at the said *Prestons* wiues house that day twelue-moneths; at which time the said *Prestons* wife promised to make them a great Feast. And if they had occasion to meete in the meane time, then should warning be giuen, that they all should meete vpon *Romleyes* Moore.

*The Examination and Euidence of* Iennet
**Device.**

**Against**

**Iames Device** *her said Brother, Prisoner at the Barre, vpon his Arraignement and Triall: Taken before* **Roger Nowel,** *and* **Nicholas Bannester** *Esquires: two of his Maiesties Iustices of Peace within the said Countie.* viz.

SHee saith, that vpon Good-Friday last there was about twentie persons, whereof only two were men, to this Examinates remembrance, at her said Grand-mothers house, called *Malking-Tower* aforesaid, about twelue of the clock: all which persons this Examinates said Mother told her were Witches, and that they came to giue a name to *Alizon Deuice* Spirit or Familiar, Sister to this Examinate, and now Prisoner, in the Castle of Lancaster: And also this Examinate saith, that the persons aforesaid had to their Dinners, Beefe, Bacon, and rosted Mutton, which Mutton, as this Examinates said brother said, was of a Weather of *Robinsons* of Barley: which Weather was brought in the night before into this Examinates mothers house, by the said *Iames Deuice* this Examinates said brother, and in this Examinates sight killed, and eaten, as aforesaid: And shee further saith, that shee knoweth the names of sixe of the said Witches, *viz.* the wife of the said *Hugh Hargreiues*, vnder Pendle: *Christopher Howget*, of Pendle, Vncle to this Examinate: and *Dick Miles* wife, of the Rough-Lee: *Christopher Iacks*, of Thorny-holme, and his Wife: and the names of the residue shee this Examinate doth not know, sauing that this Examinates Mother and Brother were both there.

*The Examination of* Elizabeth
**Device,** *Mother of the said* **Iames Device,** *of the Forrest of Pendle, taken the seuen and twentieth day of*
*Aprill aforesaid.*

**Before**

**Roger Nowel,** *and* **Nicholas Bannester**
*Esquires; as aforesaid.* **viz.**

BEing examined, the said *Elizabeth* saith and confesseth, that vpon Good-Friday last there dined at this Examinates house, those which she hath said to be Witches, and doth verily thinke them to bee Witches, and their names are those, whom *Iames Deuice* hath formerly spoken of to be there.

And shee also confesseth in all things touching the Christning of her Spirit, and the killing of Master *Lister* of Westby, as the said *Iames Deuice* confesseth. But denieth that any talke was amongst thē the said Witches, to her now remembrance, at the said meeting together, touching the killing of the Gaoler at Lancaster; blowing vp of the Castle, thereby to deliuer old *Dembdike* her Mother; *Alizon Deuice* her Daughter, and other Prisoners, committed to the said Castle for Witchcraft.

After all these things opened, and deliuered in euidence against him; Master *Couil*, who hath the custodie of the Gaole at Lancaster, hauing taken great paines with him during the time of his imprisonment, to procure him to discouer his practises, and such other Witches as he knew to bee dangerous: Humbly prayed the fauour of the Court that his voluntarie confession to M. *Anderton*, M. *Sands* the Major of Lancaster, M. *Couel*, and others, might openly bee published and declared in Court.

*The voluntarie confession and declaration of* **Iames Device,** *Prisoner in the Castle at Lancaster.*

**Before**

**William Sands,** *Maior of Lancaster,* **Iames Anderton,** *Esquire, one of his Maiesties Iustices of Peace within the Countie of Lancaster: And* **Thomas Covel,** *Gentleman, one of his Maiesties Coroners in the same Countie.* **viz.**

*IAmes Deuice,* Prisoner in the Castle at Lancaster, saith, That his said Spirit *Dandie,* being very earnest with him to giue him his soule, He answered, he would giue him that part thereof that was his owne to giue: and thereupon the said Spirit said, hee was aboue Christ Iesvs, and therefore hee must absolutely giue him his Soule: and that done, hee would giue him power to reuenge himselfe against any whom he disliked.

And he further saith, that the said Spirit did appeare vnto him after sundrie times, in the likenesse of a Dogge, and at euery time most earnestly perswaded him to giue him his Soule absolutely: who answered as before, that he would giue him his owne part and no further. And hee saith, that at the last time that the said Spirit was with him, which was the Tuesday next before his apprehension; when as hee could not preuaile with him to haue his Soule absolutely granted vnto him, as aforesaid; the said Spirit departed from him, then giuing a most fearefull crie and yell, and withall caused a great flash of fire to shew about him: which said Spirit did neuer after trouble this Examinate.

*William Sands,*
*James Anderton.*
*Tho. Couel, Coroner.*

The said *Iennet Deuice*, his Sister, in the very end of her Examination against the said *Iames Deuice*, confesseth and saith, that her Mother taught her two Prayers: the one to get drinke, which was this. *viz.*

*Crucifixus hoc signum vitam*
*Eternam.* Amen.

And shee further saith, That her Brother *Iames Deuice*, the Prisoner at the Barre, hath confessed to her this Examinate, that he by this Prayer hath gotten drinke: and that within an houre after the saying the said Prayer, drinke hath come into the house after a very strange manner. And the other Prayer, the said *Iames Deuice* affirmed, would cure one bewitched, which shee recited as followeth. *viz.*

*A Charme.*[129]

---

[129] "*A Charme.*"] Sinclair, in his *Satan's Invisible World Discovered*, informs us, that "At night, in the time of popery, when folks went to bed, they believed the repetition of this following prayer was effectual to preserve them from danger, and the house too.
"Who sains the house the night,
They that sains it ilka night.
Saint Bryde and her brate,
Saint Colme and his hat,
Saint Michael and his spear,
Keep this house from the weir;
From running thief,
And burning thief;
And from and ill Rea,
That be the gate can gae;
And from an ill weight,
That be the gate can light
Nine reeds about the house;

*Vpon Good-Friday, I will fast while I may*
*Vntill I heare them knell*
*Our Lords owne Bell,*
*Lord in his messe*
*With his twelue Apostles good,*
*What hath he in his hand*
*Ligh in leath wand:*[130]
*What hath he in his other hand?*
*Heauens doore key,*
*Open, open Heauen doore keyes,*
*Steck, steck hell doore.*
*Let Crizum child*
*Goe to it Mother mild,*[131]

Keep it all the night,
What is that, what I see
So red, so bright, beyond the sea?
'Tis he was pierc'd through the hands,
Through the feet, through the throat,
Through the tongue;
Through the liver and the lung.
Well is them that well may
Fast on Good-friday."

which lines are not unlike some of those in the present "charme," which, evidently much corrupted by recitation, is a very singular and interesting string of fragments handed down from times long anterior to the Reformation, when they had been employed as armour of proof by the credulous vulgar against the Robin Goodfellows, urchins, elves, hags, and fairies of earlier superstition. I regret that I cannot throw more light upon it. The concluding lines are not deficient in poetical spirit.

[130] "*Ligh in leath wand.*"] Leath is no doubt lithe, flexible. What "ligh in" is intended for, unless it be lykinge, which the *Promptorium Parvulorum* (vide part i. p. 304) explains by lusty, or craske, *Delicativus*, crassus, I am unable to conjecture. It is clear, that the wand in one hand is to steck, *i.e.* stake, or fasten, the latch of hell door, while the key in his other hand is to open heaven's lock.

[131] "*Let Crizum child goe to it Mother mild.*"] The chrisom, according to the usual explanation, was a white cloth placed upon the head of an infant at baptism, when the chrism, or sacred oil of the Romish Church, was used in that sacrament. If the child died within a month of its birth, that cloth was

*What is yonder that casts a light so farrandly,*[132]
*Mine owne deare Sonne that's naild to the Tree.*
*He is naild sore by the heart and hand,*
*And holy harne Panne,*
*Well is that man*
*That Fryday spell can,*
*His Childe to learne;*
*A Crosse of Blew, and another of Red,*
*As good Lord was to the Roode.*
Gabriel *laid him downe to sleepe*
*Vpon the ground of holy weepe:*[133]
*Good Lord came walking by,*
*Sleep'st thou, wak'st thou* Gabriel,
*No Lord I am sted with sticke and stake,*
*That I can neither sleepe nor wake:*
*Rise vp* Gabriel *and goe with me,*
*The stick nor the stake shall neuer deere thee.*[134]

---

used as a shroud; and children so dying were called chrisoms in the old bills of mortality.

[132] "*A light so farrandly.*"] Farrandly, or farrantly, a word still in use in Lancashire, and which is equivalent to fair, likely, or handsome. (See *Lancashire Dialect and Glossary.*) "Harne panne," *i.e.*, cranium.— *Promptorium Parvulorum*, p. 237.

[133] "*Vpon the ground of holy weepe.*"] I know not how to explain this, unless it mean the ground of holy weeping, *i.e.*, the Garden of Gethsemane.

[134] "*Shall neuer deere thee.*"] The word to dere, or hurt, says Mr. Way, *Promptorium Parvulorum*, p. 119, is commonly used by Chaucer and most other writers until the sixteenth century:
"Fyr he schal hym nevyr dere."
*Cœur de Lion*, 1638.
Fabyan observes, under the year 1194, "So fast besyed this good Kyng Richarde to vex and dere the infydelys of Sury." Palsgrave gives, "To dere or hurte a noye nuire, I wyll never dere you by my good wyll."
Ang. Sax., **derian *nocere*, derung *læsio***.

*Sweete Iesus our Lord, Amen.*
*Iames Deuice.*

What can be said more of this painfull Steward, that was so carefull to prouide Mutton against this Feast and solemne meeting at *Malking-Tower*, of this hellish and diuellish band of Witches, (the like whereof hath not been heard of) then hath beene openly published and declared against him at the Barre, vpon his Arraignement and Triall: wherein it pleased God to raise vp Witnesses beyond expectation to conuince him; besides his owne particular Examinations, which being shewed and read vnto him; he acknowledged to be iust and true. And what I promised to set forth against him, in the beginning of his Arraignment and Triall, I doubt not but therein I haue satisfied your expectation at large, wherein I haue beene very sparing to charge him with any thing, but with sufficient matter of Record and Euidence, able to satisfie the consciences of the Gentlemen of the Iury of Life and Death; to whose good consideration I leaue him, with the perpetuall Badge and Brand of as dangerous and malicious a Witch, as euer liued in these parts of Lancashire, of his time: and spotted with as much Innocent bloud, as euer any Witch of his yeares.

After all these proceedings, by direction of his Lordship, were their seuerall Examinations, subscribed by euery one of them in particular, shewed vnto them at the time of their Triall, & acknowledged by thē to be true, deliuered to the gentlemen of the Iury of Life & Death, for the better satisfaction of their consciences: after due consideration of which said seuerall examinations, confessions, and voluntary declarations, as well of themselues as of their children, friends and confederates, The Gentlemen deliuered vp their Verdict against the Prisoners, as followeth. *viz.*

## *The Verdict of Life and Death.*

WHo found *Anne Whittle*, alias *Chattox*, *Elizabeth Deuice*, and *Iames Deuice*, guiltie of the seuerall murthers by Witchcraft, contained in the Indictments against them, and euery of them.

## THE WITCHES OF SALMESBVRY.[135]

---

[135] "*The Witches of Salmesbvry.*"] Or, more properly, Samlesbury. This wicked attempt on the part of this priest, or Jesuit, Thompson, *alias* Southworth, to murder the three persons whose trial is next reported, by suborning a child of the family to accuse them of what, in the excited state of the public mind at the time, was almost certain to consign them to a public execution, has few parallels in the annals of atrocity. The plot was defeated, and the lives of the persons accused, Jennet Bierley, Ellen Bierley, and Jane Southworth, saved, by no sagacity of the judge or wisdom of the jury, but by the effect of one simple question, wrung from the intended victims on the verge of anticipated condemnation, and which, natural as it might appear, was one the felicity of which Garrow or Erskine might have envied. It demolished, like Ithuriel's spear, the whole fabric of imposture, and laid it open even to the comprehension of Sir Edward Bromley and Master Thomas Potts. This was a case which well deserved Archbishop Harsnet for its historian. His vein of irony, which Swift or Echard never surpassed, and the scorching invective of which he was so consummate a master, would have been well employed in handing down to posterity a scene of villainy to which the frauds of Somers and the stratagems of Weston were mere child's play. We might then have had, from the most enlightened man of his age, a commentary on the statute 1st James First, which would have neutralized its mischief, and spared a hecatomb of victims. His resistless ridicule would, perhaps, have accomplished at once what was slowly and with difficulty brought about by the arguments of Scot and Webster, the establishment of the Royal Society, and a century's growth of intelligence and knowledge.

*The Arraignement and Triall of* Iennet
**Bierley Ellen Bierley,** *and* **Iane
Sovthworth** *of Salmesbury, in the County of
Lancaster; for Witchcraft vpon the bodie of* **Grace
Sowerbvts,** *vpon Wednesday the nineteenth of
August: At the Assises and generall Gaole-deliuery,
holden at Lancaster.*

**Before**

*Sir* **Edward Bromley** *Knight, one of his Maiesties
Iustices of Assize at Lancaster: as hereafter followeth.*
viz.

*Iennet Bierley.
Ellen Bierley.
Iane Southworth.*

THUS haue we for a time left the Graund Witches of the Forrest of Pendle, to the good consideration of a verie sufficient Iury of worthy Gentlemen of their Coūtrey. We are now come to the famous Witches of Salmesbury, as the Countrey called them, who by such a subtill practise and conspiracie of a Seminarie Priest,[136] or, as the best in this Honorable Assembly thinke, a Iesuite, whereof this Countie

---

[136] "*A Seminarie Priest.*"] Of this Thompson, *alias* Southworth, I find no account in Dodd's *Catholic Church History*. A John Southworth is noticed, vol. iii. p. 303, who is described as of an ancient family in Lancashire, and who was executed at Tyburn, June 28th, 1655. His dying speech is to be found in the same volume, p. 360. The interval of time, as well as the difference of surname, excludes the presumption of his being identical with the person referred to in the text, the hero of this extraordinary conspiracy, and who was probably of the family of Sir John Southworth, after mentioned.

of Lancaster hath good store,[137] who by reason of the generall entertainement they find, and great maintenance they haue, resort hither, being farre from the Eye of Iustice, and therefore, *Procul a fulmine*; are now brought to the Barre, to receiue their Triall, and such a young witnesse prepared and instructed to giue Euidence against them, that it must be the Act of God that must be the means to discouer their Practises and Murthers, and by an infant: but how and in what sort Almightie God deliuered them from the stroake of Death, when the Axe was layd to the Tree, and made frustrate the practise of this bloudie Butcher, it shall appeare vnto you vpon their Arraignement and Triall, whereunto they are now come.

---

[137] "*A Iesuite, whereof this Countie of Lancaster hath good store.*"] Lancashire was, about this period, the great hot-bed of Popish recusants. From the very curious list of recusants given (Baines's *Lancashire*, vol. i. p. 541,) it would seem that Samlesbury was one of their strongholds:—
James Cowper a seminarie prieste receipted releived and mainteined att the lodge of Sir John Southworthe in Samlesburie Parke by Mr. Tho: Southworthe, one of the younger sonnes of the said Sir John. And att the howse of John Warde dwellinge in Samlesburie Park syde. And the said Prieste sayeth Masse att the said lodge and att the said Wards howse. Whether resorte, Mr. Sowthworthe, Mres. An Sowthworthe, John Walmesley servante to Sir John Southworthe, Tho. Southworthe dwellinge in the Parke, John Gerrerde, servante to Sir John Southworthe, John Singleton, John Wrighte, James Sherples iunior, John Warde of Samlesburie, John Warde of Medler thelder, Henrie Potter of Medler, John Gouldon of Winwicke, Thomas Gouldon of the same, Roberte Anderton of Samlesburie and John Sherples of Stanleyhurst in Samlesburie.—*Baines's Lancashire*, vol. i. p. 543.
Att the lodge in Samlesburie Parke there be masses daylie and Seminaries dyuerse Resorte thither as James Cowpe, Harrisson Bell and such like, The like vnlawfull meetings are made daylie att the howse of John Warde by the Parke syde of Samlesburie all wiche matters, masses, resorte to Masses, receipting of Seminaries wilbe Justifyed by Mr. Adam Sowthewortha Thomas Sherples and John Osbaldston.—*Ibid.*, p. 544.

Master *Thomas Couel*, who hath the charge of the prisoners in the Castle at Lancaster, was commaunded to bring forth the said

## *Jennet Bierley,*
## *Ellen Bierley,*
## *Jane Southworth,*

to the Barre to receiue their Triall.

## Indictment.

THe said *Iennet Bierley*, *Ellen Bierley*, and *Iane Southworth* of Salmesbury, in the Countie of Lancaster, being indicted, for that they and euery of them felloniously had practised, exercised, and vsed diuerse deuillish and wicked Arts, called *Witchcrafts*, *Inchauntments*, *Charmes*, and *Sorceries*, in and vpon one *Grace Sowerbuts*: so that by meanes thereof her bodie wasted and consumed, *Contra formam Statuti &c. Et Contra Pacem dicti Domini Regis Coronam & dignitatem &c.*

To this Indictment vpon their Arraignement, they pleaded *Not-Guiltie*; and for the Triall of their liues put themselues vpon God and their Countrey.

Whereupon Master Sheriffe of the Countie of Lancaster, by direction of the Court, made returne of a very sufficient Iurie to passe betweene the Kings Maiestie and them, vpon their liues and deaths, with such others as follow in order.

The Prisoners being now at the Barre vpon their Triall
*Grace*
*Sowerbutts*, the daughter of *Thomas Sowerbutts*, about
the age of foureteene yeares, was produced to giue
Euidence for the Kings Maiestie against them:
who standing vp, she was commaunded
to point out the Prisoners, which
shee did, and said as
followeth,
*viz*
* *
*

*The Examination and Euidence of*
**Grace Sowerbvtts,** *daughter of* **Thomas Sowerbvtts,** *of Salmesbury, in the Countie of Lancaster Husband-man, vpon her Oath,*

**Against**

**Iennet Bierley, Ellen Bierley,** *and* **Iane Sovthworth,** *prisoners at the Barre, vpon their Arraignement and Triall,* viz.

THe said *Grace Sowerbutts* vpon her oath saith, That for the space of some yeares now last past shee hath beene haunted and vexed with some women, who haue vsed to come to her: which women, shee sayth, were *Iennet Bierley*, this Informers Grand-mother; *Ellen Bierley*, wife to *Henry Bierley*; *Iane Southworth*, late the wife of *Iohn Southworth*, and one *Old Doewife*, all of Salmesburie aforesaid. And shee saith, That now lately those foure women did violently draw her by the haire of the head, and layd her on the toppe of a Hay-mowe, in the said *Henry Bierleyes* Barne. And shee saith further, That not long after the said *Iennet Bierley* did meete this Examinate neere vnto the place where shee dwellleth, and first appeared in her owne likenesse, and after that in the likenesse of a blacke Dogge, and as this Examinate did goe ouer a Style, shee picked her off:[138] howbeit shee saith shee had no hurt then, but rose againe, and went to her Aunts in Osbaldeston, and returned backe againe to her Fathers house the same night, being fetched home by her father. And she saith, That in her way home-wards shee did then tell her Father, how

---

[138] "*Picked her off.*"] Threw her off.

shee had beene dealt withall both then and at sundry times before that; and before that time she neuer told any bodie thereof: and being examined why she did not, she sayth, she could not speake thereof, though she desired so to doe. And she further sayth, That vpon Saterday, being the fourth of this instant Aprill, shee this Examinate going towards Salmesbury bote, to meete her mother, comming from Preston, shee saw the said *Iennet Bierley*, who met this Examinate at a place called the Two Brigges, first in her owne shape, and afterwardes in the likenesse of a blacke Dogge, with two legges, which Dogge went close by the left side of this Examinate, till they came to a Pitte of Water, and then the said Dogge spake, and persuaded this Examinate to drowne her selfe there, saying, it was a faire and an easie death: Whereupon this Examinate thought there came one to her in a white sheete, and carried her away from the said Pitte, vpon the comming whereof the said blacke Dogge departed away; and shortly after the said white thing departed also: And after this Examinate had gone further on her way, about the length of two or three Fields, the said blacke Dogge did meete her againe, and going on her left side, as aforesaid, did carrie her into a Barne of one *Hugh Walshmans*,[139] neere there by, and layed her vpon the Barne-floore, and couered this Examinate with Straw on her bodie, and Haye on her head, and the Dogge it selfe lay on the toppe of the said Straw, but how long the said Dogge lay there, this Examinate cannot tell, nor how long her selfe lay there: for shee sayth, That vpon her lying downe there, as aforesaid, her Speech and Senses were taken from her: and the first time shee knew where shee was, shee was layed vpon a bedde in the said *Walshmans* house, which (as shee hath since beene told) was vpon the Monday at night following: and shee

---

[139] "*Hugh Walshmans*."] The wife of Hugh Walshman, of Samlesbury, is mentioned in the list of recusants; Baines, vol. i. p. 544.

was also told, That shee was found and taken from the place where shee first lay, by some of her friends, and carried into the said *Walshmans* house, within a few houres after shee was layed in the Barne, as aforesaid. And shee further sayth, That vpon the day following, being Tuesday, neere night of the same day, shee this Examinate was fetched by her Father and Mother from the said *Walshmans* house to her Fathers house. And shee saith, That at the place before specified, called the Two Brigges, the said *Iennet Bierley* and *Ellen Bierley* did appeare vnto her in their owne shapes: whereupon this Examinate fell downe, and after that was not able to speake, or goe, till the Friday following: during which time, as she lay in her Fathers house, the said *Iennet Bierley* and *Ellen Bierley* did once appeare vnto her in their owne shapes, but they did nothing vnto her then, neither did shee euer see them since. And shee further sayth, That a good while before all this, this Examinate did goe with the said *Iennet Bierley*, her Grand-mother, and the said *Ellen Bierley* her Aunt, at the bidding of her said Grand-mother, to the house of one *Thomas Walshman*, in Salmesbury aforesaid. And comming thither in the night, when all the house-hold was a-bed, the doores being shut, the said *Iennet Bierley* did open them, but this Examinate knoweth not how: and beeing come into the said house, this Examinate and the said *Ellen Bierley* stayed there, and the said *Iennet Bierley* went into the Chamber where the said *Walshman* and his wife lay, & from thence brought a little child,[140] which this Examinate thinketh was

---

[140] "*Brought a little child.*"] The evidence against the Pendle witches exhibits meagreness and poverty of imagination compared with the accumulated horrors with which the Jesuit, fresh, it may be, from Bodin and Delrio, made his "fire burn and cauldron bubble." With respect to this old story of the magical use made of the corpses of infants, Ben Jonson, in a note on
"I had a dagger: what did I with that?
Killed an infant to have his fat;"
tells us with great gravity:

in bed with it Father and Mother: and after the said *Iennet Bierley* had set her downe by the fire, with the said child, shee did thrust a naile into the nauell of the said child: and afterwards did take a pen and put it in at the said place, and did suck there a good space, and afterwards laid the child in bed againe: and then the said *Iennet* and the said *Ellen* returned to their owne houses, and this Examinate with them. And shee thinketh that neither the said *Thomas Walshman*, nor his wife knew that the said child was taken out of the bed from them. And shee saith also, that the said child did not crie when it was hurt, as aforesaid: But shee saith, that shee thinketh that the said child did thenceforth languish, and not long after dyed. And after the death of the said child; the next night after the buriall thereof, the said *Iennet Bierley* & *Ellen Bierley*, taking this Examinate with them, went to Salmesburie Church, and there did take vp the said child, and the said *Iennet* did carrie it out of the Church-yard in her armes, and then did put it in her lap and carryed it home to her owne house, and hauing it there did

---

Their killing of infants is common, both for confection of their ointment (whereto one ingredient is the fat boiled, as I have shewed before out of Paracelsus and Porta) as also out of a lust to do murder. *Sprenger in Mal. Malefic.* reports that a witch, a midwife in the diocese of Basil, confessed to have killed above forty infants (ever as they were new born, with pricking them in the brain with a needle) which she had offered to the devil. See the story of the three witches in *Rem. Dæmonola lib. cap.* 3, about the end of the chapter. And M. Phillippo Ludwigus Elich *Quæst.* 8. And that it is no new rite, read the practice of Canidia, *Epod. Horat. lib. ode* 5, and Lucan, *lib.* 6, whose admirable verses I can never be weary to transcribe:—

Nec cessant à cæde manus, si sanguine vivo
Est opus, erumpat jugulo qui primus aperto.
Nec refugit cædes, vivum si sacra cruorem
Extaque funereæ poscunt trepidantia mensæ.
Vulnere si ventris, non quâ natura vocabat,
Extrahitur partus calidus ponendus in aris;
Et quoties sævis opus est, et fortibus umbris
Ipsa facit maneis. Hominum mors omnis in usu est.
*Ben Johnson's Works, by Gifford*, vol. vii. p. 130.

boile some therof in a Pot, and some did broile on the coales, of both which the said *Iennet* & *Ellen* did eate, and would haue had this Examinate and one *Grace Bierley*, Daughter of the said *Ellen*, to haue eaten with them, but they refused so to doe: And afterwards the said *Iennet* & *Ellen* did seethe the bones of the said child in a pot, & with the Fat that came out of the said bones, they said they would annoint themselues,[141] that thereby they might sometimes change themselues into other shapes. And after all this being done, they said they would lay the bones againe in the graue the next night following, but whether they did so or not, this Examinate knoweth not: Neither doth shee know how they got it out of the graue at the first taking of it vp. And being further sworne and examined, she deposeth & saith, that about halfe a yeare agoe, the said *Iennet Bierley, Ellen Bierley, Iane Southworth*, and this Examinate (who went by the appointment of the said *Iennet* her Grand mother) did meete at a place called Red banck, vpon the North side of the water of Ribble, euery Thursday and Sonday at night by the space of a fortnight, and at the water side there came vnto them, as they went thether, foure black things, going vpright, and yet not like men in the face: which foure did carrie the said three women and this Examinate ouer the Water, and when they came to the said Red Banck they found some thing there which they did eate. But this Examinate saith, shee neuer saw such meate;

---

[141] "*They said they would annoint themselues.*"] Ben Jonson informs us:
When they are to be transported from place to place, they use to anoint themselves, and sometimes the things they ride on. Beside Apul. testimony, see these later, *Remig. Dæmonolatriæ lib.* 1. *cap.* 14. *Delrio, Disquis. Mag. l.* 2. *quæst.* 16. *Bodin Dæmonoman. lib.* 2 *c.* 14. *Barthol. de Spina. quæst. de Strigib. Phillippo Ludwigus Elich. quæst.* 10. *Paracelsus in magn. et occul. Philosophia*, teacheth the confection. *Unguentum ex carne recens natorum infantium, in pulmenti, forma coctum, et cum herbis somniferis, quales sunt Papaver, Solanum, Cicuta*, &c. And *Giov. Bapti. Porta, lib.* 2. *Mag. Natur. cap.* 16.—*Ben Jonson's Works by Gifford,* vol. vii. p. 119.

and therefore shee durst not eate thereof, although her said Grand mother did bidde her eate. And after they had eaten, the said three Women and this Examinate danced, euery one of them with one of the blacke things aforesaid, and after their dancing the said black things did pull downe the said three Women, and did abuse their bodies, as this Examinate thinketh, for shee saith, that the black thing that was with her, did abuse her bodie.

The said Examinate further saith vpon her Oth, That about ten dayes after her Examination taken at Blackborne, shee this Examinate being then come to her Fathers house againe, after shee had beene certaine dayes at her Vnckles house in Houghton: *Iane Southworth* widow, did meet this Examinate at her Fathers house dore and did carrie her into the loft,[142] and there did lay her vppon the floore, where shee was shortly found by her Father and brought downe, and laid in a bed, as afterwards shee was told: for shee saith, that from the first meeting of the said *Iane Southworth*, shee this Examinate had her speech and senses taken from her. But the next day shee saith, shee came somewhat to her selfe, and then the said Widow *Southworth* came againe to this Examinate to her bed-side, and tooke her out of bed, and said to this Examinate, that shee did her no harme the other time, in respect of that shee now would after doe to her, and thereupon put her vpon a hey-stack, standing some three or foure yards high from the earth, where shee was found after great search made, by a neighbours Wife neare dwelling, and then laid in her bedde

---

[142] "*Did carrie her into the loft.*"] There is something in this strange tissue of incoherencies, for knavery has little variety, which forcibly reminds us of the inventions of Elizabeth Canning, who ought to have lived in the days when witchcraft was part of the popular creed. What an admirable witch poor old Mary Squires would have made, and how brilliantly would her persecutor have shone in the days of the Baxters and Glanvilles, who acquitted herself so creditably in those of the Fieldings and the Hills.

againe, where she remained speechlesse and senselesse as before, by the space of two or three daies: And being recouered, within a weeke after shee saith, that the said *Iane Southworth* did come againe to this Examinate at her fathers house and did take her away, and laid her in a ditch neare to the house vpon her face, and left her there, where shee was found shortly after, and laid vpon a bedde, but had not her senses againe of a day & a night, or thereabouts. And shee further saith, That vpon Tuesday last before the taking of this her Examination, the said *Iane Southworth* came to this Examinates Fathers house, and finding this Examinate without the doore, tooke her and carried her into the Barne, and thrust her head amongst a companie of boords that were there standing, where shee was shortly after found and laid in a bedde, and remained in her old fit till the Thursday at night following.

And being further examined touching her being at Red-bancke, shee saith, That the three women, by her before named, were carried backe againe ouer Ribble, by the same blacke things that carried them thither; and saith that at their said meeting in the Red-bancke, there did come also diuers other women, and did meete them there, some old, some yong, which this Examinate thinketh did dwell vpon the North-side of Ribble, because she saw them not come ouer the Water: but this Examinate knew none of them, neither did she see them eat or dance, or doe anything else that the rest did, sauing that they were there and looked on.

These particular points of Euidence being thus vrged against the Prisoners: the father of this *Grace Sowerbutts* prayed that *Thomas Walshman*, whose childe they are charged to murther, might be examined as a witnes vpon his oath, for the Kings Maiestie, against the Prisoners at the Barre: who vpon this strange deuised accusation, deliuered by this impudent wench, were in opinion of many of that great Audience guilty of this bloudie murther, and more worthy to die then any of these Witches.

*The Examination and Euidence of*
**Thomas Walshman,** *of Salmesbury, in the Countie of Lancaster, Yeoman.*

**Against**

**Iennet Bierley, Ellen Bierley,** *and* **Iane Sovthworth,** *Prisoners at the Barre, vpon their Arraignement and Triall, as followeth.* **viz.**

THe said Examinate, *Thomas Walshman*, vpon his oath saith, That hee had a childe died about Lent was twelue-month, who had beene sicke by the space of a fortnight or three weekes, and was afterwards buried in Salmesburie Church: which childe when it died was about a yeare old; But how it came to the death of it, this Examinate knoweth not. And he further saith, that about the fifteenth of Aprill last, or thereabouts, the said *Grace Sowerbutts* was found in this Examinates fathers Barne, laid vnder a little hay and straw, and from thence was carried into this Examinates house, and there laid till the Monday at night following: during which time shee did not speak, but lay as if she had beene dead.

*The Examination of* Iohn Singleton: *Taken at Salmesbury, in the Countie of Lancaster, the seuenth day of August*: Anno Reg. Regis Iacobi Angliæ, Franciæ, & Hiberniæ, Fidei Defensor. &c. Decimo & Scotiæ, xlvj.

**Before**

Robert Hovlden,[143] *Esquire, one of his Maiesties Iustices of Peace in the County of Lancaster.*

**Against**

Iennet Bierley, Ellen Bierley, *and* Iane Sovthworth, *which hereafter followeth.*

THe said Examinate vpon his oath saith, That hee hath often heard his old Master, Sir *Iohn Southworth*[144] Knight,

---

[143] "*Robert Hovlden, Esquire.*"] This individual would be of the ancient family of Holden, of Holden, the last male heir of which died without issue, 1792. (See Whitaker's *Whalley*, 418.)

[144] "*Sir John Southworth.*"] In this family the manor of Samlesbury remained for three hundred and fifty years. This was, probably, the John (for the pedigree contained in Whitaker's *Whalley*, p. 430, does not give the clearest light on the subject) who married Jane, daughter of Sir Richard Sherburne, of Stonyhurst, and who took a great lead amongst the Catholics of Lancashire. What was the degree of relationship between Sir John and the husband of the accused, Jane Southworth, there is nothing in the descent to show. Family bickering might have a share, as well as superstition, in the opinion he entertained, "that she was an evil woman." Of the old hall at Samlesbury, the residence of the Southworths, a most interesting account will be found in Whitaker's *Whalley*, p. 431. He considers the centre of very high antiquity, probably not later than Edward III; and observes, "There is about the house a profusion and bulk of oak that must almost have laid prostrate a forest to erect it."

now deceased, say, touching the late wife of *Iohn Southworth*, now in the Gaole, for suspition of Witchcraft: That the said wife was as he thought an euill woman, and a Witch: and he said that he was sorry for her husband, that was his kinsman, for he thought she would kill him. And this Examinate further saith, That the said Sir *Iohn Southworth* in his comming or going betweene his owne house at Salmesbury, and the Towne of Preston, did for the most part forbeare to passe by the house, where the said wife dwelled, though it was his nearest and best way; and rode another way, only for feare of the said wife, as this Examinate verily thinketh.

*The Examination of* William
Alker *of Salmesbury, in the Countie of Lancaster, Yeoman: Taken the fifteenth day of Aprill*, **Anno Reg. Regis Iacobi, Angliæ, Franciæ, & Hiberniæ, Decimo & Scotiæ, quadragesimo quinto.**

**Before**

**Robert Hovlden,** *one of his Maiesties Iustices of Peace in the County of Lancaster: Against* **Iennet Bierley, Ellen Bierley,** *and* **Iane Bierley,** *which hereafter followeth.* **viz.**

THe said Examinate vpon his oath saith, That hee hath seene the said Sir *Iohn Southworth* shunne to meet the said wife of *Iohn Southworth*, now Prisoner in the Gaole, when he came neere where she was. And hath heard the said Sir *Iohn Southworth* say, that he liked her not, and that he doubted she would bewitch him.

Here was likewise *Thomas Sowerbutts*, father of *Grace Sowerbutts*, examined vpon his oath, and many other witnesses to little purpose: who being examined by the Court, could depose little against them: But the finding of the wench vpon the hay in her counterfeit fits: wherfore I leaue to trouble you with the particular declaration of their Euidence against the Prisoners, In respect there was not any one witnes able to charge them with one direct matter of Witchcraft; nor proue any thing for the murther of the childe.

Herein, before we come to the particular declaration of that wicked and damnable practise of this Iesuite or Seminary, I shall commend vnto your examination and iudgement some points of her Euidence, wherein you shal see what impossibilities are in this accusatiō brought to this perfection, by the great care and paines of this officious Doctor, Master *Thompson* or *Southworth*, who commonly worketh vpon the Feminine disposition, being more Passiue then Actiue.

*The particular points of the Euidence of*
## Grace Sowerbutts, *viz.*[145]

## Euidence.

*THAT for the space of some yeares she hath been haunted and vexed with some women, who haue vsed to come to her.*

The Iesuite forgot to instruct his Scholler how long it is since she was tormented: it seemes it is long since he read the old Badge of a Lyer, *Oportet mendacem esse memorem*. He knowes not how long it is since they came to church, after which time they began to practise Witchcraft. It is a likely thing the Torment and Panges of Witchcraft can be forgotten; and therefore no time can be set downe.

*Shee saith that now lately these foure women did violently draw her by the haire of the head, and lay her on the top of a Hay-mow.*

Heere they vse great violence to her, whome in another place they make choise to be of their counsell, to go with them to the house of *Walshman* to murther the childe. This courtesie deserues no discouery of so foule a Fact.

*Not long after, the said* Iennet Bierley *did meet this Examinate neere vnto the place where she dwelled, and*

---

[145] "*The particular points of the Evidence.*"] What a waste of ingenuity Master Potts displays in this recapitulation, where he is merely slaying the slain, and where his wisdom was not needed. Had he applied it to the service of the Pendle witches, he would have found still grosser contrarieties, and as great absurdity. But in that case, there was no horror of Popery to sharpen his faculties, or Jesuit in the background to call his humanity into play.

*first appeared in her owne likenesse, and after that in the likenesse of a blacke Dogge.*

*Vno & eodem tempore, shee transformed her selfe into a Dogge.* I would know by what meanes any Priest can maintaine this point of Euidence.

*And as shee went ouer a Style, shee picked her ouer, but had no hurt.*

This is as likely to be true as the rest, to throw a child downe from the toppe of a House, and neuer hurt her great toe.

*She rose againe; had no hurt, went to her Aunt, and returned backe againe to her Fathers house, being fetched home.*

I pray you obserue these contrarieties, in order as they are placed, to accuse the Prisoners.

*Saterday the fourth of this instant Aprill.*

Which was about the very day the Witches of the Forrest of Pendle were sent to Lancaster. Now was the time for the Seminarie to instruct, accuse, and call into question these poore women: for the wrinkles of an old wiues face is good euidence to the Iurie against a Witch.[146] And how often will the common people say (*Her eyes are sunke in her*

---

[146] "*The wrinkles of an old wiues face is good euidence to the Iurie against a Witch.*"] *Si sic omnia!* For once the worthy clerk in court has a lucid interval, and speaks the language of common sense.

*head,* God *blesse vs from her.*) But old *Chattox* had *Fancie,*[147] besides her withered face, to accuse her.

*This Examinate did goe with the said* Iennet Bierley *her Grand-mother, and* Ellen Bierley *her Aunt, to the house of* Walshman, *in the night-time, to murther a Child in strange manner.*

This of all the rest is impossible, to make her of their counsell, to doe murther, whome so cruelly and barbarously they pursue from day to day, and torment her. The Witches of the Forrest of Pendle were neuer so cruell nor barbarous.

*And shee also saith, the Child cried not when it was hurt.*

All this time the Child was asleepe, or the Child was of an extraordinarie patience, *ô inauditum facinus*!

*After they had eaten, the said three women and this Examinate daunced euery one of them with one of the Blacke things: and after, the Blacke things abused the said women.*

Here is good Euidence to take away their liues. This is more proper for the Legend of Lyes, then the Euidence of a witnesse vpon Oath, before a reuerend and learned Iudge, able to conceiue this Villanie, and finde out the practise. Here is the Religious act of a Priest, but behold the euent of it.

*She describes the foure Blacke things to goe vpright, but not like Men in the face.*

---

[147] "*But old Chattox had Fancie.*"] A great truth, though Master Potts might not be aware of the extent of it.

The Seminarie mistakes the face for the feete: For *Chattox* and all her fellow Witches agree, the Deuill is clouen-footed: but *Fancie* had a very good face, and was a very proper Man.

*About tenne dayes after her Examination taken at Black-borne, then she was tormented.*

Still he pursues his Proiect: for hearing his Scholler had done well, he laboured she might doe more in this nature. But notwithstanding, many things are layd to be in the times when they were Papists: yet the Priest neuer tooke paines to discouer them, nor instruct his Scholler, vntill they came to Church. Then all this was the Act of God, to raise a child to open all things, and then to difcouer his plotted Tragedie. Yet in this great discouerie, the Seminarie forgot to deuise a Spirit for them.

And for *Thomas Walshman*, vpon his Oath he sayth, That his Childe had beene sicke by the space of a fortnight, or three weekes, before it died. And *Grace Sowerbutts* saith, they tooke it out of the bedde, strucke a nayle into the Nauell, sucked bloud, layd it downe againe; and after, tooke it out of the Graue, with all the rest, as you haue heard. How these two agree, you may, vpon view of their Euidence, the better conceiue, and be able to judge.

How well this proiect, to take away the liues of three innocent poore creatures by practise and villanie; to induce a young Scholler to commit periurie, to accuse her owne Grand-mother, Aunt, &c. agrees either with the Title of a Iesuite, or the dutie of a Religious Priest, who should rather professe Sinceritie and Innocencie, then practise Trecherie: But this was lawfull; for they are Heretikes accursed, to leaue the companie of Priests; to frequent Churches, heare the word of God preached, and professe Religion sincerely.

But by the course of Times and Accidents, wise men obserue, that very seldome hath any mischieuous attempt beene vnder-taken without the direction or assistance of a Iesuit, or Seminarie Priest.

Who did not condemne these Women vpon this euidence, and hold them guiltie of this so foule and horrible murder? But Almightie God, who in his prouidence had prouided meanes for their deliuerance, although the Priest by the help of the Deuill, had prouided false witnesses to accuse them; yet God had prepared and placed in the Seate of Iustice, an vpright Iudge to sit in Iudgement vpon their liues, who after he had heard all the euidence at large against the Prisoners for the Kings Majestie, demanded of them what answere they could make. They humbly vpon their knees with weeping teares, desired him for Gods cause to examine *Grace Sowerbuts*, who set her on, or by whose meanes this accusation came against them.

Immediately the countenance of this *Grace Sowerbuts* changed: The witnesses being behinde, began to quarrell and accuse one an other. In the end his Lordship examined the Girle, who could not for her life make any direct answere, but strangely amazed, told him, shee was put to a Master to learne, but he told her nothing of this.

But here as his Lordships care and paines was great to discouer the practises of these odious Witches of the Forrest of Pendle, and other places, now vpon their triall before him: So was he desirous to discouer this damnable practise, to accuse these poore Women, and bring their liues in danger, and thereby to deliuer the innocent.

And as he openly deliuered it vpon the Bench, in the hearing of this great Audience: That if a Priest or Iesuit had a hand in one end of it, there would appeare to bee knauerie, and practise in the other end of it. And that it might the better appeare to the whole World, examined *Thomas Sowerbuts*, what Master taught his daughter: in generall termes, he denyed all.

The Wench had nothing to say, but her Master told her nothing of this. In the end, some that were present told his Lordship the truth, and the Prisoners informed him how shee went to learne with one *Thompson* a Seminarie Priest, who had instructed and taught her this accusation against them, because they were once obstinate Papists, and now came to Church. Here is the discouerie of this Priest, and of his whole practise. Still this fire encreased more and more, and one witnesse accusing an other, all things were laid open at large.

In the end his Lordship tooke away the Girle from her Father, and committed her to M. *Leigh*, a very religious Preacher,[148] and M. *Chisnal*, two Iustices of the Peace, to be carefully examined. Who tooke great paines to examine her of euery particular point: In the end they came into the Court, and there deliuered this Examination as followeth.

\* \*
\*

---

[148] "*M. Leigh, a very religious Preacher.*"] Parson of Standish, a man memorable in his day. He published several pieces, amongst others the two following: I. "The Drumme of Devotion," by W. Leigh, of Standish, 1613.— 2. "News of a Prodigious Monster in Aldington, in the Parish of Standish, in Lancashire," 1613, 4to, which show him to have been an adept in the science of title-making. He was one of the tutors of Prince Henry, and was great-grandfather of Dr. Leigh, author of the *History of Lancashire*.

*The Examination of* Grace Sowerbvts,
*of Salmesburie, in the Countie of Lancaster, Spinster:
Taken vpon Wednesday the 19. of August 1612.
Annoq; Reg. Regis,* Iacobi *Angliæ, Franciæ, & Hiberniæ,
Fidei Defensoris, &c. decimo & Scotiæ,* xlvi.

## Before

**William Leigh,** *and* **Edward Chisnal,**
*Esquires; two of his Maiesties Iustices of Peace in the same
Countie: At the Assizes and generall Gaole deliuerie, holden
at Lancaster.*

## By

***Direction of Sir* Edward Bromley *Knight, one
of his Maiesties Iustices of Assize at Lancaster.***

BEing demanded whether the accusation shee laid vppon her Grand-mother, *Iennet Bierley*, *Ellen Bierley*, and *Iane Southworth*, of Witchcraft, *viz.* of the killing of the child of *Thomas Walshman*, with a naile in the Nauell, the boyling, eating, and oyling, thereby to transforme themselues into diuers shapes, was true; Shee doth vtterly denie the same; or that euer shee saw any such practises done by them.

Shee further saith, that one Master *Thompson*, which she taketh to be Master *Christopher Southworth*, to whom shee was sent to learne her prayers, did perswade, counsell, and aduise her, to deale as formerly hath beene said against her said Grand-mother, Aunt, and *Southworths* wife.

And further shee confesseth and saith, that shee neuer did know, or saw any Deuils, nor any other Visions, as formerly by her hath beene alleaged and informed.

Also shee confesseth and saith, That shee was not throwne or cast vpon the Henne-ruffe, and Hay-mow in the Barne, but that shee went vp vpon the Mow her selfe by the wall side.

Being further demanded whether shee euer was at the Church, shee saith, shee was not, but promised her after to goe to the Church, and that very willingly.

*Signum* + **Grace Sowerbuts.**

*William Leigh.*

*Edward Chisnal.*

*The Examination of* Iennet Bierley,
**Ellen Bierley,** *and* **Iane Sovthworth,**
*of Salmesburie, in the Countie of Lancaster,*
*Taken vpon Wednesday the nineteenth of August* **1612.**
*Annoq; Reg. Regis,* **Iacobi** *Angliæ, Franciæ, & Hiberniæ,*
*Fidei Defensoris, &c. decimo & Scotiæ,* **xlvi.**

### Before

**William Leigh,** *and* **Edward Chisnal,**
*Esquires; two of his Maiesties Iustices of Peace in the same*
**Countie: At the Assizes and generall Gaole deliuerie, holden**
**at Lancaster.**

### By

**Direction of Sir Edward Bromley** *Knight, one of his Maiesties Iustices of Assize at Lancaster.*

*IEnnet Bierley* being demanded what shee knoweth, or hath heard, how *Grace Sowerbuts* was brought to *Christopher Southworth*, Priest; shee answereth, that shee was brought to M. *Singletons* house by her owne Mother, where the said Priest was, and that shee further heard her said Mother say, after her Daughter had been in her fit, that shee should be brought vnto her Master, meaning the said Priest.

And shee further saith, that shee thinketh it was by and through the Counsell of the said M. *Thomson*, alias *Southworth*, Priest, That *Grace Sowerbuts* her Grand-child accused her of Witchcraft, and of such practises as shee is accused of: and thinketh further, the cause why the said *Thompson*, alias *Southworth* Priest, should practise with the Wench to doe it was, for that shee went to the Church.

*Iane Southworth* saith shee saw Master *Thompson*, alias *Southworth*, the Priest, a month or sixe weekes before she was committed to the Gaole; and had conference with him in a place called Barne-hey-lane, where and when shee challenged him for slandering her to bee a Witch: whereunto he answered, that what he had heard thereof, he heard from her mother and her Aunt: yet she, this Examinate, thinketh in her heart it was by his procurement, and is moued so to thinke, for that shee would not be disswaded from the Church.

*Ellen Bierley* saith, Shee saw Master *Thompson*, alias *Southworth*, sixe or eight weeks before she was committed, and thinketh the said Priest was the practiser with *Grace Sowerbutts*, to accuse her of Witchcraft, and knoweth no cause why he should so doe, but because she goeth to the Church.

*Signum*, + **Iennet Bierley.**

*Signum*, £ **Iane Southworth.**

*Signum*, Φ **Ellen Bierley.**

**William Leigh.**

**Edward Chisnall.**

These Examinations being taken, they were brought into the Court, and there openly in the presence of this great Audience published, and declared to the Iurie of Life and

Death; and thereupon the Gentlemen of their Iury required to consider of them. For although they stood vpon their Triall, for matter of Fact of Witchcraft, Murther, and much more of the like nature: yet in respect all their Accusations did appeare to bee practise: they were now to consider of them, and to acquit them. Thus were these poore Innocent creatures, by the great care and paines of this honorable Iudge, deliuered from the danger of this conspiracie; this bloudie practise of the Priest laid open: of whose fact I may lawfully say; *Etiam si ego tacuero clamabunt lapides.*

These are but ordinary with Priests and Iesuites: no respect of Bloud, kindred, or friendship, can moue them to forbeare their Conspiracies: for when he had laboured treacherously to seduce and conuert them, and yet could doe no good; then deuised he this meanes.

*God of his great mercie deliuer vs all from them and their damnable conspiracies: and when any of his Maiesties subiects, so free and innocent as these, shall come in question, grant them as honorable a Triall, as Reuerend and worthy a Iudge to sit in Iudgement vpon them; and in the end as speedie a deliuerance. And for that which I haue heard of them; seene with my eyes, and taken paines to Reade of them: My humble prayer shall be to God Almightie.* Vt Conuertantur ne pereant. Aut confundantur ne noceant.

To conclude, because the discourse of these three women
of Salmesbury
hath beene long and troublesome to you; it is heere placed
amongst
the Witches, by special order and commandement, to set
forth to
the World the practise and conspiracie of this bloudy
Butcher.

And because I haue presented to your view a Kalender in
the Frontispice of this Booke, of twentie notorious
Witches: I shall shew you their deliuerance in
order, as they came to their Arraignement
and Triall euery day, and as the
Gentlemen of euery Iury for
life and death stood
charged with
them.

# THE ARRAIGNMENT
*and Triall of* Anne Redferne,[149] *Daughter of* **Anne Whittle**, *alias* **Chattox,** *of the Forrest of Pendle, in the Countie of Lancaster, for Witchcraft; vpon Wednesday the nineteenth of August, at the Assises and Generall Gaole-deliuerie, holden at Lancaster,*

Before

Sir **Edward Bromley** *Knight, one of his Maiesties Iustices of Assise at Lancaster.*

## *Anne Redferne.*

SVch is the horror of Murther, and the crying sinne of Bloud, that it will neuer bee satisfied but with Bloud. So fell it out with this miserable creature, *Anne Redferne*, the daughter of *Anne Whittle*, alias *Chattox*: who, as shee was her Mother, and brought her into the World, so was she the meanes to bring her into this danger, and in the end to her

---

[149] "*The Arraignment and Triall of Anne Redferne.*"] This poor woman seems to have been regularly hunted to death by her prosecutors, who pursued her with all the dogged pertinacity of blood-hounds. Neither the imploring appeal for mercy, in her case, from her wretched mother, who did not ask for any in her own, nor the want of even the shadow of a ground for the charge, had the slightest effect upon the besotted prejudices of the judge and jury. Acquitted on one indictment, she is now put on her trial on another; the imputed crime being her having caused the death of a person, who did not even accuse her of being accessory to it, nearly eighteen years before, by witchcraft; the only evidence, true or false, being, that she had been seen, about the same period, making figures of clay or marl. Her real offence, it may well be conjectured, was her having rejected the improper advances of the ill-conditioned young man whose death she was first indicted for procuring, and to which circumstance the rancour of his relations, the prosecutors, may evidently be traced. It is gratifying to know that she had firmness of mind to persist in the declaration of her innocence to the last.

Execution, for much Bloud spilt, and many other mischiefes done.

For vpon Tuesday night (although you heare little of her at the Arraignement and Triall of old *Chattox*, her Mother) yet was shee arraigned for the murther of *Robert Nutter*, and others: and by the fauour and mercifull consideration of the Iurie, the Euidence being not very pregnant against her, she was acquited, and found Not guiltie.

Such was her condition and course of life, as had she liued, she would haue beene very dangerous: for in making pictures of Clay, she was more cunning then any: But the innocent bloud yet vnsatisfied, and crying out vnto God for satisfaction and reuenge; the crie of his people (to deliuer them from the danger of such horrible and bloudie executioners, and from her wicked and damnable practises) hath now againe brought her to a second Triall, where you shall heare what wee haue vpon Record against her.

This *Anne Redferne*, prisoner in the Castle at Lancaster, being brought to the Barre, before the great Seat of Iustice, was there, according to the former order and course, indicted and arraigned, for that she felloniously had practised, exercised, and vsed her deuillish and wicked Arts, called *Witchcrafts, Inchauntments, Charmes*, and *Sorceries*, in and vpon one *Christopher Nutter*, and him the said *Christopher Nutter*, by force of the same Witchcrafts, felloniously did kill and murther, *Contra formam Statuti &c. Et Contra Pacem &c.*

Vpon her Arraignement to this Indictment, she pleaded *Not-Guiltie*; and for the triall of her life put her selfe vpon God and the Countrey.

So as now the Gentlemen of the Iurie of Life and Death stand charged with her as with others.

*The Euidence against* Anne Redferne, *Prisoner at the Barre.*

*The Examination of* Elizabeth
**Sothernes, alias Old Dembdike,** *taken at the Fence, in the Forrest of Pendle, in the Countie of Lancaster,*
*the second day of Aprill,* **Anno Reg. Regis Iacobi, Angliæ, &c. decimo, & Scotiæ xlv.**

**Against**

**Anne Redferne (***the daughter of* **Anne Whittle, alias Chattox)** *Prisoner at the Barre:*

**Before**

**Roger Nowel** *of Reade, Esquire, one of his Maiesties Iustices of Peace within the said Countie.*

THis Examinate saith, That about halfe a yeare before *Robert Nutter* died, as this Examinate thinketh, this Examinate went to the house of *Thomas Redferne*, which was about Midsummer, as shee this Examinate now remembreth it: and there, within three yards of the East end of the said house, shee saw the said *Anne Whittle* and *Anne Redferne*, wife of the said *Thomas Redferne*, and daughter of the said *Anne Whittle*, the one on the one side of a Ditch, and the other on the other side, and two pictures of Clay or Marle lying by them, and the third picture the said *Anne Whittle* was making. And the said *Anne Redferne*, her said daughter, wrought her Clay or Marle to make the third picture withall. And this Examinate passing by them, a Spirit, called *Tibbe*, in the shape of a blacke Cat, appeared vnto her this Examinate and said, Turne backe againe, and doe as they doe. To whom this Examinate said, What are they doing? Whereunto the said Spirit said, They are making three pictures: whereupon shee asked, whose pictures they were? whereunto the said Spirit said, They are the pictures of *Christopher Nutter*, *Robert Nutter*, and *Mary*, wife of the said *Robert Nutter*. But this Examinate denying to goe backe to helpe them to make the pictures aforesaid, the said Spirit seeming to be angrie therefore, shot or pushed this Examinate into the Ditch; and so shedde the milke which this Examinate had in a Kanne, or Kitt; and so thereupon the Spirit at that time vanished out of this Examinates sight. But presently after that, the said Spirit appeared vnto this Examinate again in the shape of a Hare, and so went with her about a quarter of a myle, but said nothing vnto her this Examinate, nor shee to it.

*The Examination of* Margaret **Crooke**

**Against**

*the said* **Anne Redferne:** *Taken the day and yeare aforesaid,*

**Before**

**Roger Nowel** *aforesaid, Esquire, one of his Maiesties Iustices of the Peace in the Countie of Lancaster.*

THis Examinate, sworne & examined vpon her oath, sayth, That about eighteene or nineteene yeares agoe, this Examinates brother, called *Robert Nutter*, about Whitsontide the same yeare, meeting with the said *Anne Redferne*, vpon some speeches betweene them they fell out, as this Examinats said brother told this Examinat: and within some weeke, or fort-night, then next after, this Examinats said brother fell sicke, and so languished vntill about Candlemas then next after, and then died. In which time of his sicknesse, he did a hundred times at the least say, That the said *Anne Redferne* and her associates had bewitched him to death. And this Examinate further saith, That this Examinates Father, called *Christopher Nutter*, about Maudlintide next after following fell sicke, and so languished, vntill Michaelmas then next after, and then died: during which time of his sicknesse, hee did sundry times say, That hee was bewitched; but named no bodie that should doe the same.

*The Examination of* Iohn Nvtter,
**of Higham Booth, in the Forrest of Pendle, in the Countie of Lancaster, yeoman,**

**Against**

*the said* **Anne Redferne:** *Taken the day and yeare aforesaid,*

**Before**

**Roger Nowel** *Esquire, one of his Maiesties Iustices of Peace in the Countie of Lancaster.*

THis Examinate, sworne and examined vpon his oath, sayth, That in or about Christmas, some eighteene or nineteene yeares agoe, this Examinat comming from Burnley with *Christopher Nutter* and *Robert Nutter*, this Examinates Father and Brother, this Examinate heard his said Brother then say vnto his said Father these words, or to this effect. *Father, I am sure I am bewitched by the* Chattox, Anne Chattox, *and* Anne Redferne *her daughter, I pray you cause them to bee layed in Lancaster Castle:* Whereunto this Examinates Father answered, Thou art a foolish Ladde, it is not so, it is thy miscarriage. Then this Examinates Brother weeping, said; nay, I am sure that I am bewitched by them, and if euer I come againe (for hee was readie to goe to Sir *Richard Shuttleworths*, then his Master) I will procure them to bee laid where they shall be glad to bite Lice in two with their teeth.

Hereupon *Anne Whittle*, alias *Chattox*, her Mother, was brought forth to bee examined, who confessed the making of the pictures of Clay, and in the end cried out very heartily to God to forgiue her sinnes, and vpon her knees intreated for this *Redferne*, her daughter.

Here was likewise many witnesses examined vpon oth *Viua voce*, who charged her with many strange practises, and declared the death of the parties, all in such sort, and about the time in the Examinations formerly mentioned.

All men that knew her affirmed, shee was more dangerous then her Mother, for shee made all or most of the Pictures of Clay, that were made or found at any time.

> Wherefore I leaue her to make good vse of the little
> time she hath to repent in: but no meanes
> could moue her to repentance, for
> as shee liued, so shee
> dyed.

*The Examination of* Iames Device, *taken the day and yeare afore-said.*

**Before**

**Roger Nowel,** *and* **Nicholas Bannester,**
*Esquires: two of his Maiesties Iustices of Peace within the said Countie of Lancaster.* **viz.**

THe said Examinate vpon his oath saith, That about two yeares agoe, hee this Examinate saw three Pictures of Clay, of halfe a yard long, at the end of *Redfernes* house, which *Redferne* had one of the Pictures in his hand, *Marie* his daughter had another in her hand, and the said *Redfernes* wife, *Anne Redferne the Witch*.now prisoner at Lancaster, had an other Picture in her hand, which Picture she the said *Redfernes* wife, was then crumbling, but whose Pictures they were, this Examinate cannot tell. And at his returning backe againe, some ten Roods off them there appeared vnto him this Examinate a thing like a Hare, which spit fire at him this Examinate.

# THE ARRAIGNMENT
*and Triall of* Alice Nutter,
**of the Forrest of Pendle, in the Countie of Lancaster, for Witch-craft; upon Wednesday the nineteenth of August, at the Assizes and generall Gaole deliuerie, holden at Lancaster.**

## Before

### *Sir* Edward Bromley *Knight, one of his Maiesties Iustices of Assize at Lancaster.*

### *Alice Nutter.*[150]

---

[150] "*Alice Nutter.*"] We now come to a person of a different description from any of those who have preceded as parties accused, and on whose fate some extraordinary mystery seems to hang. Alice Nutter was not, like the others, a miserable mendicant, but was a lady of large possessions, of a respectable family, and with children whose position appears to have been such as, it might have been expected, would have afforded her the means of escaping the fate which overtook her humbler companions.
"I knew her a good woman and well bred,
Of an unquestion'd carriage, well reputed
Amongst her neighbours, reckoned with the best."
*Heywood's Lancashire Witches.*
She is described as the wife of Richard Nutter of the Rough Lee, and mother of Miles Nutter, who were in all likelihood nearly related to the other Nutters whose descent has been given. The tradition is, that she was closely connected by relationship or marriage with Eleanor Nutter, the daughter of Ellis Nutter of Pendle Forest, the grandmother of Archbishop Tillotson. That she was the victim of a foul and atrocious conspiracy, in which the movers were some of her own family, there seems no reason to doubt. The anxiety of her children to induce her to confess may possibly have originated in no impure or sinister motive, but it is difficult altogether to dismiss from the mind the suspicion that her wealth was her great misfortune; and that to secure it within their grasp her own household were passive, if not active, agents in her destruction. Any thing more childish or absurd than the evidence against her—as, for instance, that she joyned in killing Henry Mitton because he refused a penny to Old Demdike—it would not be easy, even from the records of witch trials, to

produce. As regards Alice Nutter, Potts is singularly meagre, and it is to be lamented that the deficiency of information cannot at present be supplied. Almost the only fact he furnishes us with is, that she died maintaining her innocence. It would have been most interesting to have had the means of ascertaining how she conducted herself at her trial and after her condemnation; and how she met the iniquitous injustice of her fate, sharpened, as it must have been, by the additional bitterness of the insults and execrations of the blind and infuriated populace at her execution. It is far from improbable that some of the correspondence now deposited in the family archives in the county hitherto unpublished may ultimately furnish these particulars.

Alice Nutter was doubtless the original of the story of which Heywood availed himself in *The Late Lancashire Witches*, 1634, 4to, which is frequently noticed by the writers of the 17th century—that the wife of a Lancashire country gentleman had been detected in practising witchcraft and unlawful arts, and condemned and executed. In that play there can be little hesitation in ascribing to Heywood the scenes in which Mr. Generous and his wife are the interlocutors, and to Broome, Heywood's coadjutor, the subordinate and farcical portions. It is a very unequal performance, but not destitute of those fine touches, which Heywood is never without, in the characters of English country gentlemen and the pathos of domestic tragedy. The following scene, which I am tempted to extract, though very inferior to the noble ones in his *Woman Killed by Kindness*, between Mr. and Mrs. Frankford, which it somewhat resembles in character, is not unworthy of this great and truly national dramatic writer:—

Mr. Generous. Wife. Robin, *a groom.*

*Gen.* My blood is turn'd to ice, and all my vitals
Have ceas'd their working. Dull stupidity
Surpriseth me at once, and hath arrested
That vigorous agitation, which till now
Exprest a life within me. I, methinks,
Am a meer marble statue, and no man.
Unweave my age, O time, to my first thread;
Let me lose fifty years, in ignorance spent;
That, being made an infant once again,
I may begin to know. What, or where am I,
To be thus lost in wonder?

*Wife.* Sir.

*Gen.* Amazement still pursues me, how am I chang'd,
Or brought ere I can understand myself
Into this new world!

*Rob.* You will believe no witches?

*Gen.* This makes me believe all, aye, anything;
And that myself am nothing. Prithee, Robin,
Lay me to myself open; what art thou,
Or this new transform'd creature?

*Rob.* I am Robin;
And this your wife, my mistress.

*Gen.* Tell me, the earth
Shall leave its seat, and mount to kiss the moon;
Or that the moon, enamour'd of the earth,
Shall leave her sphere, to stoop to us thus low.
What, what's this in my hand, that at an instant
Can from a four-legg'd creature make a thing
So like a wife!

*Rob.* A bridle; a jugling bridle, Sir.

*Gen.* A bridle! Hence, enchantment.
A viper were more safe within my hand,
Than this charm'd engine.—
A witch! my wife a witch!
The more I strive to unwind
Myself from this meander, I the more
Therein am intricated. Prithee, woman,
Art thou a witch?

*Wife.* It cannot be denied,
I am such a curst creature.

*Gen.* Keep aloof:
And do not come too near me. O my trust;
Have I, since first I understood myself,
Been of my soul so chary, still to study
What best was for its health, to renounce all
The works of that black fiend with my best force;
And hath that serpent twined me so about,
That I must lie so often and so long
With a devil in my bosom?

*Wife.* Pardon, Sir. [*She looks down.*]

*Gen.* Pardon! can such a thing as that be hoped?
Lift up thine eyes, lost woman, to yon hills;
It must be thence expected: look not down
Unto that horrid dwelling, which thou hast sought
At such dear rate to purchase. Prithee, tell me,
(For now I can believe) art thou a witch?

*Wife.* I am.

*Gen.* With that word I am thunderstruck,
And know not what to answer; yet resolve me.
Hast thou made any contract with that fiend,
The enemy of mankind?

*Wife.* O I have.

*Gen.* What? and how far?

*Wife.* I have promis'd him my soul.

*Gen.* Ten thousand times better thy body had
Been promis'd to the stake; aye, and mine too,
To have suffer'd with thee in a hedge of flames,
Than such a compact ever had been made. Oh—
Resolve me, how far doth that contract stretch?

*Wife.* What interest in this Soul myself could claim,
I freely gave him; but his part that made it
I still reserve, not being mine to give.

*Gen.* O cunning devil: foolish woman, know,
Where he can claim but the least little part,
He will usurp the whole. Thou'rt a lost woman.

*Wife.* I hope, not so.

*Gen.* Why, hast thou any hope?

*Wife.* Yes, sir, I have.

*Gen.* Make it appear to me.

*Wife.* I hope I never bargain'd for that fire,
Further than penitent tears have power to quench.

*Gen.* I would see some of them.

*Wife.* You behold them now
(If you look on me with charitable eyes)
Tinctur'd in blood, blood issuing from the heart.
Sir, I am sorry; when I look towards heaven,
I beg a gracious pardon; when on you,
Methinks your native goodness should not be
Less pitiful than they; 'gainst both I have err'd;
From both I beg atonement.

*Gen.* May I presume 't?

*Wife.* I kneel to both your mercies.

*Gen.* Knowest thou what
A witch is?

*Wife.* Alas, none better;
Or after mature recollection can be
More sad to think on 't.

*Gen.* Tell me, are those tears
As full of true hearted penitence,
As mine of sorrow to behold what state,
What desperate state, thou'rt fain in?

*Wife.* Sir, they are.

*Gen.* Rise; and, as I do you, so heaven pardon me;
We all offend, but from such falling off
Defend us! Well, I do remember, wife,
When I first took thee, 'twas *for good and bad*:
O change thy bad to good, that I may keep thee
(As then we past our faiths) 'till Death us sever.
O woman, thou hast need to weep thyself
Into a fountain, such a penitent spring
As may have power to quench invisible flames;

THE two degrees of persons which chiefly practise Witch-craft, are such, as are in great miserie and pouertie, for such the Deuill allures to follow him, by promising great riches, and worldly commoditie; Others, though rich, yet burne in a desperate desire of Reuenge; Hee allures them by promises, to get their turne satisfied to their hearts contentment, as in the whole proceedings against old *Chattox*: the examinations of old *Dembdike*; and her children, there was not one of them, but have declared the like, when the Deuill first assaulted them.

But to attempt this woman in that sort, the Diuel had small meanes: For it is certaine she was a rich woman; had a great estate, and children of good hope: in the common opinion of the world, of good temper, free from enuy or malice; yet whether by the meanes of the rest of the Witches, or some vnfortunate occasion, shee was drawne to fall to this wicked course of life, I know not: but hither shee is now come to receiue her Triall, both for Murder, and many other vilde and damnable practises.

Great was the care and paines of his Lordship, to make triall of the Innocencie of this woman, as shall appeare vnto you vpon the Examination of *Iennet Deuice*, in open Court, at the time of her Arraignement and Triall; by an extraordinary meanes of Triall, to marke her out from the rest.

It is very certaine she was of the Grand-counsell at Malking-Tower vpon Good-Friday, and was there present, which was a very great argument to condemne her.

---

In which my eyes shall aid: too little, all.
*Late Lancashire Witches, Act 4.*

This *Alice Nutter*, Prisoner in the Castle at Lancaster: Being brought to the Barre before the Great Seat of Iustice; was there according to the former order and course Indicted and Arraigned, for that she felloniously had practised, exercised, and vsed her diuellish and wicked Arts, called *Witchcrafts, Inchantments, Charmes* and *Sorceries*, in and vpon *Henry Mitton*: and him the said *Henry Mitton*, by force of the same Witchcrafts, felloniously did kill and murther. *Contra formam Statuti,* &c. *Et Contra Pacem,* &c.

Vpon her Arraignement, to this Indictment shee pleaded not guiltie; and for the triall of her life, put her selfe vpon God and the Countrey.

So as now the Gentlemen of the Iury of life and death stand charged with her, as with others.

*The Euidence against* Alice Nutter *Prisoner at the Barre.*

*The Examination of* Iames Device
***sonne of* Elizabeth Device:** *Taken the seuen and twentieth day of Aprill*: **Anno Reg. Regis Iacobi Angliæ, Franciæ, & Hiberniæ, Fidei Defensor. &c. Decimo & Scotiæ, xlvj.**

**Before**

**Roger Nowel** *and* **Nicholas Banester,** *two of his Maiesties Iustices of Peace in the Countie of Lancaster. Against Alice Nutter.*

THe said Examinate saith vpon his oath, That hee heard his Grand-mother say, about a yeare ago, that his mother, called *Elizabeth Deuice*, and his Grand-mother, and the wife of *Richard Nutter*, *Alice Nutter* the Prisoner.of the Rough-Lee aforesaid, had killed one *Henry Mitton*, of the Rough-Lee aforesaid, by Witchcraft. The reason wherefore he was so killed, was for that this Examinats said Grand-mother had asked the said *Mitton* a penny: and hee denying her thereof; thereupon shee procured his death as aforesaid.

*The Examination of* Elizabeth
**Device,** *mother of the said* **Iames Device.**

**Against**

**Alice Nvtter,** *wife of* **Richard Nvtter,**
**Prisoner at the Barre, vpon her Arraignement and Triall.**

**Before**

**Roger Nowel** *and* **Nicholas Banester,**
**Esquires, the day and yeare aforesaid.**

THis Examinate vpon her oath confesseth, and saith, That she, with the wife of *Richard Nutter*, called *Alice Nutter*, Prisoner at the Barre; and this Examinates said mother, *Elizabeth Sotherne*, alias *Old Demdike*; ioyned altogether, and bewitched the said *Henry Mitton* to death.

This Examinate further saith, That vpon Good-friday last, there dined at this examinats house two women of Burneley Parish, whose names the said *Richard Nutters* wife, *Alice Nutter*, now Prisoner at the Barre, doth know.

*The Examination of* Iames Device
***aforesaid.***

**Against**

***The said* Alice Nvtter,** *the daye and yeare aforesaid.*

THE said Examinate vpon his oath saith, That vpon Good-Friday about twelue of the clocke in the day time, there dined in this Examinats said mothers house, a number of persons, whereof three were men, with this Examinate, and the rest women: and that they mette there for these three causes following, as this Examinats said mother told this Examinate.

The first was for the naming of the Spirit, which *Alizon Deuice*, now Prisoner at Lancaster, had, but did not name him, because she was not there.

The second cause was, for the deliuerie of his said Grand-mother; this Examinates said sister, *Alizon*; the said *Anne Chattox*, and her daughter *Redferne*; killing the Gaoler at Lancaster, and before the next Assizes to blow vp the Castle there; to the end that the foresaid Prisoners might by that meanes make an escape, and get away: all which this Examinate then heard them conferre of.

And he also saith, The names of such Witches as were on Good-Friday at this Examinats said Grand-mothers house, and now this Examinates owne mothers, for so many of them as he doth know, were amongst others, *Alice Nutter*, mother of *Myles Nutter*, now Prisoner at the Barre. And this Examinate further saith, That all the said Witches went out of the said house in their owne shapes and likenesses; and they all, by that time they were forth of the doores, were gotten on horse-backe, like vnto Foales, some of one colour, and some of another; and *Prestons* wife was the last: and when shee got on horse-back, they all presently vanished out of this Examinates sight: and before their said parting away, they all appointed to meete at the said *Prestons* wifes house that day twelue month, at which time the said *Prestons* wife promised to make them a great feast: and if they had occasion to meete in the meane time, then should warning be giuen to meet upō Romleys Moore.

*The Examination and Euidence of*
**Iennet Device,** *daughter of* **Elizabeth Device.**

**Against**

**Alice Nvtter,** *Prisoner at the Barre.*

THe said Examinate saith, That on Good-Friday last, there was about 20. persons, whereof only two were men (to this Examinates remembrance) at her said Grand-mothers house at Malking-Tower, about twelue of the clock; all which persons, this Examinats said mother tould her, were Witches. And she further saith, she knoweth the names of six of them, *viz.* the wife of *Hugh Hargreiues* vnder Pendle, *Christopher Howgate* of Pendle, Vncle to this Examinat and *Elizabeth* his wife; and *Dick Myles* wife of the Rough-Lee, *Christopher Iacks* of Thorniholme, and his wife; and the names of the residue, she this Examinate doth not know.

AFter these Examinations were openly read, his Lordship being very suspitious of the accusation of this yong wench *Iennet Deuice*, commanded one to take her away into the vpper Hall, intending in the meane time to make Triall of her Euidence, and the Accusation especially against this woman, who is charged to haue beene at Malking-Tower, at this great meeting. Master *Couel* was commanded to set all his prisoners by themselues, and betwixt euery Witch another Prisoner, and some other strange women amongst them, so as no man could iudge the one from the other: and these being set in order before the Court from the prisoners, then was the Wench *Iennet Deuice* commaunded to be brought into the Court: and being set before my Lord, he tooke great paines to examine her of euery particular Point, What women were at Malking-Tower vpon Good-Friday? How she knew them? What were the names of any of them? And how she knew them to be such as she named?

In the end being examined by my Lord,[151] Whether she knew them that were there by their faces, if she saw them? she told my Lord she should: whereupon in the presence of this great Audience, in open Court, she went and tooke *Alice Nutter*, this prisoner, by the hand, and accused her to be one: and told her in what place shee sat at the Feast at Malking-Tower, at the great assembly of the Witches, and who sat next her: what conference they had, and all the rest of their proceedings at large, without any manner of contrarietie.

Being demaunded further by his Lordship, Whether she knew *Iohan a Style*?[152] she alledged, she knew no such womā to be there, neither did she euer heare her name.

---

[151] "*Being examined by my Lord.*"] She had evidently learned her lesson well; but this was, with all submission to his Lordship, if adopted as a test, a mighty poor one. Jennet Device must have known well the persons of the parties she accused, and who were now upon their trial, as they were all her near neighbours.

[152] "*Whether she knew Iohan a Style?*"] His Lordship's introduction of this apocryphal legal personage on such an occasion is very amusing. Had he studied Littleton and Perkins a little less, and given some attention to the Lancashire dialect, and some also to the study of that great book, in which even a judge may find valuable matter, the book of human nature, he might have been more successfull in his examination. Jack's o' Dick's o' Harry's would have been more likely to have been recognised as a veritable person of this world by Jennet Device, than such a name as Johan a Style; which, though very familiar at Westminster, would scarcely have its prototype at Pendle. But Jennet Device, young as she was, in natural shrewdness was far more than a match for his lordship.

This could be no forged or false Accusation, but the very Act of God to discouer her.

Thus was no meanes left to doe her all indifferent fauour, but it was vsed to saue her life; and to this shee could giue no answere.

But nothing would serue: for old *Dembdike*, old *Chattox*, and others, had charged her with innocent bloud, which cries out for Reuenge, and will be satisfied. And therefore Almightie God, in his Iustice, hath cut her off.

And here I leaue her, vntill shee come to her Execution, where<br>
you shall heare shee died very impenitent; insomuch as<br>
her owne children were neuer able to moue her to<br>
confesse any particular offence, or declare any<br>
thing, euen in *Articulo Mortis*: which was<br>
a very fearefull thing to all that were<br>
present, who knew shee<br>
was guiltie.<br>
\* \*<br>
\*

# THE ARRAIGNMENT
*and Triall of* Katherine Hewit,
*Wife of* Iohn Hewit, *alias* Movld-heeles,[153]
*of Coulne, in the Countie of Lancaster Clothier, for Witchcraft; vpon Wednesday the nineteenth of August, at the Assises and Generall Gaole-deliuerie, holden at Lancaster,*

## Before

*Sir* **Edward Bromley** *Knight, one of his Maiesties Iustices of Assise at Lancaster.*

## *Katherine Hewit.*

WHOo but Witches can be proofes, and so witnesses of the doings of Witches? since all their Meetings, Conspiracies, Practises, and Murthers, are the workes of Darkenesse: But to discouer this wicked *Furie*, God hath not only raised meanes beyond expectation, by the voluntarie Confession and Accusation of all that are gone before, to accuse this Witch (being Witches, and thereby witnesses of her doings) but after they were committed, by meanes of a Child, to discouer her to be one, and a Principall in that wicked assembly at Malking-Tower, to deuise such a damnable course for the deliuerance of their friends at Lancaster, as to kill the Gaoler, and blow vp the Castle, wherein the Deuill did but labour to assemble them together, and so being knowne to send them all one way: And herein I shall

---

[153] "*Katherine Hewit, alias Movld-heeles.*"] Of this person, who comes next in the list of witches, our information is very scanty. She was not of Pendle, but of Colne; and as her husband is described as a "clothier," may be presumed to have been in rather better circumstances than Elizabeth Southernes or Anne Whittle's families. She made no confession.

commend vnto your good consideration the wonderfull meanes to condemne these parties, that liued in the world, free from suspition of any such offences, as are proued against them: And thereby the more dangerous, that in the successe we may lawfully say, the very Finger of God did point thē out. And she that neuer saw them, but in that meeting, did accuse them, and by their faces discouer them.

This *Katherine Hewyt*, Prisoner in the Castle at Lancaster, being brought to the Barre before the great Seate of Iustice, was there according to the former order and course Indicted and Arraigned, for that she felloniously had practized, exercised, and vsed her Deuillish and wicked Arts, called *Witch-crafts*, *Inchantments*, *Charmes*, and *Sorceries*, in, and vpon *Anne Foulds*; and the same *Anne Foulds*, by force of the same witch-craft, felloniously did kill and murder. *Contra formam Statuti, &c. Et contra Pacem dicti Domini Regis, &c.*

Vpon her Arraignement to this Indictment, shee pleaded not guiltie; And for the triall of her life put her selfe vpon God and her Countrie.

So as now the Gentlemen of the Iurie of life and death, stand charged with her as with others.

*The Euidence against* Katherine Hewyt,
*Prisoner at the Barre.*

*The Examination of* Iames Device,
**Sonne of Elizabeth Device,** *taken the seuen and twentieth day of Aprill,* **Anno Reg. Regis Iacobi, Angliæ, Franciæ, & Hiberniæ, decimo, et Scotiæ quadragesimo quarto.**

**Before**

**Roger Nowel,** *and* **Nicholas Bannester,**
*Esquires; two of his Maiesties Iustices of Peace, in the Countie of Lancaster.*

**Against**

**Katherine Hewyt,** *alias* **Movld-heeles**
*of Colne.* viz.

THis Examinate saith, that vpon Good-Friday last, about twelue of the Clock in the day time, there dined at this Examinates Mothers house a number of persons: And hee also saith, that they were Witches; and that the names of the said Witches, that were there, for so many of them as he did know, were amongst others *Katherine Hewyt,* wife of *Iohn Hewyt,* alias *Mould-heeles,* of Colne, in the Countie of Lancaster Clothier; And that the said Witch, called *Katherine Hewyt,* alias *Mould-heeles,* and one *Alice Gray,* did confesse amongst the said Witches at their meeting at *Malkin-Tower* aforesaid, that they had killed *Foulds* wifes child, called *Anne Foulds,* of Colne:[154] And also said, that

---

[154] "*Anne Foulds of Colne. Michael Hartleys of Colne.*"] Folds and Hartley are still the names of families at and in the neighbourhood of Colne.

they had then in hanck a child[155] of *Michael Hartleys* of Colne.

And this Examinate further saith, that all the said Witches went out of the said house in their own shapes and likenesses, and by that time they were gotten forth of the doores, they were gotten on Horse-back like vnto foales, some of one colour, some of an other, and the said *Prestons* wife was the last: And when she got on Horse-back, they all presently vanished out of this Examinates sight. And before their said parting away they all appointed to meete at the said *Prestons* wifes house that day twelue Moneths: at which time the said *Prestons* wife promised to make them a great feast, and if they had occasion to meete in the meane time, then should warning be giuen that they all should meet vpon Romlesmoore.

---

[155] "*Had then in hanck a child.*"] The meaning of this term is clear, the origin rather dubious. It may come from the Scotch word, *to hanck*, i.e. to have in holdfast or secure, vide Jamieson's Scotch Dictionary, tit. hanck, or from handkill, to murder, vide Jamieson, under that word; or lastly, may be metaphorically used, from hanck, also signifying a skein of yarn or worsted which is tied or trussed up.

*The Examination and Euidence of* Elizabeth
**Device,** *Mother of the said* **Iames
Device.**

**Against**

**Katherine Hewyt,** *alias* **Movld-heeles,**
*Prisoner at the Barre vpon her Arraignement and Triall, taken the day and yeare aforesaid.* **viz.**

THis Examinate vpon her oath confesseth, that vpon Good-Friday last there dyned at this Examinates house, which she hath said are Witches, and verily thinketh to bee Witches, such as the said *Iames Deuice* hath formerly spoken of: amongst which was *Katherine Hewyt*, alias *Mould-heeles*, now Prisoner at the Barre: and shee also saith, that at their meeting on Good-Friday at *Malkin-Tower* aforesaid, the said *Katherine Hewyt*, alias *Mould-heeles*, and *Anne Gray*, did confesse, they had killed a child of *Foulds* of Colne, called *Anne Foulds*, and had gotten hold of another.

And shee further saith, the said *Katherine Hewyt* with all the rest, there gaue her consent with the said *Prestons* wife for the murder of Master *Lister*.

*The Examination and Euidence of*
**Iennet Device,**

**Against**

**Katherine Hewyt,** *alias* **Movld-heeles,**
*Prisoner at the Barre.*

THe said Examinate saith, That vpon Good-Friday last, there was about twentie persons, whereof two were men to this Examinates remembrance, at her said Grand-mothers house, called *Malkin-Tower* aforesaid, about twelue of the clock: All which persons this Examinates said mother told her were Witches, and that shee knoweth the names of sixe of the said Witches.

Then was the said *Iennet Deuice* commanded by his Lordship, to finde and point out the said *Katherine Hewyt*, alias *Mould-heeles*, amongst all the rest of the said Women, whereupon shee went and tooke the said *Katherine Hewyt* by the hand: Accused her to bee one, and told her in what place shee sate at the feast at *Malkin-Tower*, at the great Assembly of the Witches, and who sate next her; what conference they had, and all the rest of their proceedings at large, without any manner of contrarietie: Being demanded further by his Lordship, whether *Ioane a Downe* were at that Feast, and meeting, or no? shee alleaged shee knew no such woman to be there, neither did shee euer heare her name.

If this were not an Honorable meanes to trie the accusation against them, let all the World vpon due examination giue iudgement of it. And here I leaue her the last of this companie, to the Verdict of the Gentlemen of the Iurie of life and death, as hereafter shall appeare.

Heere the Iurie of Life and Death, hauing spent the most part of the day, in due consideration of their offences, Returned into the Court to deliuer vp their Verdict against them, as followeth.

# *The Verdict of Life and Death.*

WHo vpon their Oathes found *Iennet Bierley*, *Ellen Bierley*, and *Iane Southworth*, not guiltie of the offence of Witch-craft, conteyned in the Indictment against them.

*Anne Redferne*, guiltie of the fellonie & murder, conteyned in the Indictment against her.

*Alice Nutter*, guiltie of the fellonie and murder conteyned in the Indictment against her.

And

*Katherine Hewyt*, guiltie of the fellonie & murder conteyned in the Indictment against her.

Whereupon Master *Couell* was commanded by the Court to take away the Prisoners Conuicted, and to bring forth *Iohn Bulcocke, Iane Bulcocke* his mother,[156] and *Alizon Deuice*, Prisoners in the Castle at Lancaster, to receiue their Trialls.

Who were brought to their Arraignement and Triall as hereafter followeth.

---

[156] "*Iohn Bulcocke, Iane Bulcocke his mother.*"] The condition of these persons is not stated. It may be conjectured that they were of the lowest class.

THE ARRAIGNMENT
*and Triall of* Iohn Bvlcock,
*and* **Iane Bvlcock** *his mother, wife of* **Christopher Bvlcock,** *of the Mosse-end, in the Countie of Lancaster, for Witch-craft: vpon Wednesday in the after-noone, the nineteenth of August, 1612. At the Assizes and generall Gaole deliuery, holden at Lancaster.*

**Before**

*Sir* **Edward Bromley,** *Knight, one of his Maiesties Iustices of Assizes at Lancaster.*

*John Bulcock,*
and
*Jane Bulcock* **his mother.**

IF there were nothing to charge these Prisoners withall, whom now you may behold vpon their Arraignement and Triall but their poasting in haste to the great Assembly at Malking-Tower, there to aduise and consult amongst the Witches, what were to bee done to set at liberty the Witches in the Castle at Lancaster: Ioyne with *Iennet Preston* for the murder of Master *Lister*; and such like wicked & diuellish practises: It were sufficient to accuse them for Witches, & to bring their liues to a lawfull Triall. But amongst all the Witches in this company, there is not a more fearefull and diuellish Act committed, and voluntarily confessed by any of them, comparable to this, vnder the degree of Murder: which impudently now (at the Barre hauing formerly confessed;)[157] they forsweare, swearing they were neuer at the great assembly at Malking Tower; although the very

---

[157] "*At the Barre hauing formerly confessed.*"] Why is not their confession given?

Witches that were present in that action with them, iustifie, maintaine, and sweare the same to be true against them: Crying out in very violent & outragious manner, euen to the gallowes,[158] where they died impenitent for any thing we know, because they died silent in the particulars. These of all others were the most desperate wretches (void of all feare or grace) in all this Packe; Their offences not much inferiour to Murther: for which you shall heare what matter of Record wee haue against them; and whether they be worthie to continue, we leaue it to the good consideration of the Iury.

The said *Iohn Bulcock*, and *Iane Bulcock* his mother, Prisoners in the Castle at Lancaster, being brought to the Barre before the great Seat of Iustice: were there according to the former order and course Indicted and Arraigned, for that they felloniously had practised, exercised and vfed their diuellish & wicked Arts, called *Witchcrafts, Inchantments, Charmes* and *Sorceries*, in and vpon the body of *Iennet Deane*: so as the body of the said *Iennet Deane*, by force of the said Witchcrafts, wasted and consumed; and after she, the said *Iennet*, became madde. *Contra formam Statuti*, &c. *Et Contra pacem*, &c.

Vpon their Arraignement, to this Indictment they pleaded not guiltie; and for the triall of their liues put themselues vpon God and their Countrey.

---

[158] "*Crying out in very violent and outrageous manner, even to the gallowes.*"] The latter end of these unfortunate people was perhaps similar to that of Isobel Crawford, executed in Scotland the year after for witchcraft, who, on being sentenced, openly denied all her former confessions, and died without any sign of repentance, offering repeated interruption to the minister in his prayer, and refusing to pardon the executioner.

So as now the Gentlemen of the Iurie of Life and Death stand charged with them as with others.

*The Euidence against* Iohn Bulcock, *and* Jane Bulcock *his mother, Prisoners at the Barre.*

*The Examination of* Iames Device
***taken the seuen and twentieth day of Aprill aforesaid.***

**Before**

**Roger Nowel *and* Nicholas Banester,**
***Esquires, two of his Maiesties Iustices of Peace in the Countie of Lancaster.***

**Against**

**Iohn Bvlcock *and* Iane Bvlcock *his mother.***

THis Examinate saith, That vpon Good-Friday, about twelue of the clocke in the day time, there dined in this Examinates said Mothers house a number of persons, whereof three were men with this Examinate, and the rest women, and that they met there for these three causes following, as this Examinates said mother told this Examinate. The first was, for the naming of the Spirit which *Allison Deuice*, now prisoner at Lancaster had, but did not name him, because shee was not there. The second cause was, for the deliuerie of his said Grand-mother; this Examinates said sister *Allison*; the said *Anne Chattox*, and her daughter *Redferne*, killing the Gaoler at Lancaster, and before the next Assises to blow vp the Castle there, to that end the aforesaid prisoners might by that meanes make an escape, and get away: All which this Examinate then heard them conferre of.

And he also sayth, That the names of such said Witches as were on Good-Friday at this Examinates said Grand-mothers house, and now this Examinates owne mothers, for so many of them as hee did know, were these, *viz. Iane Bulcock*, wife of *Christopher Bulcock*, of the Mosse end, and *Iohn* her sonne amongst others, &c.

And this Examinate further saith, That all the said Witches went out of the said house in their own shapes and likenesses: and they all, by that they were forth of the dores, were gotten on horse-backe, like vnto Foales, some of one colour, and some of another, and *Prestons* wife was the last: and when shee got on horse-backe, they all presently vanished out of this Examinates sight.

And further he saith, That the said *Iohn Bulcock* and *Iane* his said Mother, did confesse vpon Good-Friday last at the said Malking-Tower, in the hearing of this Examinate, That they had bewitched, at the new-field Edge in Yorkeshire, a woman called *Iennet*, wife of *Iohn Deyne*, besides, her reason; and the said Womans name so bewitched, he did not heare them speake of. And this Examinate further saith, That at the said Feast at Malking-Tower this Examinate heard them all giue their consents to put the said Master *Thomas Lister* of Westby[159] to death. And after Master *Lister* should be made away by Witch-craft, then all the said Witches gaue their consents to ioyne all together, to hanck Master *Leonard Lister*, when he should come to dwell at the Cow-gill, and so put him to death.

---

[159] "*Master Thomas Lister of Westby.*"] See note on p. Y *a*.

*The Examination of* Elizabeth
**Device,** *Taken the day and yeare aforesaid,*

**Before**

**Roger Nowel** *and* **Nicholas Banester,**
*Esquires, two of his Maiesties Iustices of Peace in the Countie of Lancaster.*

**Against**

**Iohn Bvlcock,** *and* **Iane Bvlcock,** *his mother.*

THis Examinate saith vpon her oath, That she doth verily thinke, that the said *Bulcockes* wife doth know of some Witches to bee about Padyham and Burnley.[160]

And shee further saith, That at the said meeting at Malking-Tower, as aforesaid, *Katherine Hewyt* and *Iohn Bulcock*, with all the rest then there, gaue their consents, with the said *Prestons* wife, for the killing of the said Master *Lister*.

---

[160] "*The said Bulcockes wife doth know of some Witches to bee about Padyham and Burnley.*"] Precious evidence this to put the lives of two poor creatures into jeopardy.

*The Examination and Euidence of*
**Iennet Device**

**Against**

**Iohn Bvlcocke** *and* **Iane** *his mother, prisoners at the Barre.*

THe said Examinate saith, That vpon Good-Friday last there was about twentie persons, whereof two were men, to this Examinates remembrance, at her said Grand-mothers house, called Malking-Tower aforesaid: all which persons, this Examinates said mother told her were Witches, and that she knoweth the names of sixe of the said Witches.

Then was the said *Iennet Deuice* commaunded by his Lordship to finde and point out the said *Iohn Bulcock* and *Iane Bulcock* amongst all the rest; whereupon shee went and tooke *Iane Bulcock* by the hand, accused her to be one, and told her in what place shee sat at the Feast at Malking-Tower, at the great Assembly of the Witches; and who sat next her: and accused the said *Iohn Bulcock* to turne the Spitt there;[161] what conference they had, and all the rest of their proceedings at large, without any manner of contrarietie.

Shee further told his Lordship, there was a woman that came out of Craven to that Great Feast at Malking-Tower, but shee could not finde her out amongst all those women.

---

[161] "*Accused the said Iohn Bulcock to turne the Spitt there.*"] What a fact this would have been for De Lancre. With all his accurate statistics on the subject of the witches' Sabbath, he was not aware that a turnspit was a necessary officer on such occasions, as well as a master of ceremonies. This artful and well instructed jade, Jennet Device, must have borne especial malice against John Bulcock.

¶ The names of the Witches at the *Great Assembly and Feast at* **Malking-Tower,** *viz.* **vpon** Good-Friday last, 1612.[162]

---

[162] "*The names of the Witches at the Great Assembly and Feast at Malking-Tower, viz. vpon Good-Friday last, 1612.*"] In this list of fourteen individuals, Master Potts has omitted "the painful steward so careful to provide mutton," James Device, who made up the number to fifteen. Of these persons seven were not indicted: Jennet Hargraves, the wife of Hugh Hargraves, of Barley under Pendle; Elizabeth Hargraves, the wife of Christopher Hargraves; Christopher Howgate, the son of Old Demdike; Christopher Hargraves, who is described as of Thurniholme, or Thornholme, and as Christopher o' Jacks, and was husband of Elizabeth Hargraves; Grace Hay, of Padiham; Anne Crunkshey, of Marchden, or more properly, Cronkshaw of Marsden; and Elizabeth Howgate, the wife of Christopher Howgate. The two Howgates were, it may be, the "one Holgate and his wife," mentioned in Robinson's deposition in 1633. Alice Graie, or Gray, included in the list, was indicted, though no copy of the indictment is afforded by Potts, and, singular as it may seem, acquitted. Richard Miles' wife, of the Rough Lee, stated to have been present in some of the depositions, was, beyond doubt, Alice Nutter, so called as the wife of Richard and mother of Miles Nutter.

It may afford matter for speculation, whether any real meeting took place of any of the persons above enumerated, which gave occasion for the monstrous versions of the witnesses at this trial. It is far from unlikely, that on the apprehension and commitment of Old Demdike, Old Chattox, Alizon Device, and Anne Redfern to Lancaster, a meeting would take place of their near relations, and others who might attend from curiosity, or from its being rumoured that they were themselves implicated by the confessions of those apprehended, and who by such attendance sealed their dooms. In all similar fabrications there is generally some slight foundation of fact, some scintilla of homely truth, from which, like the inverted apex of a pyramid, the disproportioned fabric expands. It is possible that, from the simple occurrence of an unusual attendance at Malking Tower on Good Friday, not unnatural under the circumstances, some of the witnesses, ignorant and easily persuaded, might be afterwards led to believe in the existence of those monstrous superadditions with which the convention was afterwards clothed. However this may be, there must have been at hand for working up the materials into a plausible form, some drill sergeant of evidence behind the curtain, who had his own interest to serve or revenge to gratify. The two particulars in the narrative that one feels least disposed to question, are, that James Device stole a wether

*Elizabeth Deuice.*

*Alice Nutter.*

*Katherine Hewit*, alias *Mould-heeles.*

*John Bulcock.*

*Jane Bulcock.*

*Alice Graie.*

*Jennet Hargraues.*

*Elizabeth Hargraues.*

*Christopher Howgate.* Sonne to old *Dembdike.*

*Christopher Hargraues.*

*Grace Hay*, of Padiham.

*Anne Crunckshey*, of Marchden.

*Elizabeth Howgate.*

*Jennet Preston*, Executed at Yorke for the Murder of Master *Lister*,

---

from John Robinson of Barley, to provide a family dinner on Good Friday, and that when the meat was roasted John Bulcock performed the humble, but very necessary, duty of turning the spit.

With many more, which being bound ouer to appeare at the last Assizes, are since that time fled to saue themselues.

THE ARRAIGNMENT
*and Triall of* Alizon Device,
**Daughter of Elizabeth Device,** *within the Forrest of Pendle, in the Countie of Lancaster aforesaid, for Witch-craft.*

## *Alizon Deuice.*

BEHOLD, aboue all the rest, this lamentable spectacle of a poore distressed Pedler, how miserably hee was tormented, and what punishment hee endured for a small offence, by the wicked and damnable practise of this odious Witch, first instructed therein by old *Dembdike* her Grand-mother, of whose life and death with her good conditions, I haue written at large before in the beginning of this worke, out of her owne Examinations and other Records, now remayning with the Clarke of the Crowne at Lancaster: And by her Mother brought vp in this detestable course of life; wherein I pray you obserue but the manner and course of it in order, euen to the last period at her Execution, for this horrible fact, able to terrifie and astonish any man liuing.

This *Alizon Deuice*, Prisoner in the Castle of Lancaster, being brought to the Barre before the great Seat of Iustice, was there according to the former order and course indicted and arraigned, for that shee felloniously had practised, exercised, and vsed her Deuillish and wicked Arts, called *Witch-crafts*, *Inchantments*, *Charmes*, and *Sorceries*, in, and vpon one *Iohn Law*, a Petti-chapman, and him had lamed; so that his bodie wasted and consumed, &c. *Contra formam Statuti*, &c. *Et contra pacem dicti Domini Regis, Coronam & Dignitatem*, &c.

Vpon the Arraignement, The poore Pedler, by name *Iohn Law*, being in the Castle about the Moot-hall, attending to be called, not well able to goe or stand, being led thether by his poore sonne *Abraham Law*: My Lord *Gerrard*[163] moued the Court to call the poore Pedler, who was there readie, and had attended all the Assizes, to giue euidence for the Kings Majestie against the said *Alizon Deuice*, Prisoner at the Barre, euen now vpon her Triall. The Prisoner being at the Barre, & now beholding the Pedler, deformed by her Witch-craft, and transformed beyond the course of Nature, appeared to giue euidence against her; hauing not yet pleaded to her Indictment, saw it was in vaine to denie it, or stand vpon her justification: Shee humbly vpon her knees at the Barre with weeping teares, prayed the Court to heare her.

Whereupon my Lord *Bromley* commanded shee should bee brought out from the Prisoners neare vnto the Court, and there on her knees, shee humbly asked forgiuenesse for her offence: And being required to make an open declaration or confession of her offence: Shee confessed as followeth. *viz.*

---

[163] "*My Lord Gerrard.*"] Thomas Gerard, son and heir of Sir Gilbert Gerard, Master of the Robes 23d Elizabeth, was raised to the peerage by the title of Lord Gerard of Gerard's Bromley, in Staffordshire, 1603. He died 1618.

*The Confession of* Alizon Device,
**Prisoner at the Barre: published and declared at time of her Arraignement and Triall in open Court.**

SHe saith, That about two yeares agone, her Grand-mother, called *Elizabeth Sothernes*, alias *Dembdike*, did (sundry times in going or walking together, as they went begging) perswade and aduise this Examinate to let a Diuell or a Familiar appeare to her, and that shee, this Examinate would let him suck at some part of her; and she might haue and doe what shee would. And so not long after these perswasions, this Examinate being walking towards the Rough-Lee, in a Close of one *Iohn Robinsons*, there appeared vnto her a thing like vnto a Blacke Dogge: speaking vnto her, this Examinate, and desiring her to giue him her Soule, and he would giue her power to doe any thing shee would: whereupon this Examinate being therewithall inticed, and setting her downe; the said Blacke-Dogge did with his mouth (as this Examinate then thought) sucke at her breast, a little below her Paps, which place did remain blew halfe a yeare next after: which said Blacke-Dogge did not appeare to this Examinate, vntill the eighteenth day of March last: at which time this Examinate met with a Pedler on the high-way, called Colne-field, neere vnto Colne: and this Examinate demanded of the said Pedler to buy some pinnes of him; but the said Pedler sturdily answered this Examinate that he would not loose his Packe; and so this Examinate parting with him: presently there appeared to this Examinate the Blacke-Dogge, which appeared vnto her as before: which Black Dogge spake vnto this Examinate in English, saying; What wouldst thou haue me to do vnto yonder man? to whom this Examinate said, What canst thou do at him? and the Dogge answered againe, I can lame him: whereupon this Examinat answered, and said to the said Black Dogge, Lame him: and before the Pedler was gone fortie Roddes further, he fell downe Lame: and this Examinate then went after the said Pedler; and in a house about the distance aforesaid, he was lying Lame: and so this Examinate went begging in Trawden Forrest that day, and came home at night: and about fiue daies next after, the said Black-Dogge did appeare to this Examinate, as she was going a begging, in a Cloase neere the New-Church in Pendle, and spake againe to her, saying; Stay and speake with me; but this Examinate would not: Sithence which time this Examinat neuer saw him.

*Which agreeth* verbatim *with her owne Examination taken at* Reade, *in the Countie of Lancaster, the thirtieth day of March, before Master* Nowel, *when she was apprehended and taken.*

MY Lord *Bromley*, and all the whole Court not a little wondering, as they had good cause, at this liberall and voluntarie confession of the Witch; which is not ordinary with people of their condition and qualitie: and beholding also the poore distressed Pedler, standing by, commanded him vpon his oath to declare the manner how, and in what sort he was handled; how he came to be lame, and so to be deformed; who deposed vpon his oath, as followeth.

## The Euidence of Iohn Law,
### Pettie Chapman, vpon his Oath:

### Against

**Alizon Device,** *Prisoner at the Barre.*

HE deposeth and saith, That about the eighteenth of March last past, hee being a Pedler, went with his Packe of wares at his backe thorow Colne-field: where vnluckily he met with *Alizon Deuice*, now Prisoner at the Barre, who was very earnest with him for pinnes, but he would giue her none: whereupon she seemed to be very angry; and when hee was past her, hee fell downe lame in great extremitie; and afterwards by meanes got into an Ale-house in Colne, neere vnto the place where hee was first bewitched: and as hee lay there in great paine, not able to stirre either hand or foote; he saw a great Black-Dogge stand by him, with very fearefull firie eyes, great teeth, and a terrible countenance, looking him in the face; whereat he was very sore afraid: and immediately after came in the said *Alizon Deuice*, who staid not long there, but looked on him, and went away.

After which time hee was tormented both day and night with the said *Alizon Deuice*; and so continued lame, not able to trauell or take paines euer since that time: which with weeping teares in great passion turned to the Prisoner; in the hearing of all the Court hee said to her, *This thou knowest to be too true*: and thereupon she humblie acknowledged the same, and cried out to God to forgiue her; and vpon her knees with weeping teares, humbly prayed him to forgiue her that wicked offence; which he very freely and voluntarily did.

Hereupon Master *Nowel* standing vp, humbly prayed the fauour of the Court, in respect this Fact of Witchcraft was more eminent and apparant than the rest, that for the better satisfaction of the Audience, the Examination of *Abraham Law* might be read in Court.

*The Examination of* Abraham
**Law,** *of Hallifax, in the Countie of Yorke, Cloth-dier, taken vpon oath the thirtieth day of March, 1612.*

**Before**

**Roger Nowel,** *Esquire, aforesaid.*

BEing sworne and examined, saith, That vpon Saturday last saue one, being the one and twentieth day of this instant March, he, this Examinate was sent for, by a letter that came from his father, that he should come to his father, *Iohn Law,* who then lay in Colne speechlesse, and had the left-side lamed all saue his eye: and when this Examinate came to his father, his said father had something recouered his speech, and did complaine that hee was pricked with Kniues, Elsons and Sickles,[164] and that the same hurt was done vnto him at Colne-field, presently after that *Alizon Deuice* had offered to buy some pinnes of him, and she had no money to pay for them withall; but as this Examinates father told this Examinate, he gaue her some pinnes. And this Examinate further saith, That he heard his said father say, that the hurt he had in his lamenesse was done vnto

---

[164] "*Kniues, Elsons, and Sickles.*" In the *Promptorium Parvulorum,* p. 138, to Elsyn (elsyng$^k$) Sibula, Mr. Way appends this note: "This word occurs in the Gloss on Gautier de Bibelesworth, Arund. MS. 220, where a buckled girdle is described:—
"Een isy doyt le hardiloun (þe tunnge)
Passer par tru de subiloun (a bore of an alsene.)
"An elsyne,—acus, subula. Cath. Ang. Sibula, an elsyn, an alle or a bodkyn. Ortus. In the inventory of the goods of a merchant at Newcastle, A.D. 1571, occur, 'vj. doss' elsen heftes, 12$d$; I clowte and ½ a C elsen blades, viijs. viij$d$; xiij. clowtes of talier, needles, &c.' Wills and Inventories published by the Surtees Society, l. 361. The term is derived from the French *alene*; elson for cordwayners, alesne. Palsg. In Yorkshire and some other parts of England an awl is still called an elsen."

him by the said *Alizon Deuice*, by Witchcraft. And this Examinate further saith, that hee heard his said Father further say, that the said *Alizon Deuice* did lie vpon him and trouble him. And this Examinate seeing his said Father so tormented with the said *Alizon* and with one other olde woman, whome this Examinates Father did not know as it seemed: This Examinate made search after the said *Alizon*, and hauing found her, brought her to his said Father yesterday being the nine and twentieth of this instant March: whose said Father in the hearing of this Examinate and diuers others did charge the said *Alizon* to haue bewitched him, which the said *Alizon* confessing[165] did aske this Examinates said Father forgiuenesse vpon her knees for the same; whereupon this Examinates Father accordingly did forgiue her. Which Examination in open Court vpon his oath hee iustified to be true.

Whereupon it was there affirmed to the Court that this *Iohn Law* the Pedler, before his vnfortunate meeting with this Witch, was a verie able sufficient stout man of Bodie, and a goodly man of Stature. But by this Deuillish art of *Witch-craft* his head is drawne awrie, his Eyes and face deformed, His speech not well to bee vnderstood; his Thighes and Legges starcke lame: his Armes lame especially the left side, his handes lame and turned out of their course, his Bodie able to indure no trauell: and thus remaineth at this present time.

---

[165] "*Which the said Alizon confessing.*"] In the case of this paralytic pedlar, John Law, his mishap could scarcely be called such, as it would for the remainder of his life, be an all-sufficient stock-in-trade for him, and popular wonder and sympathy, without the judge's interposition, would provide for his relief and maintenance. The near apparent connection and correspondence of the *damnum minatum* and *damnum secutum*, in this instance, imposed upon this unfortunate woman, as it had done upon many others, and gave to her confession an earnestness which would appear to the unenlightened spectator to spring only from reality and truth.

The Prisoner being examined by the Court whether shee could helpe the poore Pedler to his former strength and health, she answered she could not, and so did many of the rest of the Witches: But shee, with others, affirmed, That if old *Dembdike* had liued, shee could and would haue helped him out of that great miserie, which so long he hath endured for so small an offence, as you haue heard.

These things being thus openly published against her, and she knowing her selfe to be guiltie of euery particular, humbly acknowledged the Indictment against her to be true, and that she was guiltie of the offence therein contained, and that she had iustly deserued death for that and many other such like: whereupon she was carried away, vntill she should come to the Barre to receiue her judgement of death.

Oh, who was present at this lamentable spectacle, that was not moued with pitie to behold it!

Hereupon my Lord *Gerard*, Sir *Richard Houghton*, and others, who much pitied the poore Pedler, At the entreatie of my Lord *Bromley* the Iudge, promised some present course should be taken for his reliefe and maintenance; being now discharged and sent away.

But here I may not let her passe; for that I find some thing more vpon Record to charge her withall: for although she were but a young Witch, of a yeares standing, and thereunto induced by *Dembdike* her Grand-mother, as you haue formerly heard, yet she was spotted with innocent bloud among the rest: for in one part of the Examination of *Iames Deuice*, her brother, he deposeth as followeth, *viz.*

*The Examination of* Iames Device,
**brother to the said Alizon Device:** *Taken vpon Oath*

**Before**

**Roger Nowel** *Esquire, aforesaid, the thirtieth day of March, 1612.*

*IAmes Deuice*, of the Forrest of Pendle, in the Countie of Lancaster, Labourer, sworne and examined, sayth, That about *Saint Peters* day last one *Henry Bulcock* came to the house of *Elizabeth Sothernes*, alias *Dembdike*, Grand-mother to this Examinate, and said, That the said *Alizon Deuice* had bewitched a Child of his, and desired her, that shee would goe with him to his house: which accordingly shee did: and thereupon shee the said *Alizon* fell downe on her knees, and asked the said *Bulcock* forgiuenesse; and confessed to him, that she had bewitched the said Child, as this Examinate heard his said sister confesse vnto him this Examinate.

And although shee were neuer indicted for this offence, yet being matter vpon Record, I thought it conuenient to joyne it vnto her former Fact.

HEre the Iurie of Life and Death hauing spent the most part of the day in due consideration of their offences, returned into the Court to deliuer up their Verdict against them, as followeth.

## The Verdict of Life and Death.

WHo vpon their Oathes found *Iohn Bulcock* and *Iane Bulcock* his mother, not guiltie of the Felonie by Witch-craft, contained in the Indictment against them.

*Alizon Deuice* conuicted vpon her owne Confession.

Whereupon Master *Couel* was commaunded by the Court to take away the Prisoners conuicted, and to bring forth *Margaret Pearson*,[166] and *Isabell Robey*, Prisoners in the Castle at Lancaster, to receiue their Triall.

Who were brought to their Arraignement and Trialls, as hereafter followeth, *viz.*

---

[166] "*Margaret Pearson.*"] This Padiham witch fared better than her neighbours, being sentenced only to the pillory. Nothing affords a stronger proof of the vindictive pertinacity with which these prosecutions were carried on than the fact of this old and helpless creature being put on her trial three several times upon such evidence as follows. Chattox, like many other persons in her situation, was disposed to have as many companions in punishment, crime or no crime, as she could compass, and denounced her accordingly: "The said Pearson's wife is as ill as shee."

# THE ARRAIGNMENT
*and Triall of* Margaret Pearson
*of Paddiham, in the Countie of Lancaster, for Witchcraft; the nineteenth of August, 1612. at the Assises and Generall Gaole-deliuerie, holden at Lancaster,*

### Before

**Sir Edward Bromley** *Knight, one of his Maiesties Iustices of Assise at Lancaster.*

## *Margaret Pearson.*

THUS farre haue I proceeded in hope your patience will endure the end of this discourse, which craues time, and were better not begunne at all, then not perfected.

This *Margaret Pearson* was the wife of *Edward Pearson* of Paddiham, in the Countie of Lancaster; little inferiour in her wicked and malicious course of life to any that hath gone before her: A very dangerous Witch of long continuance, generally suspected and feared in all parts of the Countrie, and of all good people neare her, and not without great cause: For whosoeuer gaue her any iust occasion of offence, shee tormented with great miserie, or cut off their children, goods, or friends.

This wicked and vngodly Witch reuenged her furie vpon goods, so that euery one neare her sustained great losse. I place her in the end of these notorious Witches, by reason her iudgement is of an other Nature, according to her offence; yet had not the fauour and mercie of the Iurie beene more than her desert, you had found her next to old *Dembdike*; for this is the third time shee is come to receiue her Triall; one time for murder by Witch-craft; an other time for bewitching a Neighbour; now for goods.

How long shee hath been a Witch, the Deuill and shee knows best.

The Accusations, Depositions, and particular Examinations vpon Record against her are infinite, and were able to fill a large Volume; But since shee is now only to receiue her Triall for this last offence. I shall proceede against her in order, and set forth what matter we haue vpon Record, to charge her withall.

This *Margaret Pearson*, Prisoner in the Castle at Lancaster: Being brought to the Barre before the great Seat of Iustice; was there according to the course and order of the Law Indicted and Arraigned, for that shee had practised, exercised, and vsed her diuellish and wicked Arts, called *Witchcrafts*, *Inchantments*, *Charmes* and *Sorceries*, and one Mare of the goods and Chattels of one *Dodgeson* of Padiham, in the Countie of Lancaster, wickedly, maliciously, and voluntarily did kill. *Contra formam Statuti, &c. Et Contra pacem dicti Domini Regis. &c.*

Vpon her Arraignement to this Indictment, shee pleaded not guiltie; And for the triall of her offence put her selfe vpon God and her Countrie.

So as now the Gentlemen of the Iurie of her offence and death, stand charged with her as with others.

*The Euidence against* Margaret Pearson,
*Prisoner at the Barre.*

*The Examination and Euidence of*
**Anne Whittle, *alias* Chattox.**

**Against**

**Margaret Pearson, *Prisoner at the Barre.***

THe said *Anne Chattox* being examined saith, That the wife of one *Pearson* of Paddiham, is a very euill Woman, and confessed to this Examinate, that shee is a Witch, and hath a Spirit which came to her the first time in likenesse of a Man, and clouen footed, and that shee the said *Pearsons* wife hath done very much harme to one *Dodgesons* goods, who came in at a loope-hole into the said *Dodgesons* Stable, and shee and her Spirit together did sit vpon his Horse or Mare, vntill the said Horse or Mare died. And likewise, that shee the said *Pearsons* wife did confesse vnto her this Examinate, that shee bewitched vnto death one *Childers* wife, and her Daughter, and that shee the said *Pearsons* wife is as ill as shee.

*The Examination of* Iennet Booth,
*of Paddiham, in the Countie of Lancaster, the ninth day of August 1612.*

**Before**

**Nicholas Bannester,** *Esquire; one of his Maiesties Iustices of Peace in the Countie of Lancaster.*

*IEnnet*, the wife of *Iames Booth*, of Paddiham, vpon her oath saith, That the Friday next after, the said *Pearsons* wife, was committed to the Gaole at Lancaster, this Examinate was carding in the said *Pearsons* house, hauing a little child with her, and willed the said *Margerie* to giue her a little Milke, to make her said child a little meat, who fetcht this Examinate some, and put it in a pan; this examinat meaning to set it on the fire, found the said fire very ill, and taking vp a stick that lay by her, and brake it in three or foure peeces, and laid vpon the coales to kindle the same, then set the pan and milke on the fire: and when the milke was boild to this Examinates content, she tooke the pan wherein the milke was, off the said fire, and with all, vnder the bottome of the same, there came a Toade, or a thing very like a Toade, and to this Examinates thinking came out of the fire, together with the said Pan, and vnder the bottome of the same, and that the said *Margerie* did carrie the said Toade out of the said house in a paire of tonges;[167] But what shee the said *Margerie* did therewith, this Examinate knoweth not.

---

[167] "*The said Margerie did carrie the said Toade out of the said house in a paire of tonges.*"] This toad was disposed of more easily than that of Julian Cox, as to which see Glanvil's *Collection of Relations*, p. 192:—
Another witness swore, that as he passed by Cox her door, she was taking a pipe of tobacco upon the threshold of her door, and invited him to come in and take a pipe, which he did. And as he was talking Julian said to him,

Neighbour, look what a pretty thing there is. He look't down, and there was a monstrous great toad betwixt his leggs, staring him in the face. He endeavoured to kill it by spurning it, but could not hit it. Whereupon Julian bad him forbear, and it would do him no hurt. But he threw down his pipe and went home, (which was about two miles off of Julian Cox her house,) and told his family what had happened, and that he believed it was one of Julian Cox her devils. After, he was taking a pipe of tobacco at home, and the same toad appeared betwixt his leggs. He took the toad out to kill it, and to his thinking cut it in several pieces, but returning to his pipe, the toad still appeared. He endeavoured to burn it, but could not. At length he took a switch and beat it. The toad ran several times about the room to avoid him he still pursuing it with correction. At length the toad cryed and vanish't, and he was never after troubled with it.

Dr. More's comment on the circumstance is written with all the seriousness so important a part of a witch's supellex deserves. He commences defending the huntsman, who swore that he hunted a hare, and when he came to take it up, he found it to be Julian Cox:

Those half-witted people thought he swore false, I suppose because they imagined that what he told implied that Julian Cox was turned into an hare. Which she was not, nor did his report imply any such real metamorphosis of her body, but that these ludicrous dæmons exhibited to the sight of this huntsman and his doggs the shape of an Hare, one of them turning himself into such a form, and others hurrying on the body of Julian near the same place, and at the same swiftness, but interposing betwixt that hare-like spectre and her body, modifying the air so that the scene there, to the beholders sight, was as if nothing but air were there, and a shew of earth perpetually suited to that where the hare passed. As I have heard of some painters that have drawn the sky in an huge large landskip, so lively that the birds have flown against it, thinking it free air, and so have fallen down. And if painters and juglers by the tricks of legerdemain can do such strange feats to the deceiving of the sight, it is no wonder that these airy invisible spirits as far surpass them in all such præstigious doings as the air surpasses the earth for subtilty.

And the like præstigiæ may be in the toad. It might be a real toad (though actuated and guided by a dæmon) which was cut in pieces, and that also which was whipt about, and at last snatcht out of sight (as if it had vanished) by these aerial hocus-pocus's. And if some juglers have tricks to take hot coals into their mouth without hurt, certainly it is not surprising that some small attempt did not suffice to burn that toad. That such a toad, sent by a witch and crawling up the body of the man of the house as he sate by the fire's side, was overmastered by him and his wife together, and burnt in the fire; I have heard credibly reported by one of the Isle of Ely. *Of these dæmoniack vermin, I have heard other stories also, as of a rat that followed a man some score of miles*

After this were diuers witnesses examined against her in
open Court, *viua voce*, to
proue the death of the Mare, and diuers other vild and
odious practises by her
committed, who vpon their Examinations made it so
apparant to the Iurie as
there was no question; But because the fact is of no great
importance,
in respect her life is not in question by this Indictment, and
the
Depositions and examinations are many, I leaue to trouble
you with any more of them, for being found guiltie of
this offence, the penaltie of the Law is as much as
her good Neighbours doe require, which is to
be deliuered from the companie of such a
dangerous wicked, and
malicious Witch.

\* \*
\*

---

*trudging through thick and thin along with him.* So little difficulty is there in that of the toad.—*Glanvil's Collection of Relations*, p. 200.

# THE ARRAIGNMENT
## and Triall of Isabel Robey
### in the Countie of Lancaster, for Witch-craft: vpon Wednesday the nineteenth of August, 1612. At the Assizes and generall Goale-deliuery, holden at Lancaster.

### Before

### Sir Edward Bromley, Knight, one of his Maiesties Iustices of Assizes at Lancaster.

## *Isabel Robey.*[168]


THUS at one time may you behold Witches of all sorts from many places in this Countie of Lancaster which now may lawfully bee said to abound asmuch in Witches of diuers kindes as Seminaries, Iesuites, and Papists.[169] Here

---

[168] "*Isabel Robey.*" This person was of Windle, in the parish of Prescot, a considerable distance from Pendle. The Gerards were lords of the manor of Windle. Sir Thomas Gerard, before whom the examinations were taken, was created baronet, 22nd May, 9th James I.; and thrice married. From him the present Sir John Gerard, of New Hall, near Warrington, is descended. Sir Thomas was determined that the hundred of West Derby should have its witch as well as the other parts of the county. A more melancholy tissue of absurd and incoherent accusations than those against this last of the prisoners convicted on this occasion, it would not be easy to find; who was hanged, for all that appears, because one person was suddenly "pinched on her thigh, as she thought, with four fingers and a thumb," and because another was "sore pained with a great warch in his bones."

[169] "*This Countie of Lancaster, which now may lawfully bee said to abound asmuch in Witches of diuers kindes as Seminaries, Iesuites, and Papists.*"] Truly, the county palatine was in sad case, according to Master Potts's account. If the crop of each of these was over abundant, it was from no fault of the

then is the last that came to act her part in this lamentable and wofull Tragedie, wherein his Maiestie hath lost so many Subjects, Mothers their Children, Fathers their Friends, and Kinsfolkes[170] the like whereof hath not beene set forth in any age. What hath the Kings Maiestie written and published in his *Dæmonologie*, by way of premonition and preuention, which hath not here by the first or last beene executed, put in practise or discouered? What Witches haue euer vpon their Arraignement and Trial made such open liberall and voluntarie declarations of their liues, and such confessions of their offences: The manner of their attempts and their bloudie practises, their meetings,

---

learned judges, who, in their commissions of *Oyer and Terminer*, subjected it pretty liberally to the pruning-hook of the executioner.

[170] "*This lamentable and wofull Tragedie, wherein his Maiestie hath lost so many Subjects, Mothers their Children, Fathers their Friends and Kinsfolk.*" The Lancashire bill of mortality, under the head witchcraft, so far as it can be collected from this tract, will run thus:—

1. Robert Nutter, of Greenhead, in Pendle.
2. Richard Assheton, son of Richard Assheton, of Downham, Esquire.
3. Child of Richard Baldwin, of Wheethead, within the forest of Pendle.
4. John Device, or Davies, of Pendle.
5. Anne Nutter, daughter of Anthony Nutter, of Pendle.
6. Child of John Moore, of Higham.
7. Hugh Moore, of Pendle.
8. John Robinson, *alias* Swyer.
9. James Robinson.
10. Henry Mytton, of the Rough Lee.
11. Anne Townley, wife of Henry Townley, of the Carr, gentleman.
12. John Duckworth.
13. John Hargraves, of Goldshaw Booth.
14. Blaze Hargraves, of Higham.
15. Christopher Nutter.
16. Anne Folds, of Colne.

Sixteen persons reported dead of this common epidemic, besides a countless number with pains and "starkness in their limbs," and "a great warch in their bones!" No wonder that Doctors Bromley and Potts thought active treatment necessary, with a decided preference for hemp, as the leading specific.

consultations and what not? Therefore I shall now conclude with this *Isabel Robey* who is now come to her triall.

This *Isabel Robey* Prisoner in the Castle at Lancaster being brought to the Barre before the great Seat of Iustice was there according to the former order and course Indicted and Arraigned, for that shee Felloniously had practised, exercised and vsed her Deuilish and wicked Artes called *Witchcrafts, Inchantments, Charmes and Sorceries.*

Vpon her Arraignment to this Indictment she pleaded not guiltie, and for the triall of her life, put her selfe vpon God and her Countrie.

So as now the Gentlemen of the Iurie of life and death stand charged with her as with others.

*The Euidence against* Isabel Robey
*Prisoner at the Barre.*

---

*The Examination of* Peter Chaddock
*of* **Windle, in the Countie of Lancaster: Taken at Windle aforesaid, the 12. day of Iuly 1612. Anno Reg. Regis Iacobi, Angliæ, &c. decimo, & Scotiæ xlv.**

**Before**

*Sir* **Thomas Gerrard** *Knight, and Barronet.* **One of his Maiesties Iustices of the Peace within the said Countie.**

THe said Examinate vpon his Oath saith, That before his Marriage hee heard say that the said *Isabel Robey* was not pleased that hee should marrie his now wife: whereupon this Examinate called the said *Isabel* Witch, and said that hee did not care for her. Then within two dayes next after this Examinate was sore pained in his bones: And this Examinate hauing occasion to meete Master *Iohn Hawarden* at Peaseley Crosse, wished one *Thomas Lyon* to goe thither with him, which they both did so; but as they came home-wards, they both were in euill case. But within a short time after, this Examinate and the said *Thomas Lyon* were both very well amended.

And this Examinate further saith, that about foure yeares last past, his now wife was angrie with the said *Isabel*, shee then being in his house, and his said Wife thereupon went out of the house, and presently after that the said *Isabel* went likewise out of the house not well pleased, as this Examinate then did thinke, and presently after vpon the same day, this Examinate with his said wife working in the

Hay, a paine and a starknesse fell into the necke of this Examinat which grieued him very sore; wherupō this Examinat sent to one *Iames* a Glouer, which then dwelt in Windle, and desired him to pray for him, and within foure or fiue dayes next after this Examinate did mend very well. Neuerthelesse this Examinate during the same time was very sore pained, and so thirstie withall, and hot within his body, that hee would haue giuen any thing hee had, to haue slaked his thirst, hauing drinke enough in the house, and yet could not drinke vntill the time that the said *Iames* the Glouer came to him, and this Examinate then said before the said Glouer, I would to God that I could drinke, where upon the said Glouer said to this Examinate, take that drinke, and in the name of the *Father*, the *Sonne*, and the *Holy Ghost*, drinke it, saying; The Deuill and Witches are not able to preuaile against God and his Word, whereupon this Examinate then tooke the glasse of drinke, and did drinke it all, and afterwards mended very well, and so did continue in good health, vntill our Ladie day in Lent was twelue moneth or thereabouts, since which time this Examinate saith, that hee hath beene sore pained with great warch in his bones,[171] and all his limmes, and so yet continueth, and this Examinate further saith, that his said warch and paine came to him rather by meanes of the said *Isabel Robey*, then otherwise, as he verily thinketh.

---

[171] "*With great warch in his bones.*"] Warch is a word well known and still used in this sense, *i.e.*, pain, in Lancashire.

*The Examination of* Iane Wilkinson,
**Wife of Francis Wilkinson,** *of Windle aforesaid:*
*Taken before the said Sir* **Thomas Gerrard,**
*Knight and Barronet, the day and place aforesaid.*
*Against the said* **Isabel Robey.**

THe said Examinate vpon her oath saith, that vpon a time the said *Isabel Robey* asked her milke, and shee denied to giue her any: And afterwards shee met the said *Isabel*, whereupon this Examinate waxed afraid of her, and was then presently sick, and so pained that shee could not stand, and the next day after this Examinate going to Warrington, was suddenly pinched on her Thigh as shee thought, with foure fingers & a Thumbe twice together, and thereupon was sicke, in so much as shee could not get home but on horse-backe, yet soone after shee did mend.

### The Examination of Margaret Lyon *wife of* Thomas Lyon *the yonger, of Windle aforesaid: Taken before the said Sir* Thomas Gerrard, *Knight and Barronet, the day and place aforesaid.*
### *Against the said* Isabel Robey.

THe said *Margaret Lyon* vpon her Oath saith, that vpon a time *Isabel Robey* came into her house and said that *Peter Chaddock* should neuer mend vntill he had asked her forgiuenesse; and that shee knew hee would neuer doe: whereupon this Examinate said, how doe you know that, for he is a true Christian, and hee would aske all the world forgiuenesse? then the said *Isabel* said, that is all one, for hee will neuer aske me forgiuenesse, therefore hee shall neuer mend; And this Examinate further saith, that shee being in the house of the said *Peter Chaddock*, the wife of the said *Peter*, who is God-Daughter of the said *Isabel*, and hath in times past vsed her companie much, did affirme, that the said *Peter* was now satisfied, that the said *Isabel Robey* was no Witch, by sending to one *Halseworths*, which they call a wiseman,[172] and the wife of the said *Peter* then said, to abide vpon it,[173] I thinke that my Husband will neuer mend vntill hee haue asked her forgiuenesse, choose him whether hee will bee angrie or pleased, for this is my opinion: to which he answered, when he did need to aske her forgiuenesse, he would, but hee thought hee did not need, for any thing hee knew: and yet this Examinate

---

[172] "*The said Peter was now satisfied that the said Isabel Robey was no Witch, by sending to one Halseworths, which they call a wiseman.*"] I honour the memory of this Halsworth, or Houldsworth, as I suppose it should be spelled, for he was indeed a wise man in days when wisdom was an extremely scarce commodity.

[173] "*To abide vpon it.*"] *i.e.,* my abiding opinion is.

further saith, That the said *Peter Chaddock* had very often told her, that he was very afraid that the said *Isabel* had done him much hurt; and that he being fearefull to meete her, he hath turned backe at such time as he did meet her alone, which the said *Isabel* hath since then affirmed to be true, saying, that hee the said *Peter* did turne againe when he met her in the Lane.

### *The Examination of* Margaret **Parre** *wife of* **Hvgh Parre** *of Windle aforesaid, Taken before the said Sir* **Thomas Gerard** *Knight and Baronet, the day and place aforesaid. Against the said* **Isabel Robey.**

THe said Examinate vpon her oath saith, that vpon a time, the said *Isabel Robey* came to her house, and this Examinate asked her how *Peter Chaddock* did, And the said *Isabel* answered shee knew not, for shee went not to see, and then this Examinate asked her how *Iane Wilkinson* did, for that she had beene lately sicke and suspected to haue beene bewitched: then the said *Isabel* said twice together, I haue bewitched her too: and then this Examinate said that shee trusted shee could blesse her selfe from all Witches and defied them; and then the said *Isabel* said twice together, would you defie me? & afterwards the said *Isabel* went away not well pleased.

Here the Gentlemen of the last Iurie of Life and Death hauing taken great paines, the time being farre spent, and the number of the Prisoners great, returned into the Court to deliuer vp their Verdict against them as followeth. *viz.*

## *The Verdict of Life and Death.*

WHo vpon their Oathes found the said *Isabel Robey* guiltie of the Fellonie by Witch-craft, contained in the Indictment against her. And *Margaret Pearson* guiltie of the offence by Witch-craft, contained in the Indictment against her.

Whereupon Master *Couell* was commaunded by the Court in the afternoone to bring forth all the Prisoners that stood Conuicted, to receiue their Iudgment of Life and Death.

For his Lordship now intended to proceed to a finall dispatch of the Pleas of the Crowne. And heere endeth the Arraignement and Triall of the Witches at Lancaster.

THus at the length haue we brought to perfection this intended Discouery of Witches, with the Arraignment and Triall of euery one of them in order, by the helpe of Almightie God, and this Reuerend Iudge; the Lanterne from whom I haue received light to direct me in this course to the end. And as in the beginning, I presented vnto their view a Kalender containing the names of all the witches: So now I shall present vnto you in the conclusion and end, such as stand conuicted, and come to the Barre to receiue the iudgement of the Law for their offences, and the proceedings of the Court against such as were acquitted, and found not guiltie: with the religious Exhortation of this Honorable Iudge, as eminent in gifts and graces, as in place and preeminence, which I may lawfully affirme without base flattery (the canker of all honest and worthie minds) drew the eyes and reuerend respect of all that great Audience present, to heare their Iudgement, and the end of these proceedings.

### *The Prisoners being brought to the Barre.*

THe Court commanded three solemne Proclamations for silence, vntill Iudgement for Life and Death were giuen.

Whereupon I presented to his Lordship the
names of the Prisoners in order, which
were now to receiue their
Iudgement.
\* \*
\*

¶ The names of the Prisoners at the **_Barre to receiue their Judgement_ of Life and Death.**

*Anne Whittle*, alias *Chattox.*

*Elizabeth Deuice.*

*James Deuice.*

*Anne Redferne.*

*Alice Nutter.*

*Katherine Hewet,*

*John Bulcock.*

*Jane Bulcock.*

*Alizon Deuice.*

*Isabel Robey.*

THE IVDGEMENT
OF THE RIGHT HONORABLE
**Sir Edward Bromley, Knight, one**
*of his Maiesties Iustices of Assize*
at Lancaster vpon the Witches conuicted,
as followeth.

*THERE is no man aliue more vnwilling to pronounce this wofull and heauy Iudgement against you, then my selfe: and if it were possible, I would to God this cup might passe from me. But since it is otherwise prouided, that after all proceedings of the Law, there must be a Iudgement; and the Execution of that Iudgement must succeed and follow in due time: I pray you haue patience to receiue that which the Law doth lay vpon you. You of all people haue the least cause to complaine: since in the Triall of your liues there hath beene great care and paines taken, and much time spent: and very few or none of you, but stand conuicted vpon your owne voluntarie confessions and Examinations,* Ex ore proprio. *Few Witnesses examined against you, but such as were present, and parties in your Assemblies. Nay I may further affirme, What persons of your nature and condition, euer were Arraigned and Tried with more solemnitie, had more libertie giuen to pleade or answere to euerie particular point of Euidence against you? In conclusion such hath beene the generall care of all, that had to deale with you, that you haue neither cause to be offended in the proceedings of the Iustices, that first tooke paines in these businesses, nor with the Court that hath had great care to giue nothing in euidence against you, but matter of fact; Sufficient matter vpon Record, and not to induce or leade the Iurie to finde any one of you guiltie vpon matter of suspition or presumption, nor with the witnesses who haue beene tried, as it were in the fire: Nay, you cannot denie but must confesse what extraordinarie meanes hath beene vsed to make triall of their euidence, and to discouer the least intended practice in any one of them, to touch your liues vniustly.*

*As you stand simply (your offences and bloudie practises not considered) your fall would rather moue compassion, then exasperate any man. For whom would not the ruine of so many poore creatures at one time, touch, as in apparance simple, and of little vnderstanding?*

*But the bloud of those innocent children, and others his Maiesties Subiects, whom cruelly and barbarously you haue murdered, and cut off, with all the rest of your offences, hath cryed out vnto the Lord against you, and sollicited for satisfaction and reuenge, and that hath brought this heauie iudgement vpon you at this time.*

*It is therefore now time no longer wilfully to striue, both against the prouidence of God, and the Iustice of the Land: the more you labour to acquit your selues, the more euident and apparant you make your offences to the World. And vnpossible it is that they shall either prosper or continue in this World, or receiue reward in the next, that are stained with so much innocent bloud.*

*The worst then I wish to you, standing at the Barre conuicted, to receiue your Iudgement, is, Remorse, and true Repentance, for the safegard of your Soules, and after, an humble, penitent, and heartie acknowledgement of your grieuous sinnes and offences committed both against* God *and Man.*

*First, yeeld humble and heartie thankes to Almightie* God *for taking hold of you in your beginning, and making stay of your intended bloudie practises (although* God *knowes there is too much done alreadie) which would in time have cast so great a weight of Iudgement vpon your Soules.*

*Then praise* God *that it pleased him not to surprize or strike you suddenly, euen in the execution of your bloudie Murthers, and in the middest of your wicked practises, but hath giuen you time, and takes you away by a iudiciall course and triall of the Law.*

*Last of all, craue pardon of the World, and especially of all such as you haue iustly offended, either by tormenting themselues, children, or friends, murder of their kinsfolks, or losse of any their goods.*

*And for leauing to future times the president of so many barbarous and bloudie murders, with such meetings, practises, consultations, and meanes to execute reuenge, being the greatest part of your comfort in all your actions, which may instruct others to hold the like course, or fall in the like sort:*

*It only remaines I pronounce the Iudgement of the Court against you by the Kings authoritie, which is;* You shall all goe from hence to the Castle, from whence you came; from thence you shall bee carried to the place of Execution for this Countie: where your bodies shall bee hanged vntill you be dead; And God Have Mercie Vpon Yovr Sovles; For your comfort in this world I shall commend a learned and worthie Preacher to instruct you, and prepare you, for an other World: All I can doe for you is to pray for your Repentance in this World, for the satisfaction of many; And forgiuenesse in the next world, for sauing of your Soules. And God graunt you may make good vse of the time you haue in this world, to his glorie and your owne comfort.

## *Margaret Pearson.*

THe Iudgement of the Court against you, is, You shall stand vpon the Pillarie in open Market, at *Clitheroe*, *Paddiham*, *Whalley*, and *Lancaster*, foure Market dayes, with a Paper vpon your head, in great Letters, declaring your offence, and there you shall confesse your offence, and after to remaine in Prison for one yeare without Baile, and after to be bound with good Sureties, to be of the good behauiour.

*To the Prisoners found not guiltie*
**by the Ivries.**

***Elizabeth Astley.***
***John Ramsden.***
***Alice Gray.***
***Isabel Sidegraues.***
***Lawrence Hay.***[174]

*TO you that are found not guiltie, and are by the Law to bee acquited, presume no further of your Innocencie then you haue just cause: for although it pleased God out of his Mercie, to spare you at this time, yet without question there are amongst you, that are as deepe in this Action, as any of them that are condemned to die for their offences: The time is now for you to forsake the Deuill: Remember how, and in what sort hee hath dealt with all of you: make good vse of this great mercie and fauour: and pray unto God you fall not againe: For great is your happinesse to haue time in this World, to prepare your selues against the day when you shall appeare before the Great Iudge of all.*

*Notwithstanding, the iudgement of the Court, is,* You shall all enter Recognizances with good sufficient Suerties, to appear at the next Assizes at Lancaster, and in the meane time to be of the good behauiour. All I can say to you:

---

[174] "*Elizabeth Astley, John Ramsden, Alice Gray, Isabel Sidegraues, Lawrence Hay.*"] The specific charges against these persons, with the exception of Alice Gray, do not appear, nor is it said where their places of residence were. Alice Gray was reputed to have been at the meeting of witches at Malkin's Tower, and to her the judge refers, perhaps, in particular, when he says, "Without question, there are amongst you that are as deepe in this action as any of them that are condemned to die for their offences."

## Jennet Bierley,

## Ellen Bierley,

## Jane Southworth,

is, That God hath deliuered you beyond expectation, I pray God you may vse this mercie and fauour well; and take heed you fall not hereafter: And so the Court doth order you shall be deliuered.

What more can bee written or published of the proceedings of this honourable Court: but to conclude with the Execution of the Witches,[175] who were executed the next day following at the common place of Execution, neare vnto Lancaster. Yet in the end giue mee leaue to intreate some fauour that haue beene afraid to speake vntill my worke were finished. If I haue omitted any thing materiall, or published any thing imperfect, excuse me for that I haue done: It was a worke imposed vpon me by the Iudges, in respect I was so wel instructed in euery particular. In hast I haue vndertaken to finish it in a busie Tearme amongst my other imploiments.

My charge was to publish the proceedings of Iustice, and matter of Fact, wherein I wanted libertie to write what I

---

[175] "*The Execution of the Witches.*"] We could have dispensed with many of the flowers of rhetoric with which the pages of this discovery are strewed, if Master Potts would have favoured us with a plain, unvarnished account of what occurred at this execution. It is here, in the most interesting point of all, that his narrative, in other respects so full and abundant, stops short, and seems curtailed of its just proportions. The "learned and worthy preacher," to whom the prisoners were commended by the judge, was probably Mr. William Leigh, of Standish, before mentioned. Amongst his papers or correspondence, if they should happen to have been preserved, some account may eventually be found of the sad closing scene of these melancholy victims of superstition.

would, and am limited to set forth nothing against them, but matter vpon Record, euen in their owne Countrie tearmes, which may seeme strange. And this I hope will giue good satisfaction to such as vnderstand how to iudge of a businesse of this nature. Such as haue no other imploiment but to question other mens Actions, I leaue them to censure what they please, It is no part of my profession to publish any thing in print, neither can I paint in extraordinarie tearmes.[176] But if this discouerie may serue for your instruction, I shall thinke my selfe very happie in this Seruice, and so leaue it to your generall censure.

*Da veniam Ignoto non displicuisse meretur,*
*Festinat studÿs qui placuisse tibi.*

---

[176] "*Neither can I paint in extraordinarie tearmes.*"] The worthy clerk is too modest. He is a great painter, the Tintoretto of witchcraft.

# THE ARRAIGNEMENT

## AND TRIALL OF

Iennet Preston, Of

### GISBORNE IN CRAVEN,

in the Countie of Yorke.

At the Assises and Generall Gaole-*Deliuerie holden at the Castle of Yorke* **in the Countie of Yorke, the xxvij. day of Iuly last past,** *Anno Regni Regis* **Iacobi** *Angliæ, &c. Decimo, & Scotiæ quadragesimo quinto.*

### Before

*Sir* Iames Altham *Knight,* one **of the Barons of his Maiesties Court of Exchequer; and Sir E d w a r d B r o m l e y Knight, another of the Barons of his Maiesties Court of Exchequer;** his Maiesties Iustices of Assise, Oyer and Terminer, *and generall Gaole-Deliuerie, in the Circuit of the North-parts.*

THE ARRAIGNMENT
*and Triall of* Iennet Preston
**of Gisborne in Crauen, in the Countie of Yorke, at the Assises and generall Gaole-deliuerie, holden at the Castle of Yorke, in the Countie of Yorke, the seuen and twentieth day of Iuly last past. Anno Regni Regis Iacobi Angliæ &c. Decimo & Scotiæ xlvj.**

## *Jennet Preston.*

MANY haue vndertaken to write great discourses of Witches and many more dispute and speake of them. And it were not much if as many wrote of them as could write at al, to set forth to the world the particular Rites and Secrets of their vnlawfull Artes, with their infinite and wonderfull practises which many men little feare till they seaze vpon them. As by this late wonderfull discouerie of Witches in the Countie of Lancaster may appeare, wherein I find such apparant matter to satisfie the World, how dangerous and malitious a Witch this *Iennet Preston* was, How vnfit to liue, hauing once so great mercie extended to her: And againe to reuiue her practises, and returne to her former course of life; that I thinke it necessarie not to let the memorie of her life and death die with her; But to place her next to her felloues and to set forth the Arraignement Triall and Conviction of her, with her offences for which she was condemned and executed.

And although shee died for her offence before the rest, I yet can afford her no better place then in the end of this Booke in respect the proceedings was in an other Countie;

You that were husband to this *Iennet Preston*; her friends and kinsfolkes, who haue not beene sparing to deuise so scandalous a slander out of the malice of your hearts, as that shee was maliciously prosecuted by Master *Lister* and others; Her life vniustly taken away by practise; and that (euen at the Gallowes where shee died impenitent and void of all feare or grace) she died an Innocent woman, because she would confesse nothing: You I say may not hold it strange, though at this time, being not only moued in conscience, but directed, for example sake, with that which I haue to report of her, I suffer you not to wander any further, but with this short discourse oppose your idle conceipts able to seduce others: And by Charmes of Imputations and slander, laid vpon the Iustice of the Land, to cleare her that was iustly condemned and executed for her offence; That this *Iennet Preston* was for many yeares well thought of and esteemed by Master *Lister* who afterwards died for it Had free accesse to his house, kind respect and entertainment; nothing denied her she stood in need of. Which of you that dwelleth neare them in Crauen but can and will witnesse it? which might haue incouraged a Woman of any good condition to haue runne a better course.

The fauour and goodnesse of this Gentleman Master *Lister* now liuing, at his first entrance after the death of his Father extended towards her, and the reliefe she had at all times, with many other fauours that succeeded from time to time, are so palpable and euident to all men as no man can denie them. These were sufficient motiues to haue perswaded her from the murder of so good a friend.

But such was her execrable Ingratitude, as euen this grace and goodnesse was the cause of his miserable and vntimely death. And euen in the beginning of his greatest fauours extended to her, began shee to worke this mischiefe, according to the course of all Witches.

This *Iennet Preston*, whose Arraignment and Triall, with the particular Euidence against her I am now to set forth vnto you, one that liued at Gisborne in Crauen, in the Countie of Yorke, neare Master *Lister* of Westbie, against whom she practised much mischiefe; for hauing cut off *Thomas Lister* Esquire, father to this gentleman now liuing,[177] shee reuenged her selfe vpon his sonne: who in short time receiued great losse in his goods and cattell by her meanes.

These things in time did beget suspition, and at the Assizes and Generall Gaole deliuerie holden at the Castle of Yorke in Lent last past, before my Lord *Bromley*, shee was Indicted and Arraigned for the murder of a Child of one *Dodg-sonnes*,[178] but by the fauour and mercifull consideration of the Iurie thereof acquited.

---

[177] "*Hauing cut off Thomas Lister, Esquire, father to this gentleman now liuing.*"] Thomas Lister, of Westby, ancestor of the Listers, Lords Ribblesdale, married Jane, daughter of John Greenacres, Esquire, of Worston, county of Lancaster, and was buried at Gisburn, February 8th, 1607. His son, Thomas Lister, referred to as the "gentleman now living," married Jane, daughter of Thomas Heber, Esq., of Marton, after mentioned, and was buried at Gisburn, July 10th, 1619.

[178] "*Was Indicted and Arraigned for the murder of a Child of one Dodg-sonnes.*"] One acquittal was no protection to these unhappy creatures. It caused only additional exasperation, and, sooner or later, they were brought within what Donne calls "the hungry statutes' gaping jaws." Whether superstition or malice prompted this prosecution, on the part of Mr. Lister, it is difficult to say. Some grudge he entertained, or cause of offence he had taken up against this Jennet Preston, might be her death warrant in those days, when it was penal for a woman to be old, helpless, ugly, and poor. She was not so fortunate as the females tried at York, nine years afterwards, for bewitching the children of Edward Fairfax, of Fuyston, in the forest of Knaresborough, to whom we owe the only English translation of Tasso worthy of the name. These females, six in number, were indicted at two successive assizes, and every effort was made by the
"Prevailing poet! whose undoubting mind
Believed the magic wonders which he sung,"

But this fauour and mercie was no sooner extended towardes her, and shee set at libertie, But shee began to practise the utter ruine and ouerthrow of the name and bloud of this Gentleman.

And the better to execute her mischiefe and wicked intent, within foure dayes after her deliuerance out of the Castle at Yorke, went to the great Assembly of Witches at *Malking-Tower* vpon Good-friday last: to praye aide and helpe, for the murder of Master *Lister*, in respect he had prosecuted against her at the same Assizes.

Which it pleased God in his mercie to discouer, and in the end, howsoeuer he had blinded her, as he did the King of Ægypt and his Instruments, for the brighter euidence of his own powerfull glory: Yet by a Iudiciall course and triall of the Law, cut her off, and so deliuered his people from the danger of her Deuilish and wicked practises: which you

---

to procure their conviction. Never was a more unequal contest. On the one side was a relentless antagonist, armed with wealth, influence, learning, and accomplishments, and whose family connections gave him an unlimited power in the county; and on the other, six helpless persons, whose sex, age, and poverty were almost sufficient for their condemnation, without any evidence at all. Yet, owing to the magnanimous firmness of the judge, whose name, deserving of immortal honour, I regret has not been preserved, these efforts were frustrated, and the women accused delivered from the gulph which yawned before them. The disappointment he experienced in this instance, in being defrauded, as he thought, of a conviction for which he had strained every nerve and sinew, and in not being allowed to render the forest of Knaresborough as famous as that of Pendle, cast a gloom of despondency over the remaining days of this admirable poet, who has left a narration of the whole transaction, of most singular interest and curiosity, yet unpublished. The MSS. now in my possession, and which came from Mr. Bright's collection, consists of seventy-eight closely-written folio pages. It is entitled "A Discourse of Witchcraft, as it was enacted in the family of Mr. Edward Fairfax, of Fuystone, coun. Ebor, 1621." From page 78 to 144 are a series of ninety-three most extraordinary and spirited sketches, made with the pen, of the witches, devils, monsters, and apparitions referred to in the narrative.

shall heare against her, at her Arraignement and Triall, which I shall now set forth to you in order as it was performed, with the wonderfull signes and tokens of God, to satisfie the Iurie to finde her guiltie of this bloudie murther, committed foure yeares since.

## Indictment.

THis *Iennet Preston* being Prisoner in the Castle at Yorke, and indicted, for that shee felloniously had practised, vsed, and exercised diuerse wicked and deuillish Arts, called Witchcrafts, Inchauntments, Charmes, and Sorceries, in and vpon one *Thomas Lister* of Westby in Crauen, in the Countie of Yorke Esquire, and by force of the same Witchcraft felloniously the said *Thomas Lister* had killed, *Contra Pacem &c.* beeing at the Barre, was arraigned.

To this Indictment vpon her Arraignement, shee pleaded not guiltie, and for the Triall of her life put her selfe vpon God and her Countrey.

Whereupon my Lord *Altham* commaunded Master Sheriffe of the Countie of Yorke, in open Court to returne a Iurie of sufficient Gentlemen of vnderstanding, to passe betweene our Soueraigne Lord the Kings Majestie and her, and others the Prisoners, vpon their liues and deaths; who were afterwards sworne, according to the forme and order of the Court, the prisoner being admitted to her lawfull challenge.

Which being done, and the Prisoner at the Barre to receiue her Tryall, Master *Heyber*,[179] one of his Maiesties Iustices of Peace in the same County, hauing taken great paines in the proceedings against her; and being best instructed of any man of all the particular points of Euidence against her, humbly prayed, the witnesses hereafter following might be examined against her, and the seuerall Examinations, taken

---

[179] "*Master Heyber.*"] This was Thomas Hayber, or Heber, of Marton, in Craven, Esquire, who was buried at Marton, 7th February, 1633. He was the ancestor of Bishop Reginald Heber and the late Richard Heber, Esq.

before Master *Nowel*, and certified, might openly bee published against her; which hereafter follow in order, *viz.*

## *The Euidence for the Kings Maiestie*

### Against

### Iennet Preston, *Prisoner at the Barre.*

HEreupon were diuerse Examinations taken and read openly against her, to induce and satisfie the Gentlemen of the Iurie of Life and Death, to finde she was a Witch; and many other circumstances for the death of M. *Lister*. In the end *Anne Robinson* and others were both examined, who vpon their Oathes declared against her, That M. *Lister* lying in great extremitie, vpon his death bedde, cried out vnto them that stood about him; that *Iennet Preston* was in the house, looke where shee is, take hold of her: for Gods sake shut the doores, and take her, shee cannot escape away. Looke about for her, and lay hold on her, for shee is in the house: and so cryed very often in his great paines, to them that came to visit him during his sicknesse.

## *Anne Robinson,*

## and

## *Thomas Lister,*

Being examined further, they both gaue this in euidence against her, That when Master *Lister* lay vpon his death-bedde, hee cryed out in great extremitie; *Iennet Preston* lyes heauie vpon me, *Prestons* wife lies heauie vpon me; helpe me, helpe me: and so departed, crying out against her.

These, with many other witnesses, were further examined, and deposed, That *Iennet Preston*, the Prisoner at the Barre, being brought to M. *Lister* after hee was dead, & layd out to be wound vp in his winding-sheet, the said *Iennet Preston* comming to touch the dead corpes, they bled fresh bloud presently,* in the presence of all that were there present: Which hath euer beene held a great argument to induce a Iurie to hold him guiltie that shall be accused of Murther, and hath seldome, or neuer, fayled in the Tryall.

---

*" *The said Iennet Preston comming to touch the dead corpes, they bled fresh bloud presently.*"] On the popular superstition of touching the corpse of a murdered person, as an ordeal or test for the discovery of the innocence or guilt of suspected murderers, the reader cannot better be referred than to the very learned and elaborate essay in Pitcairne's *Criminal Trials*, vol. iii. p. 182-189. Amongst the authors there quoted, Webster is omitted, who, (see *Displaying of supposed Witchcraft*, p. 304,) discusses the point at considerable length, and with an earnest and implicit faith singularly at variance with his enlightened scepticism in other matters. But there were regions of superstition in which even this Sampson of logic became imbecile and powerless. The rationale of the bleeding of a murdered corpse at the touch of the murderer is given by Sir Kenelm Digby with his usual force and spirit:

To this cause, peradventure, may be reduced the strange effect which is frequently seen in England, when, *at the approach of the Murderer, the slain body suddenly bleedeth afresh*. For certainly the Souls of them that are treacherously murdered by surprise, use to leaue their bodies with extreme unwillingness, and with vehement indignation against them that force them to so unprovided and abhorred a passage! That Soul, then, to wreak its evil talent against the hated Murderer, and to draw a just and desired revenge upon his head, would do all it can to manifest the author of the fact! To *speak* it cannot—for in itself it wanteth the organs of voice; and those it is parted from are now grown too heavy, and are too benummed, for to give motion unto: Yet some change it desireth to make in the body, which it hath so vehement inclination to; and therefore is the aptest for it to work upon. It must then endeavour to cause a motion in the subtilest and most fluid parts (and consequently the most moveable ones) of it. This can be nothing but the blood, which then being violently moved, *must needs gush out at those places where it findeth issue!*

In the two following Scotch cases of witchcraft, this test was resorted to. The first was that of

Marioun Peebles,[180] *alias* Pardone, spouse to Swene, in Hildiswick, who was, on March 22, 1644, sentenced to be strangled at a stake, and burnt to ashes, at *the Hill of Berrie*, for Witchcraft and Murder. Marion and her husband having 'ane deadlie and venefical malice in her heart' against Edward Halero in Overure, and being determined 'to destroy and put him down,' being 'transformed in the lyknes of ane pellack-quhaill, (the Devill changing her spirit, quhilk fled in the same quhaill,') and the said Edward and other four individuals being in a fishing-boat, coming from the Sea, at the North-banks of Hildiswick, 'on ane fair morning, did cum under the said boat, and overturnit her with ease, and drowned and devoired thame in the sey, right at the shore, when there wis na danger wtherwayis.' The bodies of Halero and another of these hapless fishermen having been found, Marion and Swene 'wir sent for, and brought to see thame, and to lay thair hands on thame, ... dayis after said death and away-casting, quhaire thair bluid was evanished and desolved, from every natural cours or caus, shine, and run; the said umquhill Edward *bled at the collir-bain or craig-bane*, and the said ...,[181] *in the hand and fingers, gushing out bluid thairat*, to the great admiration of the beholders—and revelation of the judgement of the Almytie! And by which lyk occasionis and miraculous works of God, made manifest in Murders and the Murderers; whereby, be

---

[180] See Dr. Hibbert's "History of Orkney," &c., to which this remarkable Trial is appended.
[181] The name left blank.

many frequent occasiones brought to light, and the Murderers, be the said proof brought to judgment, conuict and condemned, not only in this Kingdom, also this countrie, but lykwayis in maist forrin Christiane Kingdomis; and be so manie frequent precedentis and practising of and tuitching Murderis and Murdereris, notourlie known: So, the forsaid Murder and Witchcraft of the saidis persons, with the rest of their companions, through your said Husband's deed, art, part, rad,[182] and counsall, is manifest and cleir to all, not onlie through and by the foirsaid precedentis of your malice, wicked and malishes[183] practises, by Witchcraft, Confessionis, and Declarationis of the said umquill Janet Fraser, Witch, revealed to her, as said is, and quha wis desyrit by him to concur and assist with you to the doing thereof; but lykways *be the declaration and revelation of the justice and judgementis of God, through the said issuing of bluid from the bodies!*' &c.

A similar and very remarkable instance is related in the following Triall: In the Dittay of Christian Wilson, alias *the Lanthorne*,[184] accused of Murder, Witchcraft, &c., (which is founded upon the examinations of James Wilson, Abraham Macmillan, William Crichton, and Fyfe and George Erskine, &c. led before Sir William Murray of Newtoun, and other Commissioners, at Dalkeith, Jun. 14, 1661,) it is stated, that 'Ther being enimitie betuixt the said Christiane and Alexander Wilsone, her brother, and shoe having often tymes threatned him, at length, about 7 or 8 monthes since, altho' the said Alexander was sene that day of his death, at three houres afternoone, in good health, walking about his bussnesse and office; yitt, at fyve howres in that same night,

---

[182] Rede; advice.

[183] Malicious.

[184] The name given at her baptism by the Devil. From "Collection of Original Documents," belonging to the Society of Antiquaries of Scotland, MS. As a specimen of the other charges, take the following: "Williame Richardsone, in Dalkeith, haiving felled ane hen of the said Cristianes with ane stone, and wpone her sight thereof did imediatly threatne him, and with ane frowneing countenance told him, that he 'should newer cast ane vther stone!' And imediatly the said Williame fell into ane franicie and madnes, and tooke his bed, and newer rose agane, but died within a few dayes: And in the tyme of his sicknes, he always cryed owt, that the said Cristiane was present befor him, in the likeness of ane grey catt! And some tyme eftir his death, James Richardsone, nephew to the said Williame, being a boy playing in the said Cristiane her yaird, and be calling her Lantherne, shoe threatned, that, if he held not his peace, shoe sowld cause him to die the death his nephew (uncle) died of!' Whairby it would appeare that shoe tooke wpon hir his nepheas (uncle's) death."

he was fownd dead, lying in his owne howse, naked as he was borne, with his face torne and rent, without any appearance of a spot of blood either wpon his bodie or neigh to it. And altho' many of the neiboures in the toune (Dalkeith) come into his howse to see the dead corpe, yitt shoe newar offered to come, howbeit her dwelling was nixt adjacent thairto; nor had shoe so much as any seiming greiff for his death. Bot the Minister and Bailliffes of the towne, taking great suspitione of her, in respect of her cairiage comand it that shoe showld be browght in; bot when shoe come, shoe come trembling all the way to the howse—bot *shoe refuised to come nigh* the corps *or to* tuitch *it* saying, that shoe "nevir tuitched a dead corpe in her lyfe!" Bot being arnestly desyred by the Minister, Bailliffes, and hir brother's friends who was killed, that shoe wold "bot *tuitch the corpes softlie*," shoe granted to doe it—but before shoe did it, the Sone being shyning in at the howse, shoe exprest her selfe thus, humbly desyring, that "as the Lord made the Sone to shyne and give light into that howse, that also *he wald give light to discovering of that Murder*!" And with these words, shoe tuitcheing *the wound of the dead man, verie saftlie*, it being whyte and cleane, without any spot of blod or the lyke!—yitt imediatly, *whill her fingers was wpon it*, the blood rushed owt of it, to the great admiratioune[185] of all the behoulders, who tooke it for *discoverie of the Murder*, according to her owne prayers.—For ther was ane great lumpe of flesh taken out of his cheik, so smowthlie, as no rasor in the world cowld have made so ticht ane incisioune, wpon flesh, or cheis—and ther wes no blood at all in the wownd—nor did it at all blead, altho' that many persones befor had tuitched it, whill[186] shoe did tuitche it! And the howse being searched all over, for the shirt of the dead man, yitt it cowld not be found; and altho' the howse was full of people all that night, ever vatching the corpes;[187] neither did any of them tuitch him that night—which is probable[188]—yitt, in the morneing, his shirt was fownd tyed fast abowt his neck, as a brechame,[189] non knowing how this come to pass! And this Cristian did immediatlie transport all her owne goods owt of her own howse into her dowghter's, purposing to flie away—bot was therwpon apprehendit and imprisoned.'—*Pitcairn's Criminal Trials*, vol. iii. p. 194.

---

[185] Wonder; amazement.
[186] Until. That is, many previous trials had been made of other persons suspected, or of those who were near neighbours, perhaps living at enmity with the deceased, who had voluntarily offered themselves to this solemn ordeal, or had been called upon thus publicly to attest their innocence of his blood.
[187] Holding the lyke-wake.
[188] Can be proved, by testimony or probation.
[189] The large collar which goes about a draught-horse's neck.

But these were not alone: for this wicked and bloud-thirstie Witch was no sooner deliuered at the Assises holden at Yorke in Lent last past, being indicted, arraigned, and by the fauor and mercie of the Iurie found not guiltie, for the murther of a Child by Witch-craft: but vpon the Friday following, beeing Good-Friday, shee rode in hast to the great meeting at Malking-Tower, and there prayed aide for the murther of M. *Thomas Lister:* as at large shall appeare, by the seuerall Examinations hereafter following; sent to these Assises from Master *Nowel* and other his Maiesties Iustices of Peace in the Countie of Lancaster, to be giuen in euidence against her, vpon her Triall, *viz.*

*The Examination and Euidence of*
**Iames Device,** *of the Forrest of Pendle, in the Countie of Lancaster, Labourer, taken at the house of* **Iames Wilsey,** *of the Forrest of Pendle in the Countie of Lancaster, the seuen and twentieth day of Aprill*, **Anno Reg. Regis Iacobi Angliæ, &c. Decimo ac Scotiæ quadragesimo quinto.**

**Before**

**Roger Nowel** *and* **Nicholas Banester,** *Esquires, two of his Maiesties Iustices of the Peace within the Countie of Lancaster*, **viz.**

THis Examinate saith, That vpon Good-Friday last about twelue of the clocke in the day-time, there dined in this Examinates said mothers house a number of persons, whereof three were men, with this Examinate, and the rest women: and that they met there for these three causes following (as this Examinates said mother told this Examinate): First was for the naming of the Spirit, which *Alizon Deuice*, now Prisoner at Lancaster, had, but did not name him, because shee was not there. The second cause was for the deliuery of his said Grand-mother, this Examinates said sister *Alizon*, the said *Anne Chattox*, and her daughter *Redferne*: Killing the Gaoler at Lancaster; and before the next Assizes to blow vp the Castle there; to that end the aforesaid Prisoners might by that meanes make an escape and get away. All which this Examinate then heard them conferre of. And the third cause was, for that there was a woman dwelling in Gilburne Parish, who came into this Examinates said Grand-mothers house, who there came, and craued assistance of the rest of them that were then there, for the killing of Master *Lister* of Westby: because, as she then said, he had borne malice vnto her, and had thought to haue put her away at the last Assizes at Yorke; but could not. And then this Examinat heard the said woman say, that her power was not strong enough to doe it her selfe, being now lesse then before time it had beene.

And he also further saith, that the said *Prestons* wife had a Spirit with her like vnto a white Foale, with a blacke-spot in the forehead. And further, this Examinat saith, That since the said meeting, as aforesaid, this Examinate hath beene brought to the wife of one *Preston* in Gisburne Parish aforesaid, by *Henry Hargreiues* of Goldshey, to see whether shee was the woman that came amongst the said Witches, on the said last Good-Friday, to craue their aide and assistance for the killing of the said Master *Lister*: and hauing had full view of her; hee this Examinate confesseth, That shee was the selfe-same woman which came amongst the said Witches on the said last Good-Friday, for their aide for the killing of the said Master *Lister*; and that brought the Spirit with her, in the shape of a White Foale, as aforesaid.

And this Examinate further saith, That all the said Witches went out of the said house in their owne shapes and likenesses, and they all, by that they were forth of the doores, were gotten on horse-backe like vnto Foales, some of one colour, some of another, and *Prestons* wife was the last; and when she got on horse-backe, they all presently vanished out of this Examinats sight: and before their said parting away, they all appointed to meete at the said *Prestons* wifes house that day twelue-month; at which time the said *Prestons* wife promised to make them a great feast; and if they had occasion to meet in the meane time, then should warning bee giuen that they all should meete vpon Romles-Moore. And this Examinate further saith, That at the said feast at Malking-Tower, this Examinat heard them all giue their consents to put the said Master *Thomas Lister* of Westby to death: and after Master *Lister* should be made away by Witchcraft, then al the said Witches gaue their consents to ioyne altogether to hancke Master *Leonard Lister*,[190] when he should come to dwell at the Sowgill, and so put him to death.

---

[190] "*Master Leonard Lister.*"] This Leonard Lister was the brother of Master Thomas Lister, for whose murder Jennet Preston was indicted; and married Ann, daughter of —— Loftus, of Coverham Abbey, county of York.

*The Examination of* Henrie Hargreives
**of Goldshey-booth, in the Forrest of
Pendle, in the Countie of Lancaster Yeoman, taken the
fifth day of May,** Anno Reg. Regis Iacobi Angliæ,
&c. Decimo, ac Scociæ quadragesimo quinto.

**Before**

**Roger Nowel, Nicholas Bannester,
*and* Robert Holden,** *Esquires; three of his
Maiesties Iustices of Peace within the said Countie.*

THis Examinat vpon his oath saith, That *Anne Whittle*, alias *Chattox*, confessed vnto him, that she knoweth one *Prestons* wife neere Gisburne, and that the said *Prestons* wife should haue beene at the said feast, vpon the said Good-Friday, and that shee was an ill woman, and had done Master *Lister* of Westby great hurt.

*The Examination of* Elizabeth
**Device,** *mother of* **Iames Device,** *taken before*
**Roger Nowel** *and* **Nicholas Banester,**
*Esquires, the day and yeare aforesaid,* viz.

THe said *Elizabeth Deuice* vpon her Examination confesseth, That vpon Good-Friday last, there dined at this Examinats house, which she hath said are Witches, and doth verily thinke them to be Witches; and their names are those whom *Iames Deuice* hath formerly spoken of to be there.

She also confesseth in all things touching the killing of Master *Lister* of Westby, as the said *Iames Deuice* hath before confessed.

And the said *Elizabeth Deuice* also further saith, That at the said meeting at Malking-Tower, as aforesaid, the said *Katherine Hewyt* and *Iohn Bulcock*, with all the rest then there, gaue their consents, with the said *Prestons* wife, for the killing of the said Master *Lister*. And for the killing of the said Master *Leonard Lister*, she this Examinate saith in all things, as the said *Iames Deuice* hath before confessed in his Examination.

*The Examination of* Iennet Device,
***daughter of* Elizabeth *late wife of* Iohn
Device, *of the Forrest of Pendle, in the Countie of
Lancaster,*
*about the age of nine yeares or thereabouts, taken
the day and yeare aboue-said:*

**Before**

**Roger Nowel *and* Nicholas Banester,**
*Esquires, two of his Maiesties Iustices of Peace in
the Countie of Lancaster.*

THe said Examinate vpon her Examination saith, that vpon Good-friday last there was about twenty persons, whereof only two were men, to this Examinats remembrance, at her said Grand-mothers house, called Malking-Tower aforesaid, about twelue of the clocke: all which persons, this Examinates said mother told her were Witches, and that she knoweth the names of diuers of the said Witches.

---

AFter all these Examinations, Confessions, and Euidence, deliuered in open Court against her, His Lordship commanded the Iurie to obserue the particular circumstances;[191] first, Master *Lister* in his great extremitie,

---

[191] "*His Lordship commanded the Iurie to obserue the particular circumstances.*"] The judge in this case was Altham, who seems even to have been more superstitious, bigotted, and narrow-minded than his brother in commission, Bromley. Fenner, who tried the witches of Warbois, and Archer, before whom the trial of Julian Cox took place, are the only judges I can meet with, quite on a level with this learned baron in grovelling absurdity, upon whom "Jennet Preston would lay heavy at the time of his death," whether she

to complaine hee saw her, and requested them that were by him to lay hold on her.

After he cried out shee lay heauie vpon him, euen at the time of his death.

But the Conclusion is of more consequence then all the rest, that *Iennet Preston* being brought to the dead corps, they bled freshly. And after her deliuerance in Lent, it is proued shee rode vpon a white Foale, and was present in the great assembly at *Malkin Tower* with the Witches, to intreat and pray for aide of them, to kill Master *Lister*, now liuing, for that he had prosequuted against her.

And against these people you may not expect such direct euidence, since all their workes are the workes of darkenesse, no witnesses are present to accuse them, therefore I pray God direct your consciences.

> After the Gentlemen of the Iurie of Life and Death had spent the most part of the day, in consideration of the euidence against her, they returned into the Court and deliuered vp their Verdict of Life and Death.
> \* \*
> \*

---

had so lain upon Mr. Thomas Lister or not, if bigotry, habit, and custom did not render him seared and callous to conscience and pity.

## *The Verdict of Life and Death.*

WHo found *Iennet Preston* guiltie of the fellonie and murder by Witch-craft of *Thomas Lister*, Esquire; conteyned in the Indictment against her, &c.

Afterwards, according to the course and order of the Lawes, his Lordship pronounced Iudgement against her to bee hanged for her offence. And so the Court arose.

---

HERE was the wonderfull discouerie of this *Iennet Preston*, who for so many yeares had liued at Gisborne in Crauen, neare Master *Lister*: one thing more I shall adde to all these particular Examinations, and euidence of witnesses, which I saw, and was present in the Court at Lancaster, when it was done at the Assizes holden in August following.

My Lord *Bromley* being very suspicious of the accusation of *Iennet Deuice*, the little Wench, commanded her to looke vpon the Prisoners that were present, and declare which of them were present at *Malkin Tower*, at the great assembly of Witches vpon Good-Friday last: shee looked vpon and tooke many by the handes, and accused them to be there, and when shee had accused all that were there present, shee told his Lordship there was a Woman that came out of Crauen that was amongst the Witches at that Feast, but shee saw her not amongst the Prisoners at the Barre.

What a singular note was this of a Child, amongst many to misse her, that before that time was hanged for her offence, which shee would neuer confesse or declare at her death? here was present old *Preston* her husband, who then cried out and went away: being fully satisfied his wife had Iustice, and was worthie of death.

To conclude then this present discourse, I heartilie desire you, my louing Friends and Countrie-men, for whose particular instructions this is added to the former of the wonderfull discouerie of Witches in the Countie of Lancaster: And for whose particular satisfaction this is published; Awake in time, and suffer not your selues to be thus assaulted.

Consider how barbarously this Gentleman hath been dealt withall; and especially you that hereafter shall passe vpon any Iuries of Life and Death, let not your conniuence, or rather foolish pittie, spare such as these, to exequute farther mischiefe.

Remember that shee was no sooner set at libertie, but shee plotted the ruine and ouerthrow of this Gentleman, and his whole Familie.

Expect not, as this reuerend and learned Iudge saith, such apparent proofe against them, as against others, since all their workes, are the workes of darkenesse: and vnlesse it please Almightie God to raise witnesses to accuse them, who is able to condemne them?

Forget not the bloud that cries out vnto God for reuenge, bring it not vpon your owne heads.

Neither doe I vrge this any farther, then with this, that I would alwaies intreat you to remember, that it is as great a crime (as *Salomon* sayth, *Prov.* 17.) to condemne the innocent, as to let the guiltie escape free.

Looke not vpon things strangely alledged, but iudiciously consider what is justly proued against them.

And that as well all you that were witnesses, present at the Arraignement and Triall of her, as all other strangers, to whome this Discourse shall come, may take example by this Gentlemen to prosecute these hellish Furies to their end:[192] labor to root them out of the Commonwealth, for the common good of your Countrey. The greatest mercie extended to them, is soone forgotten.

God graunt vs the long and prosperous cotinuance of these Honorable and Reuerend Iudges, vnder whose Gouernment we liue in these North parts: for we may say, that God Almightie hath singled them out, and set him on his Seat, for the defence of Iustice.

> And for this great deliuerance, let vs all pray to
> God Almightie, that the memorie of
> these worthie Iudges may bee
> blessed to all Posterities.[193]

---

[192] "*Take example by this Gentlemen to prosecute these hellish Furies to their end.*"] It is marvellous that Potts does not, like Delrio, recommend the rack to be applied to witches "in moderation, and according to the regulations of Pope Pius the Third, and so as not to cripple the criminal for life." Not that this learned Jesuit is much averse to simple dislocations occasioned by the rack. These, he thinks, cannot be avoided in the press of business. He is rather opposed, though in this he speaks doubtfully and with submission to authority, to those tortures which fracture the bones or lacerate the tendons. Verily, the Catholic and the Protestant author might have shaken hands; they were, beyond dispute, *pœne Gemelli*.

[193] "*Posterities.*"] Master Potts, of the particulars of whose life nothing is known, made, as far as can be discovered, no further attempt to acquire fame in the character of an author. No subject so interesting probably again occurred, as that which had diversified his legal pursuits "in his lodgings in Chancery-lane," from the pleasing recollections associated with his Summer Circuit of

# *FINIS.*

---

1612. He was not, however, the only person of the name of Pott, or Potts, who distinguished himself in the field of Witchcraft. The author of the following tract, in my possession, might have garnished it with various flowers from the work now reprinted, if he had been aware of such a repository: "Pott (Joh. Henr.) De nefando Lamiarum cum Diabolo coitu." 4to. Lond. 1689. The other celebrated cases of supposed witchcraft occurring in the county of Lancaster, besides those connected with the foregoing republication, are, the extraordinary one of Ferdinand, Earl of Derby, who died at Latham in 1594, for which the reader is referred to Camden's *Annals of Elizabeth*, years 1593, 1594; Kennet, 2. 574, 580; or Pennant's *Tour from Downing to Alston Moor*, p. 29;—the case of Edmund Hartley, hanged at Lancaster in 1597, for bewitching some members of the family of Mr. Starkie, of Cleworth, which will be fully considered in the proposed republication of the Chetham Society, which gives the history of that event;—and lastly, that of a person of the name of Utley, (Whitaker, p. 528; Baines, vol. i. p. 604,) who was hanged at Lancaster about 1630, for having bewitched to death Richard, the son of Ralph Assheton, Esq., Lord of Middleton, of whose trial, unfortunately, no report is in existence. Webster also mentions two supposed witches as having been put to death at Lancaster, within eighteen years before his *Displaying of supposed Witchcraft* was published; and which occurrence, not referred to by any other historian, must therefore have taken place about the year 1654.

www.ingramcontent.com/pod-product-compliance
Lightning Source LLC
Chambersburg PA
CBHW071656160426
43195CB00012B/1488